Praise for *The Promise of Not-Knowing*

"And what if the answer to our heritage of culture wars—which have so effectively colonized and policed the sacred—were to bracket our drive for victory, to open the chance for a new spirit, a new spirituality? And what if the New Testament itself were released from the old cultural inheritance to incite this new exodus from war, and this on the merest promise of spiritual renewal? Caution, reader: With this *new* New Testament reading in hand you may just find yourself bereft of weapons, without the identity forged by culture wars, and instead nothing but newly awake and alive in ways you just could not have known before. This book is a risky masterpiece."

WARD BLANTON, reader in biblical cultures and European thought,
University of Kent, and author of several books, including *A Materialism
for the Masses: Saint Paul and the Philosophy of Undying Life*

"David Fredrickson is calling Christians to rid themselves of certainty and cerebrality in reading the New Testament. His mastery of Greek and his knowledge of ancient Greek poets convince the reader that the New Testament should be read for its emotion, 'madness,' and passion. If twenty-first-century Christians can do this, they will not only discover a whole new world of divine hospitality but a whole new sense of the humanity and hopefulness of the New Testament."

AMY MARGA, professor of systematic theology, Luther Seminary

"What if reading a text is like reading a face? As we read, our understanding of that person grows, as do the mystery and dignity of their life. We feel connected to them, responsible to them, drawn to give of ourselves to them, even as they remain unknown to us. With trenchant probes into the Gospels and Paul's letters, Fredrickson shows how faith, hope, and love spring from this new reading of the New Testament."

NED WISNEFSKE, Schumann Professor of Lutheran Theology, Roanoke College

THE PROMISE OF NOT-KNOWING

THE PROMISE OF NOT-KNOWING

A *New* New Testament Reading

David E. Fredrickson

Fortress Press
Minneapolis

THE PROMISE OF NOT-KNOWING
A *New* New Testament Reading

Cover design: Brice Hemmer
Cover art: "Christ Appearing to the Disciples" by Rembrandt Harmenszoon van Rijn (1606–69), etching (1646) © Bnf.

Print ISBN: 978-1-4514-9631-4
eBook ISBN: 978-1-5064-7999-6

Contents

Acknowledgments

I wish to thank Neil Elliott and Scott Tunseth for their patience, encouragement, and just the right words to help me say what I wanted to say. And thanks to Elvis Ramirez for wrangling my wayward manuscript into good shape. Echoes of conversations with many of my faculty colleagues at Luther Seminary might be detected throughout the book, but I say these names out loud: Gary Simpson, Cameron Howard, Dirk Lange, and Amy Marga. To the hundreds of students over the years, and also my colleagues, thank you for telling me what you think! And my gratitude goes out to the Luther Seminary Library for its efficiency and friendliness. Finally, chapter Five in the present volume builds on an essay that appeared in Mark A. Throntveit and Rolf A. Jacobson, ed., *"Worship the Lord with Gladness": Essays in Honor of Frederick J. Gaiser* (St. Paul: Word & World, 2017). It is used here with permission. I am grateful for *Word & World*'s hospitality to my thoughts over the last three decades.

Introduction

It, And, and a *New* New

I WAS SHAKEN by an earthquake once. A tiny one for West Coasters, but for one born and raised in Iowa, where the land seldom rattles and the ground beneath one's feet behaves itself . . . well, it was quite a thing. I write "earthquake" now, but in that strange moment, I had no word for an event that, to this day, resists my efforts to understand it. I was sitting in a restaurant with colleagues gathered from around the United States for a conference on the use of case studies in the teaching of religion. Looking back, I think an unexpected case study on religion might have happened to me. Then, however, I had no words. I was stunned. *Something* happened. But what was that something?

I did not then, nor do I now, have words for it. I write "words for it" as if the word *it* itself presented no difficulties. *It* is very difficult to talk about, mostly because I fear (or do I hope?) the moment I talk about *it*, *it* will slip from my memory. In fact, that disappearance has already started. *It* began to withdraw the moment we put the dishes back in order and finished dessert with nervous laughter. In the hours after, to calm my nerves, I assigned to the word *it* the job of representing something inexplicable. I want now to confess (inappropriately personifying *it*, I also confess) my belief that *it* does not like, I can only imagine, to be talked about and resents being represented by two measly letters. *It* feels underappreciated to find *it*self repeated with the technology of ink on paper or electrons shooting across a screen. *It* dislikes being one topic of conversation among many.

Most of all, *it* would be offended if I were to name *it* "God," even though the name of God has a big reputation—not, however, without mixed reviews. For a reason (or reasons) I do not understand, I can't bring myself to call a moment of perplexity an experience of God, as if I knew a divine someone out there were trying to get through to me with a message relevant to my life.[1] I didn't and I don't. If *it* was anything, *it* was the blank, unrepresentable, inexpressible, unanticipated split-second interruption in the flow of my thoughts and conversation. *Split-second*—that is a wonderful term, since for a moment, I was living in a cut, a tear in the fabric of time as we usually think about time, as a sequence of possibilities becoming realities, like a rope unwinding from the past through the present to the future.[2] I was speechless. There was not a single word in my head that I could throw out like a lasso to secure *it* so I might drag *it* back to me and comprehend *it*. There was no next, no prior, and most of all, no present—just an impersonal blank occupying the space called *me*.

You see how I can't stop talking about the very thing that evades my talk, but I am not alone. In traditional, theological language, there is a connection between my fascination with *it* and the allure of apophatic theology.[3] Apophatic theologians assert that God is beyond language, but then they go on to speak a great deal about the One they worship who exists beyond being and beyond the power of language to name. I am attracted to the writings of apophatic theologians, though irritated by their (and my) inability to keep from talking about what we know we cannot talk about. I admire them because they quite effectively pull the rug out from under the kataphatic theologians, those thinkers who have come up with definite ideas about God, all the way from the supreme being or the ground of being to the divinity behind the prosperity gospel.[4] Apophaticism makes it extremely problematic to say anything about God, even to put the word *God* into a sentence as I have just done. Symeon the New Theologian (949–1042 CE) was an exemplary practitioner of apophatic theology and puts these words in the unnameable One's mouth as he navigates (rather too artistically for my tastes) the impossibility of speaking about God: "By nature I am inexpressible, infinite, / Without need, unapproachable, invisible to all, / Intangible, unfeelable, immutable by essence."[5] Please notice, however, that unlike Symeon and other apophatic theologians, I am not applying the name *God* to that which is beyond language and beyond being.[6] Indeed, I feel guilty about using the phrase "that which is beyond language and beyond being" in the prior sentence as if I knew something definite about the nature of *that which* or that there even is a *that which* beyond being. Yet I have no choice but to use words lest and until I finally fall completely silent. If this book were about *it*—which can't be touched by language—then obviously it would be quite short, finished by now if I were being honest with you in my claim that *it* evades language.

Or the book could be very long—that is, it could be if I lied about *it*. I could pretend to know all about *it* and fool you, having first fooled myself, into thinking not that *it* is radically other than anything and everything else but that *it* is the biggest, most powerful, and most intelligent being in the universe, and on that cool California evening, that being itself was sending me a message by sending an earthquake my way. Keeping up the pretense, I could say that He is there for you too with a message I will deliver in the next hundred and some pages, if you pay attention. Or perhaps I could keep on dropping hints that I know the so-called *deposit of faith* given by Christ to the disciples and transmitted by the church down to this very day—that is, the essentials of what Christianity has to say about God, Christ, the Spirit, the church, and so on.

I do know the essentials, by the way, but only infrequently do I find deposited in them the *it* of which I am trying (not) to speak. And least of all do I find in the essentials the innumerable *it*s stirring the souls of those who are otherwise than Christian and to whom I feel an overwhelming responsibility to keep their *it*s safe from the violent strains of sure and certain knowledge within my own religious tradition. Indeed, with the Christian essentials in mind, I could cover the writings of the New Testament. I could assume that the writers of the New Testament all think of God in the same way, with only a few differences around the edges owing to changing historical circumstances. I could show a straight path leading from the words and sentences in the New Testament to the being of God whom we already know from the so-called *deposit of faith* or from our heartfelt intuitions.

But I won't. In the twenty-first century, a severe credibility problem undermines reading the New Testament as a witness to the one metaphysical God. That is why I have written this book. To put it bluntly, for an increasing number of people (myself included), the God named in the official confessions of the various branches of Christianity—each branch having its own take on the metaphysical God as the supreme being or the ground of being or the promoter of prosperity for believers, the one whom Scripture supposedly reveals at every turn in the grand sweep of the biblical narrative from Genesis to Revelation—this God, for more and more people, turns out to be very difficult to put any faith in.[7] John D. Caputo puts his finger on one important reason God, as traditionally conceived by metaphysical thinkers (and, honestly, who isn't one?), is unworthy of belief:

> If you think of God in terms of power, you will be regularly, systematically confounded by—let us say, to put it politely—the unevenness of God's record on behalf of the poor and the oppressed, the irregularity of help that God gives when my enemy oppresses me. Beyond obfuscation and mystification, it is in the end an outright blasphemy to say that God has some mysterious divine purpose when an innocent child is abducted, raped, and murdered.[8]

Again, to be blunt, Where was the God who supposedly prospers the good and punishes the evil, this supreme being? Where was this God of control during the Holocaust, to cite but one example of a horror that so exceeds imagining that for me to take rhetorical advantage of it, as I am doing by citing it as an example for the point *I* want to make, detracts from its singularity and insults those who have been shaken by it? (*It*, perhaps?)[9]

There is another approach I could take whose violence is more overt than the survey method. It begins by discounting any experience you have had of *it*. In this approach, I would try to bully you into thinking that you have never experienced *it*, have never known *it*—that *it* has revealed *it*self to a few people who have letters after their names, like PhD or MDiv, or titles before their names, like Reverend or Father or Professor. Over the generations since the first and only revelation that God ever gave of himself, I might argue, only a few (s)elected individuals have received training and certification to instruct others. Well, I too have proper credentials, although those who bestowed them on me are possibly having second thoughts right now. But credentials do me no good. They do not help me with the one thing I really care about. They do not guarantee that I won't turn the *it* of which I am simultaneously speaking and trying not to speak into the God of the philosophers and the God of ecclesiastical hierarchy. In fact, my credentials egg me on to do that very thing, since one gets a degree in the first place and advances in a discipline by knowing *things*, and what higher academic or churchly credential could there be than the one awarded for knowing the greatest thing of all, God?

So again, this book is not about *it*. I don't know what *it* is (and the word *is* is likely the most misleading word I could ever associate with *it*), but for some reason (once again, one that I don't know), I can't seem to stop talking about *it* even though I should remain silent. Silent, not only because language falls short when it refers to *it*, but also because language insults *it* by the very act of referring. Reference makes *it* an object pointed at by a sign. You can sympathize with *it*. How do *you* like to be pointed at?[10] How do you like to be talked about in the third person when you are sitting right there?

No, this book is not about *it* for one simple reason: because *it* was, and still is (but only as long as the memory endures), my *it*. Not that I own *it*. No more than I own the memory of my deceased parents, whose faces I find more and more difficult to recall even with the aid of photographs. In the matter of *it*, owning is just not an option. But more than that, you could not experience my *it*, no matter how much I wrote, unless you became me, and I am not prepared to give that up. If I seem a little selfish with my *it*, flip the situation around, and you will see how safe your *it* is from me or from anyone else analyzing, explaining, reducing, making a case study of, laughing at, idolizing, or ignoring your split second(s) of nonknowing in the nonpresence of *it*.[11] When, for example, one of your seconds has been split by news (good or bad) and you live suspended over an abyss—holding on to the ragged edges of the past and future, an abyss called *presence* that the Western intellectual tradition, Christianity included, foolishly has thought to be full of tranquility when God experiences God's own self, according to some big-name theologians and philosophers—that moment, *your* split second, this book does not aim to take from you.[12] So to keep all our *it*s safe, I will try to avoid talking about *it* as if *it* could be known, as if *it* were just another name for God.

Instead, I want to think about what happened a second or two into that tremor in California when I got in the way of *it* between dinner and dessert. Now, upon reflection, I realize that I missed a chance for something new to come my way. How did that happen? So there I was, stunned as my chair rocked back and forth. Instead of leaving my mind open to the openness spreading out before me, however, and the truly staggering possibility that others (some dear to me, some not so much) wake up each morning to their world, which they might experience as an abyss of meaninglessness or horror, my first thought was to complain of disorder and untidiness. *Who is playing a joke on me?* I asked myself, supposing someone had sneaked up behind me, grabbed the back of my chair, and started to shake it wildly. The validity of this explanation lasted only as long as it took me to see my colleagues at the table—along with their plates, their silverware, and the whole room—churning about. In that restaurant and on that night, I tamed *it*, branded, labeled, domesticated, calculated, and evaluated *it*. By doing all these things, I acted unjustly toward *it*. For a split second, I had been given an opportunity, by whom or what I have no idea, to feel in my gut how constructed my world is and how constructed I myself am. For a split second, I had the chance to feel just how illusory the ego is, how fabricated is the *I* that seems to constitute *me* as the same entity through time. Where was that *I*, though, when *it* showed up without words, calling me out of this self-involvement I take so seriously and call *my* life as if I owned it?

If this were a book on psychoanalysis, I would explore how past experiences had influenced me so that my first reaction was to think the shaking earth was all about *me*, that someone was messing with *me*. But this book is about reading the New Testament, and one of its main ideas is that the *new* in New Testament is ruined very quickly by readers like me who are in a rush to explain the inexplicable and represent the unrepresentable. In this book, I will assume that under the influence of habitual Western ways of reading, we are all in a rush to explain the *it*s of our lives as we encounter them in texts; other persons; the stars on a cloudless, moonless Montana night; or the vulnerability and hope written on the face of a migrant or refugee waiting, waiting, waiting for something new here in the land I arrogantly and with unfathomable ignorance call my own. Instead of rushing to explain the inexplicable, I wish to stop writing, take a breath, and take in the words of David Wood, who introduces an essay on hospitality (I wish I had read it before *it* struck) in this way: "This essay adumbrates the intriguing possibility that the world (as we call it) may be populated with beings of various sorts that in all sorts of different ways, open worlds, open unto worlds, and open our eyes to possible worlds, by interrupting this one."[13]

Starting Again

Officially, my title is Professor of New Testament, but *teacher of early Christian literature* is what I often say when strangers discover I work at a theological seminary and politely inquire what I am a professor of. I tell this little lie, since I know the reputation these twenty-seven books called the New Testament have in the world around me. I love the word *new*, and *testament* fascinates me with its connotations of truthful witnessing and a gift that cannot possibly be repaid, as in *last will and testament*, but when I read the hideous things that have been said by Christians in the name of the New Testament about women, LGBTQIA+ persons, Jews, Muslims—the list of people, animals, languages, lands, and waters (and the list goes on) whose irremediable ruin has been instigated or ignored by readers and proclaimers of the New Testament—when that long list unfolds before me and I begin a journey of taking responsibility for the religion into which I was born, I am overwhelmed with sadness, and I feel a great necessity to repent.[14] Or just quit. For this reason, I have been casting about in the last few years for another way of understanding the *new* in *New Testament*. There is something wrong with the old, established way of explaining the *new*, the explanation that has, with the exception of a few saintly, restless souls, satisfied the Christian church for nearly two thousand years and justified the exclusion from Christianity's heart of all of that is other than Christian.

New first acquired what would become its traditional meaning when Christians set up a competition between two religions, Judaism and Christianity. (Note how in a gesture of presumed superiority, Christians to this day often leave Muslims out of the contest of the religions as I just did, though they certainly have a legitimate claim to be there, if competition is in fact what any of us who still value religion should really want to be up to.) The competition comes down to this: a contest to see which religion can claim the most recent updates on God and God's plans for humans living in God's creation. In other words, Christians have claimed over the centuries that the divine self-revelation they think is contained in the New Testament exceeds and makes obsolete the divine self-revelation in the Old Testament. Not only is this Christian understanding of *new* arrogant; it is dangerous for Jews and Muslims, or anyone else who has not received the latest bulletin explaining God's mind. That danger is why I am searching for a new way to read the New Testament. The old *new* has hurt a lot of people, and that puts the situation far too mildly.

Even before this collection of early Christian writings came to be called the *New Testament*, the unknown author of one of its latest documents, Hebrews, framed the relationship between Judaism and Christianity in terms of the information about God that each had in its possession. According to Hebrews 1 and 3, the knowledge Christians have about God is better than Jewish knowledge because it comes from the Son of God and not from Moses or even from angels. In fact, the old testament (here not the collection of writings but the so-called old covenant between God and Israel) was faulty from the start, as the author of Hebrews points out for his readers: "For if that first covenant had been faultless, there would have been no need to look for a second one" (Heb 8:7). And in a statement that blithely builds on the logic of racism in the name of Christ, the fault was not with the covenant itself but with the disobedient people of Israel who impudently refused to live by God's rules (8:8–12). Then come the chilling words that in following centuries would be used to justify the exclusion of Jews from Christendom and nearly exterminate them in Europe: "In speaking of 'a new covenant,' he has made the first one obsolete. And what is obsolete and growing old will soon disappear" (8:13). God is the "he" whose thoughts the author presumes to know so well. Knowledge like that is frightening. Certain about that which will soon disappear, a reader might ask, *So why not help that which is obsolete on its way out?* The true believer runs the logic of this brand of *new* to its horrifying conclusion. That train of thought drives me to search for a way to understand the *new* in *New Testament* that does not depend on relegating Judaism to the dustbin of history, as the author of Hebrews thinks God did to the Jews or as later Christians would do to Jews—to say nothing of ignoring Islam altogether or demonizing it.

Hebrews' belief in the obsolescence of Judaism caught on with Christians in later centuries. With an appalling lack of sympathy, Eusebius (ca. 260–340 CE), bishop of Caesarea and prominent Christian historian, pointed out the consequences Jews suffered for stubbornly hanging on to their old covenant/testament (here meaning their scripture). Yet Eusebius thought these dated and mostly irrelevant writings had one thing going for them: the old covenant predicted the new covenant and all the evils that the Jews would bring upon themselves for having, as he puts it, "laid godless hands on Christ":

> The most ancient Hebrew oracles present all these things definitely about One Who would come in the last times, and Who would undergo such sufferings among men, and they clearly tell the source of their foreknowledge. They bear witness to the Resurrection from the dead of the Being Whom they revealed, His appearance to His disciples, His gift of the Holy Spirit to them, His return to heaven, His establishment as King on His Father's throne and His glorious second Advent yet to be at the consummation of the age. In addition to all this you can hear the wailings and lamentations of each of the prophets, wailing and lamenting characteristically over the calamities which will overtake the

Jewish people because of their impiety to Him Who had been foretold. How their kingdom, that had continued from the days of a remote ancestry to their own, would be utterly destroyed after their sin against Christ; how their fathers' Laws would be abrogated, they themselves deprived of their ancient worship, robbed of the independence of their forefathers, and made slaves of their enemies, instead of free men; how their royal metropolis would be burned with fire, their venerable and holy altar undergo the flames and extreme desolation, their city be inhabited no longer by its old possessors but by races of other stock, while they would be dispersed among the Gentiles through the whole world, with never a hope of any cessation of evil, or breathing-space from troubles. And it is plain even to the blind, that what they saw and foretold is fulfilled in actual facts from the very day the Jews laid godless hands on Christ, and drew down on themselves the beginning of the train of sorrow.[15]

It should now be clear why readers of the New Testament in the twenty-first century have a responsibility to examine their presuppositions about the word *new* in the title of the smaller testament. If the *new* in the New Testament depends on Eusebius's imagination, then we must break free from his sort of newness and discover another one that is life-affirming *for all*—or dispense with the word *new* altogether.

Perhaps we should give Eusebius another chance. In the following passage, the venom *seems* to have drained from his pen. Here he claims that the *new* in New Testament is actually older than the old testament itself. Christianity, he asserts, is no different from what the saints before Moses knew about God and how they conducted themselves in the light of their knowledge:

I have now proved that the old covenant and the law given by Moses was only applicable to the Jewish race, and only to such of them as lived in their own land. It did not apply to other nations of the world nor to Jews inhabiting foreign soil. And I have shown

that the ideal of the new covenant must be helpful to the life of all
nations: the members of its kingdom are to be restricted in no way
whatever. Considerations of country, race or locality, or anything
else are not to affect them in any way at all. The law and life of
our Saviour Jesus Christ shows itself to be such, *being a renewal of the
ancient pre-Mosaic religion*, in which Abraham, the friend of God, and
his forefathers are shown to have lived. And if you cared to compare
the life of Christians and the worship introduced among all nations
by Christ with the lives of the men who with Abraham are witnessed
to by Scripture as holy and righteous, you would find one and the
same ideal.[16]

According to Eusebius, the two covenants, or testaments, work like this:
the old covenant is a matter of local, specific, and temporally limited laws
for the Jews only, but the new covenant is a universally applicable law.[17]
The thing to notice in Eusebius's approach is that both covenants are
law. The new law is better than the old because it can be applied to all
people at all times. For that reason, Jesus, who in Eusebius's view advocates
the law of love, is a better lawgiver than Moses.[18] Now all of this universal-
ity is quite convenient for Eusebius, a prominent designer of Christianity
as the religion of empire after the conversion of Constantine in 312. An
empire needs universals as it attempts to erase the singularity, difference,
and strangeness of each and every *other* swept up in the sovereign's drive
to assimilate diverse others to itself. If *new* only means that the other is
acceptable as long as the other is the same as me or similar enough and
that all lives must conform to one law, then Eusebius and the representa-
tives of the Christianity he has influenced have, in my opinion, run out of
chances, even if every other word coming out of their mouths is *love*.

A *New* New?

Even if Eusebius does not deserve another chance, there may still be a way
to save the *new* in the New Testament, but we will have to think outside

of the box into which he and the author of Hebrews and countless other interpreters have tried to confine our thoughts. I do not think this is going to be easy. Not at all. In fact, I do not know if it is even possible to think our way out. There is a voice in my head warning me that just when I think I have broken through the box of traditional thinking, I have gotten there with the help of the very intellectual tradition I am trying to escape. But that makes me want to try all the harder.[19] The first step in opening the box a bit is to think about the box itself. We owe our way of thinking to the same Greek philosophic tradition that got itself written into the Letter to the Hebrews and into the texts of Eusebius. Thinking inside this box is primarily a matter of explaining things and events by observing how they repeat what has happened before.[20] Greek philosophical thinking is essentially the movement from the known to the unknown and the effort to convert the unknown into the known. In other words, to know in a philosophical way is to become certain of what *it* is when earthquakes in California sneak up on us.

Something—I don't know what—tells me we ought to leave *it* unexplained if explanation is a matter of pointing to *it*s cause or *it*s purpose. Thinking in the West has become the reduction of a certain *something* that is other to our individual or collective experience to a *certain* something that we have already experienced and aim to possess and control. Just think of the phrases *oh, I get it* and *now I have it*. Both phrases reveal that inheritors of the Western intellectual tradition think of knowledge as the subject's control of an object. So thinking about *new* is going to be frustrating for anyone who has grown up in this tradition. *New* is new precisely by escaping our efforts to fit it into what we already are certain of.[21] This new is scary, I do not deny it, but then again, an encounter with it might turn out to be exhilarating too. This book proceeds from a hope in the latter possibility and a realism about the former.

This book also asks a question guaranteed to make some readers fearful that I am walking on thin ice (and they would be right): What if the *new* in *New Testament* referred to something other than the repetition of the same? Repetition puts us off its scent by disguising itself under the perfume of good things—like *improvement*, as in Hebrews, or *renewal/restoration*, as in Eusebius. But what if we resist Hebrews' call to personal, moral improvement and refuse to believe Eusebius's seductive falsehood that life would be restored—indeed, made great again—by returning to the original law, as if there were such a thing? What if we held out for something else, something worthy of the name *new*?

And no, I don't know what it is.

Why I Love the Little Word *And*

Here is a different angle to come at the problem of the new. The Greek word for "new" is *kainos*, and the Greek word for "and" is *kai*. This means that every time Greek speakers in the first century wanted to say *new*, they had to say *and* first. In other words, *and* was structurally necessary for *new*. No *kainos* without *kai*. And (and *kai* in Greek) is a wonderfully inclusive word, since it does not spurn what comes before it. In fact, it couldn't even be *and* without every word written or spoken before it, but just as *and* respects its past, it also says yes to whatever words are yet to come. Now, although I know that language does not have a mind of its own, nor does it possess a sense of humor, I cannot keep from thinking someone is playing a game with *kai* and *kainos*. (Remember, though, I also thought the earthquake was a rude trick on me.) I, for one, am desperate enough to go along with the whimsy of language, if that is what it takes to find a *new* new, one that frees us from repeating the past but *also* drives us to welcome the past and honor it with gratitude even as we say yes to what (we cannot possibly know) is to come.[22]

The peculiarity of *kainos*'s structure takes hold when we see letters written on a surface or we hear the articulation of a voice. What about the conceptual level? Were ancient Greeks aware they were saying *and* as they made their way through to *kainos*? I doubt it, but the key word here is *aware*. Whether written or spoken, language has subtle ways of shaping our minds and moving our emotions that neither writers nor readers can control. What I am proposing is this: let's play along with the game language plays with *kai* (unfortunately, this only works in Greek) and the move language makes on us with the phrase *kainē diathēkē* (New Testament). We ought to say no to Eusebius and his anti-Jewish understanding of *new* (but not no to the past in general!). And we ought to let *kainos* entice us to journeys whose ends we do not know, to borrow words from a prayer I have heard in church. Ends, I would add, we do not want to know, since if we ever were to know *the* end, if we ever were in a position to purchase the complete, we would forfeit the new.

Doing without Augustine

Back to reading the New Testament. I want to explore a famous reading of one of its most famous verses. It was Christmas in the North African town of Hippo. Augustine was the preacher. To no one's surprise, he based his sermon on "And the Word became flesh" (John 1:14). And predictably, he expounded the doctrine of the incarnation. What is noteworthy, however, is that in the middle of all his theological talk, Augustine embraced a theory of language that was quite philosophic. It was not, of course, the first time a Christian theologian ran to philosophy to avert disaster, nor would it be the last, but this time the preacher's intensity was remarkable, and reading the New Testament—indeed, the act of reading in cultures influenced by Christianity—has been marked by Augustine's fervent endorsement ever since.

The interpretive problem, for which an ancient philosophical understanding of language was the solution, was the word "became" in John 1:14. Augustine wants there to be no mistake. The divine Word took on flesh and did not actually become flesh:

> Let no-one, therefore, believe that the Son of God was changed or transformed into the Son of man; but rather let us believe that He, remaining the Son God, was made the Son of man, without loss of His divine substance and by a perfect *assumption* [my emphasis]

of the human substance. Nor do the words, *The Word was God* and, *The Word was made flesh*, signify that the Word was made flesh in such a way that It ceased to God.[23]

Augustine solved the confusion of human and divine natures in the way Christian writers before him had: he asserted the word "became" really meant "took on" or "assumed."[24] While no Greek words in John 1:14 justify "took on," this replacement for "became" had the theological advantage of protecting God's eternal nature from the finitude of flesh (*sarx*). Judging from the hundreds of times in the first thousand years biblical commentators have misquoted John 1:14 by substituting "took on" for "became," one might reasonably conclude these four words ("The Word became flesh") were more than a little frightening. What about them has so unsettled the experts? The problem was that the word "became" (*egeneto* in Greek) raised the impossible possibility that the Word, identified in John 1:1 as divine, crossed the border between the eternal and the temporal and became flesh—indeed, was transformed into flesh.[25] No wonder Augustine encouraged his listeners to think "take on" when they heard "became." To think otherwise invited a colossal theological disaster: God sullied beyond recognition by human flesh.

On this occasion, however, Augustine did not trust that the traditional strategy would protect his hearers from the danger of "became." He worried the usual trick of substituting "took on" for "became" might not prevent his listeners from wondering whether immortality had been infected by mortality in the Word's incarnation. Therefore, to protect the Word from the flesh, Augustine turned to a philosophic theory of the voice's relation to the mind's thoughts and applied it to the incarnate Word:

Take the word which we carry in our thoughts: it goes over into voice when we give expression to it by way of mouth; yet it is not transformed into voice, but, while the word is preserved entirely intact, the voice in which it finds expression is taken in addition to it. . . . Thus, when the word becomes voice, it is not changed into voice; but, remaining in the light of the mind, having assumed the voice bound to flesh, it goes forth to the one who hears it, and does not leave the one who thinks it. I am not referring to the word itself as thought of in silence—be that in Greek, in Latin, or in any other language; but to the thing itself which is to be said, in its state anterior to any differentiation by language, when in the chamber of the heart it in a way shows itself naked to the one whose intellect grasps it; and when it proceeds to go forth, it is clothed in the voice of the speaker.[26]

This passage is worth pondering. In it, Augustine binds both the Christian doctrine of the incarnation and the church's theory of reading to an ancient understanding of language that a growing number of readers of the New Testament in the twenty-first century wish to do without.[27] Especially problematic for postmodern interpreters is the part where the word bundles itself up in the voice, travels to the ear of another person, and is deposited safely in the listener's mind. And then, in Augustine's opinion, the best thing of all happens: the voice itself disappears, leaving the immaterial word intact and unsullied by the voice's materiality. The voice conveys the word to its intended destination but has no effect whatsoever on the word in the split second it takes for the word to get from the speaker's head through the exterior world to the hearer. As a recent scholar observes, "The uttered word is the vehicle that delivers to the outside the product or handiwork of internal reason."[28] The voice lets its passenger off and drives away into oblivion, no longer threatening to infect the word with the world through which it passes and by means of which it travels. The word arrives at its destination as pristine as it left the speaker's mind.[29] If we transfer this theory of language to the incarnation, as Augustine wanted his hearers to do, then Jesus's flesh is no longer required once believers have taken the divine Word into their hearts, since at that moment, the act of communication is complete. If refreshment is required for weaker minds, the church as an institution could just as easily take over the duty of transporting the Word.

In fact, the-flesh-that-Jesus-was, if it just hangs around with nothing to do but to live and die as all flesh does, would threaten the divinity of the Word.

Under no circumstances, according to Augustine and the vast majority of Christian theologians since, is it permitted to think that in becoming flesh, the Word was actually changed by its fleshly experience. It would be blasphemous to think that the incarnate Word experienced a split-second event (or perhaps many fracturing moments over a life cut short by Roman violence), the kind of event that once in California shook some of the certainty out of me and ultimately shakes it out of all of us who are born and die. Blasphemous or not, what if we were to think the thought Augustine didn't want his hearers to think? What happens when we dare think of John 1:14 with the literal sense of "became"?

My point is that the Christian tradition, with its habitual gloss of "assumed" flesh for "became" flesh, has gotten in the way of reading John 1:14. These words could have been a stunning moment in early Christian literature when *God* was thought otherwise than as another name for the immaterial, sovereign, controlling agent of the material world. But Augustine made sure it didn't happen; he linked incarnation to a dubious theory of language in such a way that to question the latter is to attack the former. In other words, he wrapped the incarnate Word up in a phonocentric theory of language that poststructuralist philosophers, literary theorists, and a growing number of New Testament interpreters have called into question. I will describe the nature and importance of phonocentrism at appropriate moments in the pages to follow.

So Then What Might Happen When We Read?

Perhaps the title of this book says too much. Anyone reading the New Testament in the twenty-first century already knows how to read, obviously. Yet this title not only entices browsers in bookstores or their digital counterparts with the (false) promise of a manual on how to read the New Testament but also, I hope, hints at another way of reading, a way that is unsteady and quite unsure of itself. It is a way of reading that does not secure itself by turning to the theory of language Augustine embraced to ensure the incarnation would not infect God. Perhaps it is not even a *way* at all.

Is there really something so special about the twenty-first century, it might be asked, that established ways of reading need to be challenged and new ones explored? I think so, but I want to tread carefully here lest I dismiss readers' experiences in the previous two millennia. I hope it becomes apparent in this book that I value the readings of the past even as I contest the insights of scholars, preachers, monks, nuns, skeptics, the devout, the disinterested, the keenly interested, and all the rest who have tried to make sense of the earliest Christian writings. I care what they thought, but more importantly, I honor that they were moved as they tried to make sense of what they were reading. So if the title of this book gives an *I know better than them* impression, then it definitely says too much. I don't *know* better.

And strange as it sounds, *not-knowing* is actually the point of this book. More than anything else, *not-knowing* is, I believe, the key to reading the New Testament today. As I will emphasize in the following chapters, there is more to the experience of reading than coming to know something or receiving information. The *more* I have in mind exists in the shock of encountering an "other" who (or which) eludes the reader's urge to assimilate them/it (remember *it?*) to an already known world, a familiar horizon, or the repeatability of language. What if reading the New Testament—reading anything, for that matter—meant giving an unexpected other a chance to take place and to change the world you thought was an unchangeable given? What if we thought of reading as a way of preparing for what postmodernism calls an *event*?

An *event* might loosely (and paradoxically) be defined as the incoming of an unimagined and unimaginable future that if it ever happened would not be an *event*.[30] By emphasizing reading's opening to otherness, to the event, however, I am not suggesting we should throw the historical-critical method out the window. The latter is the intellectual apparatus that has rescued the New Testament from proof-texting dogmaticians, and if an encounter with an "other" is to occur in the context of reading—and there is no guarantee that it will—it must do so in, with, and under the normal practices of reading. One such practice in the last one hundred years has been the historical-critical method. Indeed, the only way an unanticipated and unanticipatable event can occur is under the cover of what Jacques Derrida called a *habitual structure*. I take Derrida's phrase *habitual structure* to mean such things as eyes moving from left to right (in many but not all languages, of course); making sense of sentences, paragraphs, plots, argumentations; attending to the author's possible intention and the original audiences' possible reception (i.e., what sense they made of the writing); literary genre; historical and cultural contexts; and so on.[31] These are the topics of most introductions to the New Testament. They will not be ignored in this book, but the event that I am dreaming about (and strictly speaking, if I were *thinking* about it, it would not be an event) cannot be preprogrammed. That is to say, there is no method, practice, or habit to guarantee that an event will be experienced, or even to define what precisely might be experienced as an event.

Derrida challenged the assumption that writing is a communication technology and not much more. Something other than coming-to-know might happen when we read. The uncertain and mysterious "some" in "something" is crucial and, yes, maddening too. Not the familiar journey from printed word to referred-to-thing, such an event would be the coming-to-us of an indescribable feeling, the sense of an otherness beyond our knowing. This is not to say that words do not refer to objects *out there*, to people, ideas, institutions, or past, present, or future possible events. They certainly do, or it would make no sense to scribble *baking soda* and *peanut butter* on a scrap of paper before heading to the grocery store. Nevertheless, one of Derrida's points about language was that *reference* itself, both as a concept and as a practice that we cannot do without, is a bit of a bully. Why?

Because to refer is to objectify. It does not matter if the referred-to-things are people, places, ideas, rivers, languages, institutions, or past, present, or future events. Referred-to-things are captured, colonized, limited, and known-by-us-the-readers things. Derrida wanted to hope that referred-to-things were other than that, other than what his or our referring

held them to be, and indeed other than our imaginations could conceive
them to be. *Deconstruction* is one of his words for hoping for the advent
of the unimaginable even as we admit that words referring to things are
all we have to work with as we prepare ourselves to welcome the other.
Derrida writes,

> Certainly, deconstruction tries to show that the question of reference
> is much more complex and problematic than traditional theories sup-
> posed. It even asks whether our term "reference" is entirely adequate
> for designating the "other." The other, which is beyond language and
> which summons language, is perhaps not a "referent" in the normal
> sense which linguists have attached to this term. But to distance one-
> self thus from the habitual structure, to challenge or complicate our
> common assumptions about it, does not amount to saying that there
> is *nothing* beyond language.[32]

Caputo quotes this passage to defend Derrida from his (mis)interpreters
who think the philosopher eliminated reference entirely from words so that
freewheeling readers can say texts mean whatever they want them to mean.
Caputo writes, "[Derrida's] delimitation of reference is motivated not by
subjectivism or skepticism but by a kind of hypersensitivity to otherness,
by a profound sensitivity to the other of language and of the possibility
of something different, something 'impossible.'"[33] Two phrases stand out
for me in these two quotations. One is Derrida's "habitual structure," a
reference to the normal practice of reading from antiquity onward and
still with us today. The other is Caputo's phrase *hypersensitivity to otherness*,
which refers to Derrida's protest against reducing the other to an example
or instance of the same.

A great deal of attention in this book will be given to identifying the
assumptions we make as we read—and more importantly, the assumptions
different writers in the New Testament want their readers (including us)
to have. A good place to start spotting these assumptions is to consider the
Greek word for "read" (*anaginōskein*), a combination of "to know" (*ginōskein*)

and "again" (*ana*). This one word speaks volumes about the way ancient Greeks and the inheritors of their intellectual achievements thought about reading: we read expecting to know again what the writer had been thinking. Or, if it is a note we make for our own use, we read to know again what we had been thinking. Reading with the expectation of knowing again is one of the habitual structures that the *hypersensitivity to otherness* that Caputo detects in Derrida's writings challenges. Hypersensitivity cracks open the door of reading, perhaps only a bit, to an unknown and unknowable other.

Another assumption for both ancient Greek and contemporary English readers is that writing is a technology built on the platform of a phonetic alphabet.[34] I want to be clear: thinking of writing as a technology is not an erroneous idea. Quite the opposite. Writing is a marvelous technological achievement, for through it, the human voice can be transferred to letters and stored on a surface for later reactivation and listening. Writing allows authors to transfer their thoughts (or what they think they are thinking) from their heads into the letters on the pages. These thoughts are later retrieved by readers who, silently or aloud, pronounce the words formed by the letters they read.

Writing as a technology thus preserves the past.[35] It makes cultural traditions available to all who learn to read, as Eurydice of Hierapolis, Alexander the Great's grandmother, discovered to her joy when she took up education in the interest of supporting her children's studies. A portion of an inscription that she dedicated to the Muses attests to the technological power of writing: "And by her [Eurydice's] diligence attained to learn / Letters [*grammata*], wherein lies buried all our lore [*mnēmeia logōn*]."[36] Writing makes it possible for later readers at great distances of time and space and even after the death of the author and the demise of original readers to know again the author's thoughts. The ancient Greeks attributed this technology to nature's wisdom and not to their own: "Nature, loving the duties of friendship, invented instruments by which absent friends can converse, pens, paper, ink, handwriting, tokens of the heart that mourns afar off."[37]

In sum, the ancients did not have cell phones, but they did have pens and papyri. The invention of writing gave them the power to store thoughts, transport them, and resurrect them from dried ink to live once again in readers' minds and on their tongues. For the ancient Greeks and nearly everyone thinking about writing since, to read is to reconstitute words authors spoke to themselves before storing those thoughts for later retrieval. Writing allows us to know again what an author was thinking, to follow the reference lines that go from their mind to referred things. That is what happens when we read, or so it seems to us who have been enchanted by the *habitual structure* of reading.

I will return often to this ancient theory of reading, examining it from various perspectives and observing not only how it has shaped the practice of interpreting texts—including, of course, the reading of the New Testament—but also how it has shaped theology, morality, and politics. What is important to consider now, however, is that the idea of writing *only* as an information technology and reading *only* as hearing the author's voice to know again the author's thoughts were concepts challenged in the twentieth century by philosophers and literary critics who believed that something other than receiving information happens, or has a chance of happening, when we read. Something might happen in addition to, and perhaps at odds with, the transfer of thoughts and the production of meaning. Reading can open us to something that we had never planned to think, feel, or imagine. Without warning, literature shakes us, sets us to trembling, surprises, haunts, shocks, and renders us speechless.[38] We are moved by something—we cannot quite put a finger on what—that hitches a ride with the words we read but refuses to be named by them. Reading a text in a language that one has known for decades is like gazing on the face of a loved one and suddenly realizing that you know nothing of how they *feel* the world, how it is for this other whose face you have supposedly learned to read to be a body-mind in that particular spot that is them and at that particular moment that is their life. And you never can know, no matter how carefully you read her face or listen to his voice, since in order to know the other, to know their experience as *they* experience it, you would have to occupy them, replace them with yourself. To know them fully, you would have to *be* them, and that would be a kind of murder. Thus this uncrossable gap between you and the other resists you even as it beckons you, summons you, to make your way across.[39]

Similarly, when you read a writer's words, you rejoice that a world comes into being just from ink on a page. You share the ancient Greeks' amazement and gratitude over writing, although awe might turn into shock and then perhaps even terror. This world, which comes into being by written signs containing the author's thoughts, begins to withdraw. It begins to hide itself. You realize that all the *things* writing refers to outside the text are actually other *words*.[40] Choose any word you want and look it up in a dictionary. What will you find? The thing itself? Obviously not. You will find more words, and if you track them down in other entries in the dictionary, you still will not find the things as they are in themselves, only more words. With words pointing to other words pointing to still more words, an infinite otherness stretches out before you that occupies no space and endures in no time, worlds/words without end to which reading, the kind of reading I have in mind that is not simply the decoding and the retrieval of what once might have been thought, says a faltering *Amen*. There's no use pretending that when we read, we are guaranteed untroubled passage to the author's mind without a wind blowing in from only God knows where to take us off to only God knows where (and what does *God* refer to anyway?). What I am saying is this: reading cannot be, must not be, reduced to knowing again the author's thoughts you are able to retrieve from writing, marvelous though that retrieval is.

The semicrazed rhetoric of the previous paragraph hints at the reason most introductory books to the New Testament avoid poststructuralism or deconstruction—two names for trying, *really trying*, to think what is impossible to be thought, to read expecting and hoping to have one's world shaken by the otherness that haunts everything familiar. Broadly speaking, introductions to the New Testament respond to their readers' desire to enter the New Testament and to take meaningful insights or useful applications from it. They honor readers and the questions they bring, like the person struggling with addiction who asks, *How might I get my life back?* or the church leader who asks, *How might I guide the lives of others?* or the individual or community puzzled over vocational goals wondering, *What is God's intention for me (us)?* I do not wish to dishonor these questions. Nevertheless, the issue I struggle with is that we have inherited a mindset that says *usefulness* is the touchstone of truth and meaning and the primary reason for reading. Yet the reduction of a text to its usefulness is one more example of the *habitual structure* that a deconstructive approach seeks to avoid, a structure in which practicality enjoys a privilege over mystery, knowing wins out over not-knowing, and control triumphs over hope.[41] My goal in what follows is to give mystery, not-knowing, and hope a chance.

CHAPTER 1

Masters of (Not Caputo's) Hermeneutics

THE AMERICAN PHILOSOPHER John D. Caputo and Plato, his ancient Greek counterpart, agree on one thing: giving oneself to uncertainty is dangerous, madness even. For his part, Caputo hopes readers will take the risk. His interpretation of interpretation, which is what he thinks hermeneutics is, does not chart a path around perplexity.[1] Rather, to read—not only texts but also life itself—is to move into the flux of experience by preparing with all the tools of reason for that which reason cannot prepare us for, an unprogrammed future.[2] When we are faithful to the other of language (remember *it?*), we read (and write too) without knowing beforehand where words might take us, and we say yes, with all the foreboding of no, to a future that when it arrives, if it ever arrives, will have come as an absolute surprise.[3]

Plato, however, would have condemned Caputo's hermeneutics as a disaster, a charge to which Caputo offers no defense. Such openness to the unknowable destroys the path to certainty that in Plato's thinking is the interpreter's job to disclose. Speaking through the figure of Socrates, Plato demanded that teachers know what they are talking about before they instruct others. Instruction that does not proceed from knowledge is dangerous. The learner's safety is at stake:

> However when I'm not confident and at the same time I'm trying to find the right way to express myself, as indeed I am right now, it is nerve-racking and tricky [*sphaleron*], not in fear of being thought

of as ridiculous, for that really is childish; but afraid of being misled [*sphaleis*] in the truth not only myself, but also, having dragged my friends down with me, I shall find myself in a position which is the last place in which one ought to be deceived [*sphallesthai*]. . . . You see, I really do suppose it a lesser misdemeanor to become the involuntary murderer of someone than to lead people astray about principles of what is fine and good and just.[4]

I begin this chapter with Socrates's (Plato's) concern for the learner's certainty (*asphaleia*) because it reappeared in the preface to the Gospel of Luke (1:1–4) and went on to define the act of reading among Christians ever since. Peppered with terms found in other prefaces of the time and composed of clauses elegantly arranged with the most important word reserved for the end, the opening four verses of Luke–Acts present a knowledgeable "I" guiding an uncertain "you," Theophilus, into certainty (*asphaleia*), here misleadingly translated by the NRSV as "truth":

Since many have undertaken to set down an orderly account of the events that have been fulfilled among us, just as they were handed on to us by those who from the beginning were eyewitnesses and servants of the word, I too decided, after investigating everything carefully from the very first, to write an orderly account for you, most excellent Theophilus, so that you may know the truth [*asphaleia*; or, better, "certainty" or "safety"] concerning the things about which you have been instructed. (Luke 1:1–4)[5]

This sentence did not disappoint first-century Christian readers aspiring to rhetorical display, since it compliments them for *paideia*, the education that enabled them to follow artfully spun-out words and subtle literary allusions. Here is one example of the pat on the reader's back the preface extends; that word that so concerned Socrates, "safety" (*asphaleia*), arrives on the page in the periodic style of the classical age just at the right time (in Greek word order only) to conclude both the sentence and the thought.

Indeed, *asphaleia* is the central thought, not only of the preface but also of Luke–Acts itself. The root *sphal* signifies slipping, stumbling, tripping up, falling, or being overthrown.[6] With the alpha privative in place (the Greek letter *a* means "not"), *asphaleia* means certainty, security, and assurance of safety. The author of Luke–Acts knew how to get to safety, how to get there in style, and how to get others there too. Most excellent Theophilus was in good hands.

The Author of Luke–Acts as a Master of Hermeneutics

It is difficult to believe that Theophilus alone is the intended audience. In fact, observing that the name *Theophilus* is made up of *theos* (God) and *philos* (friend), Origen of Alexandria (ca. 184–234 CE) argues the name refers to all believers, since by religious right, they can confidently claim the title *friend of God.*[7] Like Origen, I proceed in this chapter under the assumption that the name Theophilus represents a group of persons rather than an individual, although to avoid pedantry, I frequently yield to the author's fiction of a real live Theophilus. In any case, even though it appears that I am repeating Origen's opinion about a broad readership, there is a difference. I add to his speculation some reflections on social standing and the production of literature in ancient society. In the first century, wealthy patrons supported authors, who returned the favor by mentioning the names of their sponsors in the opening pages of their works. The name Theophilus, I propose, represents elite Christian converts in a position to sponsor literature; in this case, the patron-supported writing is the two-volume history of Jesus's words and deeds (the Gospel of Luke) and the expansion of the church (Acts).

I do not know if there ever was a Theophilus. I suspect not. But Luke 1:1–4 encouraged readers (and still does if you think of yourself as a member of the patronal class and share its anxieties) to put themselves into Theophilus's fictive shoes and thus be guided by the author along the path to certainty. Nor do I think friendship with God defined the spiritual or emotional condition of the readers represented by the name Theophilus. What did? Scholars of Luke–Acts have discovered cultural and intellectual forces that shaped the lives of elite converts to the Way in the late first century.[8] If we wish to understand the theory of reading promoted by Luke–Acts, we must appreciate these pressures, which might be summed up as a demand for converts to display facility in classical Greek education and culture—in a word, *paideia*. I will discuss this demand below.

In this chapter, I propose that the author of Luke–Acts commended to converts of Theophilus's social standing a way of interpretation, a hermeneutics, based on divine providence. Only the thought of an orderly universe could keep them safe from the criticism aimed at them by the cultured despisers of Christianity. In Luke–Acts, certitude is the goal of reading. This is not surprising, since in the first century, certainty was a hot topic everywhere Rome's imperial power was felt. Competition for recognition and favors from powerful officials consumed the daily lives of elite males and made them uncertain of themselves and of their public self-presentations. For example, consider the young men aspiring to positions of political leadership. In Rome, the Stoic philosopher Epictetus taught philosophy to them so that they might stabilize their lives. He did so until the emperor Domitian (ruled 81–96 CE) banished him to Nicopolis, where again he took on students, some of whom would go on to become officials in the imperial government. First, however, they had to learn how to control their emotions and present themselves as confident and well educated. The point of the comparison is this: Epictetus demonstrated a concern for their *asphaleia* just as the author of Luke–Acts was committed to supplying a solid foundation for Theophilus. Epictetus was the more severe of the two, however, since he was not above ridiculing his students for their weak grasp of philosophy:

Why, then, are they [laypeople] stronger than you are? Because their rotten talk is based on judgements, but your fine talk comes merely from your lips; that's why what you say is languid and dead, and why a man may well feel nausea when he hears your exhortations and your miserable "virtue," which you babble to and fro. . . . Therefore, until these fine ideas of yours are firmly fixed within you, and you have acquired some power which will guarantee you security [*asphaleian*] my advice to you is to be cautious about joining issue with the laymen; otherwise, whatever you write down in the lecture-room will melt away by day like wax in the sun.[9]

Although he approaches his student more tactfully than Epictetus did, the author of Luke–Acts leaves little doubt that Theophilus is not yet where he needs to be to stay sane and safe in the competitive social world of the Roman Empire. Theophilus is told he does not yet know what he needs to know in the way that he needs to know it. Like Epictetus's students, who apparently were easily talked out of their philosophic convictions, Theophilus is not yet safe. Where there is no divine plan, there will be no safety.

This is not to say Theophilus is ignorant of literature and philosophy. Quite the opposite. Nevertheless, as I will discuss at the end of this chapter, there was great social pressure on individuals in the first century to be perceived as educated and to speak well in public, especially before influential superiors. This pressure fueled anxiety and, in the opinion of the leading medical experts of the day, led to madness. The demand for *paideia* explains why allusions to classical and Hellenistic literature and philosophy circulate throughout Luke–Acts, complimenting readers for the sophistication. I will point out these allusions as we make our way through Luke and Acts, but one of them, Acts 26:14, testifies to the desire of first-century elites in the Roman Empire to show off their *paideia*.[10] This verse occurs in the last of three accounts of Paul's conversion (Acts 9:1–19; 22:1–22; 26:1–23), each episode an example of another ancient literary device, the dream/vision report.[11] Paul (i.e., the author's version of Paul) is on his way to Damascus to persecute the church. A bright light stops him in his tracks, and he hears an authoritative voice: "When we had all fallen to the ground, I heard a voice saying to me in the Hebrew language, 'Saul, Saul, why are you persecuting me?'" (Acts 26:14). It is Jesus who speaks, and he repeats a saying familiar to literary-minded, first-century readers: "It is hard for you to kick against the goads" (26:14 NIV). Pindar or Aeschylus might have been the source, but more likely, the saying came from *The Bacchae* (794–95), a late fifth-century BCE play written by Euripides.[12] The saying refers to the personal disaster of opposing the predestining will of God. It brings to mind a horse's futile resistance to the will of its rider (divine necessity) and the wound the rider's spurs inflict on the recalcitrant beast. In the fourth century, the Roman emperor Julian imagines what the Greek general Pericles would have said about the proper response to necessity:

> The whole world is my city and fatherland, and my friends are the gods and lesser divinities and all good men whoever and wherever they may be. Yet it is right to respect also the country where I was born, since this is the divine law, and to obey all her commands and not oppose them, or as the proverb says kick against the pricks [*pros kentra laktizein*]. For inexorable, as the saying goes, is the yoke of necessity. But we must not even complain or lament when her commands are harsher than usual, but rather consider the matter as it actually is.[13]

The irrationality of opposing the divine will was a core teaching of the Stoic philosophers.[14] Thus with a literary flourish, Acts 26:14 touches upon a philosophic dogma about divine providence well known to educated readers, and it does so in service of Luke–Acts' overall purpose: to demonstrate to Theophilus that Jesus's deeds, his suffering, and the growth of the early Christian movement were neither random nor insignificant events but the fulfillment of God's plan in history.

The point of this detour through the writings of Euripides, Julian, and the Stoics is this: Theophilus (i.e., the figure the author constructs to address elite converts) knew ancient literature, perhaps better than any of us ever will.[15] For this reason, then, we should take special note of a faintly condescending word in the preface: "instructed" (*katēchēthēs*). It hints at a gap in Theophilus's education in matters pertaining to the life of Jesus.[16] Instructional outcomes in the churches of the first century are not well known, and it would be anachronistic to assume they were the same as the educational goals of the third and fourth centuries. Whatever catechesis there was early on, however, it is doubtful that it consisted of advanced study.[17] At the time of the composition of Luke–Acts, instruction may only have been the teaching of basic facts, the *pragmata* (events) that the author mentions in Luke 1:1. We cannot know for certain, but in the first century, catechesis does not seem to have taken up the *why* question. If this was the case, then Theophilus was not yet an interpreter of facts, and this deficiency would have existed in spite of his familiarity with classical literature and philosophic commonplaces. Lacking a theory to tie together the facts and give them a unified meaning, he was not prepared to answer the Way's critics or silence his own misgivings. He needed an intellectual structure to supply him with the certainty of a rational explanation.

What a learner like Theophilus still needed to know was the meaning of events furnished by a *competent historian*. That presumptuous phrase is the self-description of an ancient historian, Dionysius of Halicarnassus (ca. 60 BCE to sometime after 7 CE), who organized the history of Rome from a god's-eye view.[18] We will return to Dionysius in a moment, but first, Theophilus's lack of hermeneutical grounding must be examined further. We can appreciate Theophilus's predicament better if we look closely at Apollos in Acts 18:24–26, who, in spite of his considerable learning and eloquence, also comes up short. Although "instructed [*katēchēmenos*] in the Way of the Lord," Apollos does not frame his instruction in "the things concerning Jesus" accurately enough (v. 25). Theophilus and Apollos have much in common. Both are followers of Jesus at the catechetical level. Both possess only the bare events of Jesus's life. Both lack the superstructure that gives meaning and certainty to the facts they have in hand. The narrative voice does indeed praise Apollos for teaching "the things concerning Jesus." This phrase refers to a list of the facts about Jesus that his followers should know.[19] Uninterpreted occurrences ("the things"), however, do not guarantee certitude. The events of Jesus's career culminating in his resurrection lack the power to show the divine will working in and through them. To

be catechized, then, is to have received instruction about historical occurrences and to be able to answer the *who, where,* and *when* questions, but
the hermeneutics of Luke–Acts concerns itself with the all-important *why*
question.[20] To read for safety, Theophilus needed an expert who knew
why events occur. As for Apollos, at the end of this chapter, we will revisit
his situation.

The reading theory of Luke–Acts was a response to a crisis in the
early Christian movement. Late in the first century, influential Romans
and Greeks began to take notice of Christian converts. Clear on what
constituted a legitimate religion in the Roman Empire, these observers
thought the followers of Jesus were not making the grade. No longer were
the Christians regarded as Jews. This change is important because Greek
and Roman intellectuals respected the Jews for their rational, imageless
worship; possession of an ancient book; moral seriousness; geographical
center (Jerusalem); and long national history. Without the cover of Judaism's reputation as a legitimate religion, early Christians were perceived
as uneducated persons of a low social class whose beliefs and practices had
no public importance and lacked a foundation in reason.[21]

To correct this impression, and to give Theophilus the confidence
that presumably comes from knowing God's will, the author of Luke–
Acts turned to the Stoic doctrine of divine providence to tell the story of
Jesus and the church. What is the evidence of Stoic influence on the author's
theology? For one thing, the word *dei* (it is necessary) occurs forty-two times
in Luke–Acts; the phrase "plan of God" occurs seven times.[22] These two
features in themselves are telling, and I will introduce more evidence for
Stoic influence in the following pages. For now, my point is this: the author
of Luke–Acts was not interested in listing events—even tragic events, like
the death of Jesus, or amazing ones, like a resurrection—unless these events
were interpreted as signs of an overarching divine intention. Everything
happens for a purpose, and the historian's task is to gather the facts and
present them to readers under the guiding thought that everything happens
for a reason. That is why the author does not allow events just to be events.

They are events "that have been fulfilled" (Luke 1:1). Events do not just happen. They are the realizations of divine intent.[23]

Other ancient historians also introduced their writings by referring to divine providence. For example, Dionysius of Halicarnassus wrote in order to reduce his fellow Greeks' resentment over Rome's rise as the world's leading power.[24] He criticized earlier attempts at writing the history of Rome and complained of the mere retelling of events (*pragmata*), much as the author of Luke–Acts obliquely criticizes the Gospel of Mark (among other unspecified narratives) with the phrase "since many have undertaken" (Luke 1:1).[25] Any chronicler can record what happened, Dionysius notes, but it requires a *competent historian* to say why it happened. He attributes Rome's rise to the virtues of its people and to Fortune's gift:

> So far as I am able, I shall omit nothing worthy of being recorded in history, to the end that I may instill in the minds of those who shall then be informed of the truth the fitting conception of this city,—unless they have already assumed an utterly violent and hostile attitude toward it,—and also that they may neither feel indignation at their present subjection, which is grounded on reason (for by an universal law of Nature, which time cannot destroy, it is ordained that superiors shall ever govern their inferiors), nor rail at Fortune for having wantonly bestowed upon an undeserving city a supremacy so great and already of so long continuance, particularly when they shall have learned from my history that Rome from the very beginning, immediately after its founding, produced infinite examples of virtue in men whose superiors, whether for piety or for justice or for life-long self-control or for warlike valour, no city, either Greek or barbarian, has ever produced. . . . And it is a fact that all those Romans who bestowed upon their country so great a dominion are unknown to the Greeks for want of a competent historian. For no accurate history of the Romans written in the Greek language has hitherto appeared, but only very brief and summary epitomes.[26]

Just as Dionysius's appeal to *reason* softened the hard feelings of Greek readers, the author of Luke–Acts moves Theophilus away from learning about mere events to a more accurate knowledge of the same events gathered under the plan of God by a competent historian—that is, a master of hermeneutics.[27]

We still live in the age of hermeneutics inaugurated by Luke–Acts along with Dionysius's history of Rome and other ancient writings. It is an age in which we read to discover meaning, and meaning is equated with the certainty that comes from knowing the connectedness of any particular fact to the overarching system in which that fact occurs and makes its occurrence necessary. In other words, we have grown accustomed to an ancient tradition of reading that finds safety in the idea of divine programming in history.[28]

Philip the Guide

A brief episode in Acts illustrates hermeneutics as a path to safety. In Acts 8:26–40, we read about Philip's encounter with an Ethiopian court official. Having made a trip to Jerusalem, the official turns the chariot around and heads back home. Philip overhears the official reading a text from Isaiah and asks the question that would define Christian hermeneutics in the coming centuries: "Do you understand what you are reading?" (v. 30). To which the official responds, "How can I, unless someone guides me?" (v. 31). The verb "guide" (*hodēgeō*) ought to catch our attention because it captures what in the West so many interpreters, both inside and outside the Christian church, think it means to interpret a text. *Hodēgeō* contains the noun *hodos* (way, road, and path). To guide is to lead the reader along a path to the author's intention.

Now, why is it so important to dwell on this word "guide," which the author of Luke–Acts places on the lips of the Ethiopian eunuch? As I said, the guide's job is to get the traveler (or the reader) from the beginning of the journey (the written words) to the end (the writer's intended meanings). The story illustrates the necessity of having a master of hermeneutics at one's side, an expert who knows and shows the way:

Now the passage of the scripture that he was reading was this:

> "Like a sheep he was led to the slaughter,
>   and like a lamb silent before its shearer,
>   so he does not open his mouth.
>   In his humiliation justice was denied him.
>   Who can describe his generation?
>   For his life is taken away from the earth."

The eunuch asked Philip, "About whom, may I ask you, does the prophet say this, about himself or about someone else?" Then Philip began to speak, and starting with this scripture, he proclaimed to him the good news about Jesus. (Acts 8:32–35)

The court official does everything right yet gets nowhere. He works through the text from beginning to end. He asks a question about the text's reference. And most of all, he presumes the phonocentric theory of reading: that the text is an object open before him, with the author's voice encoded in the phonetic letters that bring the author's original ideas to life as he reads aloud in the chariot. But this story shows that reading Scripture, even when well read, might fail to reveal the author's intention. The story shows that experts are required. They are the Christian guides, the masters of hermeneutics, the members of a society who know the origin and the end of a text's intentions and are able to lead others on the path to knowledge and certainty. Philip is a founding member of this society.

The Paul of Acts

Yet Philip's reputation pales in comparison to that of Paul—that is, the Paul whom the author of Luke–Acts invented. A word about the circumstances of this invention. After his death, Paul's name was detached from the corpus of his undisputed writings and reattached to letters and narrative accounts promoting theologies of power and control. This is a great irony.

The weak apostle, who wanted to know nothing but Christ crucified (1 Cor 1:23; 2:2), was resurrected in the book of Acts as an advocate of divine providence. This transformation takes center stage in Acts 13–28, after Paul's brief appearance at the stoning of Stephen in 7:58. Just as he uses the figure of Jesus in the Gospel of Luke, in Acts, the author uses the figure of Paul to promote his hermeneutical program of reading for certainty.

Two passages showcase Luke's Paul as an expert practitioner of hermeneutics: Acts 14:8–18 and 17:16–34. Here is a point well worth noting: both passages display Paul's interpretive expertise at the expense of the religion of others. Lukan hermeneutics has a competitive spirit about it and takes advantage of the power of ridicule. That is the thing about certainty; to have it, one needs to undercut rival claims to knowledge. Not having the truth in its entirety, not having "the definite plan and foreknowledge of God" (Acts 2:23), puts Theophilus's possession of truth at risk.

In the first passage, the author pokes fun at the gullible residents of Lystra when they mistake Paul and Barnabas for gods. This strategy of ridicule repeats itself in the rest of Acts, where it is "the crowd" or "the mob" that speaks for the religion of others, with the implication that only elites have access to true religion. The rabble is stuck with the beliefs of its own infantile and confused imaginings. There in Lystra, after Paul had healed a lame man, the crowd "shouted in the Lycaonian language, 'The gods have come down to us in human form!' Barnabas they called Zeus, and Paul they called Hermes, because he was the chief speaker [*ho hēgoumenos tou logou*; literally, 'the one who leads out the word']" (14:11–12).[29] In the crowd's mind, Paul is Hermes, the messenger god of the Greek divinities. Of all the immortals to mistake Paul for, why confuse him with Hermes? What sense does this ludicrous error make in the author's overall presentation of Paul in Luke–Acts? Some background on Hermes is useful in answering this question.

First, Greek myth suggests a link between Hermes and the act of literary interpretation, which was conceptualized as leading meaning out of texts.[30] Indeed, Hermes is why interpretation was named "hermeneutics" in the first place, although the god's reputation for deception, illustrated by his secretive leading out of Apollo's prized cattle from their safe confinement, complicates his reputation as the straightforward conveyer of divine intentions.[31] Thus Hermes "leads out" in two contrasting ways: (1) as an exegete, he draws out and delivers meaning from texts; (2) as a trickster, he deceitfully misappropriates property that the owner thought was safe. The way the episode unfolds has the simpletons of Lystra unwittingly draw attention to Paul as a master of hermeneutics when they call him Hermes, although conceivably, the joke may have been on the author. Who can say that the residents of Lystra were not thinking of Hermes and those stolen cows when they worshipped Paul? In any case, the NRSV's translation "chief speaker" does not say what the Greek *ho hēgoumenos tou logou* does, which ought to be translated as "he who leads [or guides] out the word." The author of Luke–Acts wants readers to know that even though he was not a god, Paul nevertheless shares in Hermes's reputation as a powerful *leader of the word*.[32] Paul guides thoughts as they make their way from the divine mind to the human mind.

This story ends with a preview of Paul's Areopagus speech in Acts 17, which, as we will see below, is the most sophisticated derision of others' religious beliefs in the book of Acts. Here in Lystra, however, Paul merely calls the objects of the inhabitants' worship "worthless" and starts down the road of hermeneutics as the science of proving Christianity's exclusive claim to the knowledge of God:

> Friends, why are you doing this? We too are only human, like you. We are bringing you good news, telling you to turn from these worthless things to the living God, who made the heavens and the earth and the sea and everything in them. In the past, he let all nations go their own way. Yet he has not left himself without testimony: He has shown kindness by giving you rain from heaven and crops in their seasons; he provides you with plenty of food and fills your hearts with joy. (Acts 14:15–17 NIV)

This is a condensed version of what Paul will say to the Athenians in Acts 17:16–34. The basic argument of both speeches goes like this: God once permitted the diverse peoples on earth to organize their lives in "their own way [*hodos*]."[33] Those days are over. Now the only valid *hodos* is the one Paul proclaims, appropriately named *the Way* (see Acts 9:2; 16:17; 18:25–26; 19:9, 23; 22:4; 24:14, 22). *The Way* is the only way. How does Paul know this? As a master of hermeneutics, he sees that the natural world is itself legible. Creation is readable and reveals the author's intent.[34] For a competent reader like Paul, nature is an open book. The author of Luke–Acts suggests to Theophilus (and to readers whom he represents) that if he were to read the book of nature with care, observing the unchanging patterns ("in their seasons") of creation, and if he were grateful for the divine benefactor's gifts ("rain from heaven and crops" and "plenty of food"), he could move from the text (i.e., the cosmos) to the author's/creator's mind. That would be a religion the most excellent Theophilus could be proud of, since despite the author's claim that Christianity is the only way, this new religion nevertheless reproduces many of the monotheistic beliefs of the intellectual class in the first century, most notably the belief in divine providence.

Not long after the Lystra affair and without time to prepare a speech—an extemporaneous performance of this kind only added to the apostle's aura of divine inspiration—Paul entered Athens and embellished what he had said in Lystra when his uncritical hearers mistook him for Hermes: "While Paul was waiting for them [his associates] in Athens, he was deeply distressed to see that the city was full of idols" (Acts 17:16). Paul does not go looking for a fight, but he ends up blasting Greek religions—indeed, any religion that does not have a single agent as the origin of the cosmos, its administrator, and its perfecter.[35] The translation "deeply distressed" does not convey as clearly as the Greek word (*parōxyneto*) the irritation that moved Paul to speak. Theophilus likely swelled with pride, as the spokesperson of the Way at the Areopagus reduces the ideas of philosophers (only Epicurean views, actually, since Stoic doctrine forms the speech's backbone) and the beliefs of laypeople alike to rubble. If this does not sound like the Paul of Romans 15:1–6, who begs his readers to bear the weaknesses of others, or

the Paul of Romans 1:14, who describes himself as a debtor to the foolish
and to the wise, it is because the Paul of Luke–Acts is the creation of the
author. The author inserts this Paul into Acts for a rhetorical purpose, to
make Theophilus's knowledge safe.[36]

Paul joins in dialogue first with Jews and then with Stoics and Epicureans; incidentally, this is the only time in the New Testament these
two famous philosophical schools are mentioned by name: "So he argued
[*dielegeto*] in the synagogue with the Jews and the devout persons, and also
in the marketplace every day with those who happened to be there.
Also some Epicurean and Stoic philosophers debated [*syneballon*] with him"
(Acts 17:17–18). The translation "argued" is too strong; *dialegein* meant
"to discuss" or "to arrive at conclusions by discussion."[37] The second term
for discourse, *symballein* (see Luke 2:19), had a range of meanings that could
accommodate debate and tilted toward a competitive effort: literally, to
"throw together" opinions.[38] So far, then, it looks like Paul is, by ancient
standards, playing nice.

That changed, however, when a particularly humiliating insult is thrown
Paul's way, all the more stinging because it is spoken with Attic elegance
and hints at the Christian reputation in the late first century for ineptitude
in matters of philosophy. In other words, although ostensibly aimed at
Paul, this insult reflects the criticism of Christians discussed at the beginning of this chapter as an uneducated mob lacking a rational foundation
for their way of life: "Some said, 'What does this babbler want to say?'"
(Acts 17:18). Rather than "babbler," as the NRSV has translated, they
call Paul a "seed picker" (*spermologos*; YLT), a small bird seen often in the
Athenian marketplace picking up crumbs and other fragments.[39] As human
seed pickers, followers of the Way had no knowledge of what they were
talking about; like little birds flitting about, they carried pieces of this and
that in their mouths but had no overarching theory or metanarrative to
ground their beliefs.

Before Paul has a chance to answer a charge that threatened to put
Theophilus to shame if it could be made to stick, the author of Luke–Acts takes
control of the situation. First, he puts a remark on the lips of the Athenians

that betrays their ignorance of world events; next, in a rare move, the narrator's voice breaks into the narrative to emphasize the crowd's ignorance:

> "He seems to be a proclaimer of foreign divinities" (This was because he was telling the good news about Jesus and the resurrection.) So they took him and brought him to the Areopagus and asked him, "May we know what this new teaching is that you are presenting? It sounds rather strange to us, so we would like to know what it means."
> (Acts 17:18–20)

Then in a second remarkable aside directed to the reader of Luke–Acts, whether Theophilus or any other reader over the centuries, the narrator makes a snide remark of his own: "Now all the Athenians and the foreigners living there would spend their time in nothing but telling or hearing something new" (17:21). The openness of the Athenians to something new in religion might have pleased the Paul of the undisputed letters. Indeed, this Athenian curiosity ought to be a model for any reader of the *New* Testament in the twenty-first century, especially in the United States and Europe, where xenophobia and violence in the name of religion are daily realities. But with this remark about the "new," the author of Luke–Acts is not complimenting the Athenians.[40] In verse 18, he explains that the Athenians foolishly thought "Jesus" and "resurrection" were names for a male god (Jesus) and his female consort (Anastasis). The latter is the Greek word for "resurrection." The author thus increases Theophilus's certitude with respect to his own religion by demeaning others; that is, the Athenians are represented as so dim-witted to believe Paul proclaims a new divine couple arising from the East, like Isis and Osiris.[41] Then the author tells the reader what the Athenians' real problem is: they have an insatiable desire for whatever is new (a puzzling criticism when we consider the title of the book—the New Testament—that would eventually house Luke–Acts).[42]

The Athenians then whisk Paul off to the Areopagus, the traditional site of rendering justice in ancient Athens. Paul begins his speech with a compliment, or so it appears. Hidden within his praise of the Athenians, however, is an insult: "Then Paul stood in front of the Areopagus and said, 'Athenians, I see how extremely religious [*deisidaimonesterous*] you are in every way'" (Acts 17:22). The word *deisidaimonesteros* also meant "superstitious"; it pointed to fear of the gods—excessive, paranoiac fear.[43] So which of the two did Paul mean: religion or superstition? That is likely the wrong question, since *Paul* is the literary construction of the author and as such had no intended meanings. A better question is, How does the ambivalence built into *deisidaimonesteros* suit the author's rhetorical strategy?[44] I believe the author wrote in a way that Theophilus might hear Paul, the spokesperson for the Way, outshine the Athenians in the matter of witty insults. Indeed, Paul, a master of hermeneutics (and if it were not for Jesus, Paul in Acts would be *the* master—unless of course one counts the author), is just getting started with clever and insulting wordplay.

The author of Luke–Acts goes on to show Theophilus that he can trust Paul to denigrate Greek religious beliefs and bolster Christianity's exclusive claim to truth. Paul first quotes Stoic theology to his audience. Then he plays his trump card, the resurrection of Jesus from the dead. We consider Paul's allusion to Stoic theology first.[45]

If ancient readers were to have stumbled across a scrap of papyrus with Acts 17:24–29 written on it, and nothing else, they might have thought they were reading a Stoic text dealing with the nature of God.[46] This is especially true of verses 24–29, where Paul's polemic against idolatry reproduces the contemporary philosophic critique of the gods. That critique boils down to this: popular conceptions of divinity fail to measure up to the supreme god's impassibility, unity, and monarchical rule.[47] Like the deity of the Stoics, the God of Acts 17:24–27 created the cosmos, organized it spatially and temporally, and needs nothing from it but permeates the space in which everything lives and moves, and it is from God that humans originated.[48] All of this is basic Stoic teaching. Nevertheless, the point of Paul's philosophical fireworks is not to dazzle the crowd with his knowledge of Stoic doctrine; rather, Paul proves the main charge against Christianity—that it lacks an intellectual superstructure—is mistaken. Thus in Acts 17:24–27, Paul once again shows himself to be a master at hermeneutics. He has not read the famous Stoics: Zeno, Chrysippus, Posidonius, or Cleanthes. He has no need to. He reads nature itself, and he reads it as if it were a book. The intention of the divine author is as plain as the regularity of the seasons: God desires the Athenians, and the rest of humanity to repent their idolatry.

Yet reading the book of nature at the Areopagus—that is, reasoning back (or, better, "up") from organized social and physical structures and temporal regularities to the one Creator, Organizer, and Regulator of the universe—is not enough to make the case for belief in Jesus. Standing there in the crowd listening to Paul but unconvinced are the Stoics, living proof that something more than the legibility of nature is required to bring persons to the one true religion. Never having heard of Jesus, their school of philosophy had been reasoning its way to the divine monarch (Zeus, Nature, Father, Fate, etc.) for hundreds of years. Paul only repeats the Stoic theo-logic. It was time, therefore, for the Paul of Acts to play his trump card—the resurrection of Jesus, which, as we will see below, has no special explanatory power, according to Luke 24. But here it does: "In the past God overlooked such ignorance, but now he commands all people everywhere to repent. For he has set a day when he will judge the world with justice by the man he has appointed. He has given proof [*pistin*] of this to everyone by raising him from the dead" (Acts 17:30–31 NIV). It is one of the great ironies in the history of Christianity that the word *pistis*, which here is appropriately translated as "proof," in other contexts also is translated as "faith," as in the famous Pauline phrase "For we walk by faith [*pisteōs*], not by sight" (2 Cor 5:7). For the Paul of the genuine Epistles, faith and hope, love, justice, gift, and messiah are what they are by their always-yet-to-come structures—that is, each is an event in Caputo's and Derrida's sense of the term. That is why sight removes the possibility of faith. That is why "hope that is seen is not hope" (Rom 8:24). That is why "love worketh no ill to her/his neighbor," as the KJV so beautifully states (Rom 13:10; translation modified). Yet for the Paul of the Areopagus speech, whom the author of Luke–Acts fabricated for Theophilus's certainty, *pistis* means no longer "faith" but "proof." And master of hermeneutics that he is, Luke's Paul reads the resuscitation of Jesus's dead body as proof of God's plan to appoint him judge of the world. The future has already been determined: a man once dead but now alive proves that all other religious beliefs except Stoic understandings of divine providence will fall under the condemnation of God's reanimated representative.

Conclusion: Madness and Hermeneutics in Luke 24

Turn for a moment to Mark 16:8, which many scholars are convinced is that Gospel's final verse. Silence, fear, and madness end the story: "So they went out and fled from the tomb, for terror [*tromos*, 'trembling'] and amazement [*ekstasis*, 'displacement of the mind'] had seized them; and they said nothing to anyone, for they were afraid."[49] The author of Luke–Acts did not tolerate the open-endedness and ambiguity of this ending. Luke 24 is a rewrite of Mark 16 promoting the doctrine of divine providence. Luke's Jesus returns from the dead to a scene of profound uncertainty and, with the help of two men dressed in white, explains how to read the Bible (Luke 24:6–7, 25–27, 44–47). Speaking rationally (I will return to this phrase below), Jesus and the two men/angels talk louder than Mark's trembling, ecstatic, and fearful women, whose bodies gesture toward another hermeneutics, one that lacks the strength to speak from knowledge, if it speaks at all, and withdraws from certainty. The women's way of silence, I believe, their way of fear and trembling, their way of not using reason to avoid the flux of experience is something like the hermeneutics practiced by Caputo, but that will be the topic for the following chapters of this book.

Now this chapter must come to an end. It began with Luke's promise to secure the matters pertaining to Jesus in which Theophilus had been instructed (Luke 1:1–4). It concludes with an examination of Luke 24, where the author delivers on his promise by thoroughly revising Mark's resurrection narrative. Here Jesus, *the* master of hermeneutics, finally speaks about the reading of Scripture.

The context of Jesus's words in Luke 24 about reading is very important. Luke forms that context by expanding the madness motif in Mark 16:8. Luke 24 has the followers of Jesus tarry in their insanity for forty-nine verses, and then, in a radical departure from the Gospel of Mark, Luke's risen Jesus appears and talks his followers out of their madness. In other words, Jesus heals their insanity with hermeneutics. In three vignettes, Mary Magdalene, Joanna, Mary the mother of James, and other unnamed women (Luke 24:1–11); Cleopas and his partner (24:13–32); and Peter, along with other disciples (24:33–49), display symptoms of madness as ancient doctors constructed the malady. With their minds severely impaired, they are unable to believe what was plainly before their eyes. If we skim Luke 24, we might catch a glimpse of how madness inhibits perception and belief:

> While they were perplexed [*aporeisthai*] . . . were terrified [*emphobōn*] . . . bowed their faces to the ground . . . seemed to them an idle tale [*lēros*] . . . amazed at what had happened [*thaumazōn to gegonos*] . . . eyes were kept [*ekratounto*] from recognizing him . . . stood still, looking sad [*skythrōpoi*] . . . astounded [*exestēsan*] us . . . how foolish you are, and how slow of heart [*bradeis tē kardia*] to believe . . . hearts burning [*ē kardia ēmōn kaiomenē*] within us . . . startled and terrified [*ptoēthentes* and *emphoboi*] . . . frightened [*tetaragmenoi*] . . . doubts arise in your heart [*dialogismoi anabainousin*] in their joy they were disbelieving and still wondering [*thaumazontōn*].

Madness? Really? I understand why readers might question my assertion that insanity is in play in Luke 24, since the NRSV's translation does not reflect the ancient terminology of insanity running through the chapter. I will discuss that terminology below.

But assume for a moment I am right, that madness does run through Luke 24. Then the question becomes, Why would the author have shaped the characters' mental states in this way? I will argue that he does so for three reasons: (1) to define hermeneutics as the therapeutic application of the doctrine of divine necessity to diseased/irrational minds; (2) to give Theophilus certainty; and (3) to claim that Christian belief, because it is based on divine reason, meets the standards of a legitimate religion in the Roman Empire. Luke–Acts' hermeneutics of divine necessity—not Caputo's hermeneutics, certainly!—heals madness by setting aside uncertainty. Divine providence is the key that unlocks Scripture and opens minds.

After two attempted cures, one by a pair of male figures in bright clothing (24:4) later identified as angels (24:23) and another by Jesus (24:26–27), the master of hermeneutics finally succeeds at restoring his followers' sanity (24:44–47). Events pertaining to Jesus and to the church's expansion in Acts happen *necessarily*, since they were spoken of / written about beforehand. To read the Scriptures, or to listen to Jesus, is to know the inevitability of past events and the definite form of future ones:

> Remember how he told you, while he was still in Galilee, that the Son of Man must [*dei*, "it is necessary"] be handed over to sinners, and be crucified, and on the third day rise again. (24:6–7)

> Then he said to them, "Oh, how foolish you are, and how slow of heart to believe all that the prophets have declared! Was it not necessary [*edei*] that the Messiah should suffer these things and then enter into his glory?" Then beginning with Moses and all the prophets, he interpreted [*diermēneusen*] to them the things about himself [*ta peri heautou*] in all the scriptures.[50] (24:25–27)

> Then he said to them, "These are my words that I spoke to you while I was still with you—that everything written [*panta ta gegrammena*] about me in the law of Moses, the prophets, and the psalms must [*dei*, 'it is necessary'] be fulfilled." Then he opened their minds to understand the scriptures, and he said to them, "Thus it is written, that the Messiah is to suffer and to rise from the dead on the third day, and that repentance and forgiveness of sins is to be proclaimed in his name to all nations, beginning from Jerusalem." (24:44–47)

As I have already mentioned, *dei* (it is necessary) occurs forty-two times in Luke–Acts, and in nearly every instance, it refers to divine necessity. This single word gathers the disparate events that made up Jesus's career, including his resurrection, into a series of events planned from the start and executed by the Divine Mind. Thus the author of Luke–Acts frames the Messiah and the growth of the church within the Stoic, deterministic understanding of history.[51] Divine necessity is the key to understanding Jesus and Scripture, and it rescues believers from the madness caused by uncertainty.

Luke 24:50–53 provides the reader with proof that Jesus restores his followers' minds. Even more than curing their insanity, by speaking rationally to them, he prepares them to speak rationally in verse 53 and in the book of Acts, thus allaying suspicion that the Christian movement lacks a rational foundation. The key term in these verses is *eulogeō*. The NRSV offers "bless" as a translation, and while this is not incorrect, it fails to communicate two crucial connotations of the word. The term refers both to a sound mind (*logos*) and to speech (*logos*) that is rational and persuasive: "Then he led them out as far as Bethany, and, lifting up his hands, he blessed [*eulogēsen*] them. While he was blessing [*eulogein*] them, he withdrew from them and was carried up into heaven. And they worshiped him, and returned to Jerusalem with great joy; and they were continually in the temple blessing [*eulogountes*] God" (24:50–53).[52] Once the Scriptures have been opened to the disciples and their minds opened to the Scriptures, they know the divinely ordained events of the past and future and can speak prudently of the God who has preplanned them. The followers of Jesus are now prepared to bring reason (*logos*) to the Roman Empire. And readers are now prepared to enjoy the certitude that comes from their success in Acts.

Earlier I asked you to assume that Luke 24 portrays the followers of Jesus as suffering madness. I will conclude this chapter by justifying that assumption. In both ancient medicine and the literature that borrowed medical terminology (tragedy, comedy, philosophy, and Jewish and early Christian writings), madness, or displacement of the mind (*ekstasis*), took two forms: *mania* and *melancholia*.[53] *Melancholia* referred generally to a depressed mood, although some physicians recognized manic-like episodes in melancholics, and nonmedical writers often blurred the distinction between the two terms.

With respect to Luke 24, more critical than the line separating *melancholia* and *mania* is the physiological explanation of madness—namely, excessive amounts of black bile. One of the body's four humors, black bile is cold and dry, and healthy bodies produce it in harmless amounts. Overheated blood, however, produces too much black bile, which in turn pollutes the mind, and madness ensues.[54] From the Hippocratic writings of the fifth and fourth centuries BCE to the physician Galen in the second century and beyond, excessive heat was the key factor in the explanation of mental illness.

In the first century CE, however, an emerging form of *melancholia* sheds light on Luke 24. I am referring to scholarly melancholy, a condition identified close in time to the composition of Luke–Acts by the physician Rufus of Ephesus.[55] He writes,

> The affects of the rational kind of soul are things such as excessive thinking, learning by heart, study, research, doubting, and exploring the meaning of things; or suspicions, conjectures, fantasies, and correct or incorrect opinions. When the soul plunges into one of any of these states—some of which are faculties and others accidents—, and draws close to it, then this often brings about the disease known as melancholy, and one easily succumbs to it.[56]

Although Aristotle had linked *melancholia* with genius, and ancient physicians noted that the rigors of the life of study (bad diet, little sleep, etc.) might produce madness, Rufus drew particular attention to the danger that wrestling with uncertainty poses.[57] Those who think too much about difficult problems, he continues,

> are truly close to melancholic delusion because they frequently doubt and think, and excessively search and distinguish. For they—through zealously pursuing their ideas, and regretting things which escape their intellect such as grasping the proof which they call "*apodeixis*"; attaining the true realities; and deducing the valid argument derived

from the concept called "*sullogismós*" in Greek, that is to say, soundness of the thought together with the predication—are rendered sad and made to succumb to the ailment of melancholy.[58]

In short, Rufus discovered the darkness of not-knowing will drive you crazy. A few decades later, Galen, almost certainly borrowing from Rufus, made the same point: nothing is more fearful and more conducive to madness than the dark.[59]

What was going on in the first century that made uncertainty so danger-ous? It turns out that scholarly melancholy can be correlated with a specific set of social conditions. Simon Swain has shown that Rufus observed a rela-tion between melancholic symptoms and the pressure on elites to present themselves as classically educated, intelligent, and well spoken in public, especially before rulers. Swain explores the writings of Plutarch and others to illustrate how Rufus had uncovered an important social-psychological phenomenon in the first century: "Although Rufus' emphasis on thinking as a cause or symptom of melancholy . . . is distinctive, it accords very well with an age which placed such great stress on male self-presentation as intelligent and possessing education or culture (*paideia*)."[60] Swain's recon-struction of the social context of scholarly melancholia makes possible a fresh approach to the interpretations of several passages in Luke–Acts in addition to Luke 24.

Take, for example, Acts 26. Here the Roman governor Festus calls upon something like Rufus's diagnostic insight of scholarly melancholia to dismiss the intensity of Paul's missionary zeal: "While he [Paul] was making this defense, Festus exclaimed, 'You are out of your mind [*mainē*], Paul! Too much learning is driving you insane [*ta polla se grammata eis manian peritrepei*]!' But Paul said, 'I am not out of my mind [*ou mainomai*], most excellent Festus, but I am speaking the sober truth'" (Acts 26:24–25). What a boon for Theophilus to discover that a high-ranking Roman offi-cial listened to Paul speak and concluded that the apostle had been driven mad by too much education and literature! And here is another example of scholarly melancholy in Luke–Acts. From Rufus's medical perspective, the case history of Apollos written up in 18:24–26 would have been a cause for alarm:

> Now there came to Ephesus a Jew named Apollos, a native of Alexandria. He was an eloquent man, well-versed in the scriptures. He had been instructed in the Way of the Lord; and he spoke with burning enthusiasm [*zeōn tō pneumati*] and taught accurately the things concerning Jesus . . . but when Priscilla and Aquila heard him, they took him aside and explained the Way of God to him more accurately.

To the untrained eye, Apollos is an educated and enthusiastic man who wields the Bible to promote Jesus, although he lacks knowledge of the divine plan. Rufus, however, would have observed several worrying social and physiological conditions. Apollos hails from a city noted for intellectual achievement, written words have captured his attention, and he disputes with others about the meaning of texts. Rufus would have been especially concerned about Apollos's overheated spirit (*pneuma*). The phrase *boiling in the spirit* refers to the physiology of madness. As touched on above, ancient doctors thought the excessive heating of black bile or the boiling (*zesis*) of blood or *pneuma* caused insanity.[61]

Apollos's symptoms point to insanity, but Priscilla and Aquila know what to do. As masters of hermeneutics in their own right, they cool Apollos's fever by explaining to him "the way of God"—and the next words are crucial for our understanding of Lukan hermeneutics—"more accurately." "More accurately" means Priscilla and Aquila frame the facts of Jesus's career with a higher-order fact: God providentially guides history.[62] Knowledge of the divine plan explains away the maddening randomness of history and quells overheated spirits. This Lukan approach to reading texts and interpreting life first appeared in the preface to the Gospel of Luke. In this chapter, I have traced the motif of the plan through Philip to Paul, and now Priscilla and Aquila have joined the group. The story of (not Caputo's) hermeneutics in Luke now culminates with two men in white and Jesus talking the insane followers of Jesus out of their diseased minds.

The First Vignette (Luke 24:1–12). The women are perplexed (*aporeisthai*) when they do not find Jesus's body (24:4). *Aporia* literally means "without a way." To feel as if there is no way forward is a symptom of insanity, according to Rufus, Galen, and other ancient physicians.[63] Unable to make sense of the absence of Jesus's corpse, they run into a wall similar to the one Cleopas and his partner will run into. The women react with fear (*emphobōn*; 24:5), an emotion not so different from the gloominess of the two travelers on the way to Emmaus (24:17). In fact, as one scholar has recently argued, in paradoxagraphical literature (tales of strange and astonishing events—and if a dead man's return to life does not count, then what would?), *phobos* should be translated as "dread," an emotion linked to fear of the unknown and melancholy.[64] Similarly, a face bent toward the ground could very well be a sign of madness, not reverence.[65]

The men in bright clothing attempt a hermeneutical cure (24:6–7), with a hint of success (24:9), but there is no unambiguous demonstration of restored reason until 24:50–53. The disciples, by labeling what the women say as *lēros* (delirium; 24:11; a better translation than the NRSV's "idle tale"), imply they have lost their minds.[66] But Theophilus, by now a knowing reader, might have drawn a different conclusion: that it is the disciples themselves who are mad in their failure to see the hand of God in what the women communicate.[67] Rather than fitting Jesus's resurrection into an overarching scheme of divine providence, Peter confirms the bare facts of the women's account and merely experiences amazement (*thaumazōn*; 24:12) over the event, not belief in its divine origin. From the Lukan perspective, amazement hinders belief (see 24:41). In fact, amazement (the Greek word has a connection to "dread") is itself a symptom of insanity.[68]

The Second Vignette (Luke 24:13–35). The metaphor of the "way" (*hodos*) winds its way throughout this episode (24:32, 35). At one level, the two disciples know where they are going. Yet at a deeper level, they are quite lost, since they are unable to make sense of the events in Jerusalem. Their conversation, described in technical terms referring to philosophic dialogue, reveals the futility of seeking the meaning of events without the guidance of an expert:

Now on that same day two of them were going to a village called
Emmaus, about seven miles from Jerusalem, and talking with
[*hōmiloun*] each other about all these things that had happened. While
they were talking [*homilein*] and discussing [*syzētein*], Jesus himself came
near and went with them, but their eyes were kept from recognizing
him. And he said to them, "What are you discussing [*antiballete*] with
each other while you walk along [*peripatountes*]?" (Luke 24:13–17)

The two talk and talk but do not arrive at certainty (*asphaleia*).[69] Their
conversation resembles a philosophic dialogue in which partners "seek
together" (a literal translation of the philosophic term *syzētein* in 24:15),
exchange views, and test each other's claims. Their dialogue seeks to arrive
at truth.[70] In 24:17, Jesus refers to their verbal exchange as the throwing
back and forth (*antiballō*) of words, a term that in the first century pointed
to philosophic dialogue.[71] Its root *ball* suggests raising objections in a competitive spirit, much as two people play catch, each participant intent on
throwing the ball more accurately or with greater force than the other.[72]
Finally, note how the disciples talk while walking (*peripatountes*), a practice that alludes to the Peripatetics, followers of Aristotle. The name reflects
the famous habit of its members doing philosophy while strolling.[73] While
I am not suggesting the disciples are Aristotelians, by now it is clear that
philosophy's quest for truth—the scholarly part of Rufus's melancholy—is
the interpretive horizon of this vignette. The disciples' conversation is a
serious examination of the events pertaining to Jesus. Nevertheless, it drives
Cleopas and his partner into the gloomy depths of melancholy. The stage
has been set for the master of hermeneutics to interrupt their failed inquiry
and point them in the right direction.

   The first hint of their melancholy comes in 24:16: "Their eyes were kept
[*ekratounto*] from recognizing him." As I mentioned above, ancient insanity was fundamentally an impairment of perception. Sanity, on the other
hand, prevails when the mind (*dianoia*) and the external object remain open
to each other.[74] A blocked mind leads to hallucinations, sluggishness, and
as in this vignette, failure to recognize familiar persons.[75] The stranger's

question stops them in their tracks: "They stood still" (24:17). Their stationary pose is itself another symptom of melancholy, since it externalizes the inner experience of an *aporia* (see 24:4).

In Luke 24:17, we encounter the strongest evidence of scholarly melancholia. The two disciples stand still with gloomy faces (*skythrōpoi*). The word *skythrōpos* connoted the emotion of "dread" as well as "grief" or "sadness."[76] It also suggested vexation and even anger.[77] The *skythrōpos* individual was obsessed with the unknown, darkness, and death.[78] Unable to peer into the future but driven to look anyway, the *gloomy person* was irritable and bitter.[79] Red in the face, too, owing to overheated blood.[80] What is particularly interesting for this study is that a gloomy countenance was a symptom of Rufus's scholarly melancholy.[81] In the first and second centuries CE, philosophers in general were regarded as a somber bunch, especially those who did not believe in divine providence. Atomists like Epicurus were rumored by philosophers who did believe in providence to be both sullen and mad because of their unbelief.[82] Heraclitus (ca. 535–ca. 475 BCE) is another example of the bad reputation unfairly attached to materialist philosophers.[83] Known as the weeping philosopher, Heraclitus was often paired with the laughing philosopher, Democritus (ca. 460–370 BCE). Like Epicurus, both Heraclitus and Democritus denied that a god guides the universe; the latter philosopher laughed over people stumbling through life's events, and the former was quite glum as humans drowned in the flux of experience. The way the author of Luke–Acts tells the story, the two disciples advance no further than Heraclitus, since they are overcome by the randomness of the things pertaining to Jesus. All they have are bare events. They are without a divine design. They lack the *asphaleia* the author promised to Theophilus. And it has taken a toll on their sanity.

Jesus plays along with their failure to recognize him. Theophilus must have chuckled as the two disciples recite for Jesus the facts about Jesus as they try in vain to work out the meaning of events without knowing the plan of God. The list culminates with Jesus's resurrection from the dead—an amazing event, to be sure—confirmed by a male (24:12) and not based on the testimony of women alone, a telltale of the narrator's sexism. Nevertheless, the resurrection of Jesus is only an event among others and not self-interpreting. For this reason, news of his rising from the dead does not calm their minds, quite the opposite: "Moreover, some women of our group astounded [*exestēsan*] us" (24:22). A more accurate translation is this: the women "caused us to stand outside of ourselves." *Existēmi* refers to a displacing of the mind; to stand apart from or outside of oneself is the nature of insanity.[84] Jesus confirms they have taken leave of their senses. He addresses them with a phrase having comic overtones: "Oh, how foolish [*anoētoi*] you are" (24:25). Literally, "O, mindless ones."[85] To say someone lacks a mind is to say they are insane.[86] The same was true of slow hearts ("slow of heart to believe"; 24:25); the disciples' madness prevents them from perceiving/believing what Moses and the prophets wrote about God's intention in Jesus's suffering, death, and resurrection.[87] In the last suggestion of madness in this vignette ("Were not our hearts burning within us?" 24:32), the two disciples summarize their earlier encounter with Jesus on the way to Emmaus. Recall Apollos's *boiling in the spirit*; we should be wary of modern interpreters' explanation of heat imagery that points to positive emotions.[88] In medicine, philosophy, and literature, a burning heart signifies vehement emotions (e.g., rage or erotic desire) that are so extreme as to cross into madness.[89] This is basic ancient physiology: heat cooks the blood surrounding the heart and produces excessive black bile.[90] Later, when cooled, black bile leads to a depressed state called melancholy. Mania is linked to black bile in its heated state.[91]

   The Third Vignette (Luke 24:33–49). Their madness persists: "They were startled [*ptoēthentes*] and terrified [*emphoboi*]" (24:37). The idea of fluttering (*ptoia*) as a condition of the soul is important in the history of ancient philosophy's association of vehement emotion and madness. The founder of the Stoic school, Zeno of Citium (334–ca. 262 BCE), defined emotion (*pathos*) as the fluttering of the soul.[92] Once again, Jesus confirms for readers that their minds are deeply disturbed: "Why are you frightened [*tetaragmenoi*]?" (24:38). Like *ptoia*, the Greek word *tarassō* connotes the madness of frantic indecision and reminds readers of the women's perplexity in 24:4.[93] In a similar move, Jesus's next words circle back to the two disciples as they futilely threw words back and forth on the way to Emmaus, only now the dialogue is internal to those who fret over the events: "Why do doubts [*dialogismoi*] arise in your hearts?" (24:38).[94] And then, for the last time, the point is made that emotion—even joy!—is an obstacle to belief: "While in their joy they were disbelieving and still wondering [better, 'marveling,' *thuamazontōn*; see 24:12]" (24:38).

We have finished with the madness of Jesus's disciples in Luke 24. Derived from the Stoic doctrine of divine providence, Lukan hermeneutics offers itself as rational therapy of uncertainty. In the next chapter, we turn to the Paul of the undisputed letters and explore his reading theory. Unlike the author of Luke–Acts and his fellow masters of hermeneutics, the Paul of the genuine letters *proceeds* from madness and does not attempt to cure it. Paul's goal in the act of reading is not certainty. Indeed, reading a genuine Pauline epistle has no goal. Rather, his letters open readers to an absence and an emptiness from which a politics of respect and hospitality has a chance to emerge. This Pauline madness is not the absence of reason or the frustration of not-knowing despite much learning; rather, it flows from longing (*pothos*), a grief joined to desire for an absent other. As we will see next, longing is, paradoxically, a nonvoluntary but not unwilled hollowing out of the self, a feeling of being overwhelmed by the uncertainty that accompanies everyone and everything longed for. Longing has no interest in healing madness but intensifies it with promises of a newness over which no one is master.

CHAPTER 2

Penelope's Tears

PAUL WROTE LETTERS to tell readers what to do and what to think. As substitutes for his physical presence, letters allowed him to manage his churches from a distance. Accordingly, we read his letters in the twenty-first century to know what he was thinking so that we might live as he would have us live.

That paragraph is a caricature of the way many Christian interpreters have read Paul's letters. Exaggerated, to be sure, it nevertheless gets at the way readers have viewed Paul and his letters, whether they admire his strong leadership or despise his patriarchal bullying. The thread running through these opposing opinions is the assumption that, for Paul, letters were instruments of authority. While admiring interpreters have renamed Paul's style *apostolic authority* and praise him for bold leadership, his critics are skeptical of this move, and I would count myself among the latter group if I thought Paul had been bent on establishing authority, whether his or God's. I resonate with their suspicions that when we read Paul's writings, we read what Elizabeth A. Castelli identifies as one of the "master narratives of Western culture," by which she means writing that reduces difference to sameness and oppresses women, sexual minorities, and outsiders.[1] For suspicious scholars, writing "apostolic" before "authority" only serves to insulate the master narrative from critique. With that I agree.

And so I find myself in an awkward position. I do not think Paul's genuine letters were intended to enforce his authority, or God's, or Christ's, but I understand why so many interpreters like Castelli think so, and I agree wholeheartedly with their desire to expose the authoritarianism of Western master narratives. Nevertheless, I want to hold out for another way of seeing Paul, one that regards him as a radically antiauthoritarian thinker. I know this is a tall order. Paul has a formidable reputation, but there may be a way. I argue in this chapter that the key to interpreting Paul is to focus on the emotions that saturate his letters.[2] One emotion in particular, longing (*pothos*), runs through them. Longing is quite at odds with authority. The ancients defined it as a mixture of love and grief.[3] It is a crucial theme in Paul's Letter to the Philippians, one of his most antiauthoritarian writings and the focus of this chapter. We will examine how it contests authority below.

The primacy of emotion holds, however, only for the *genuine* Pauline letters. There are thirteen letters in the New Testament associated with Paul's name, fourteen if we count Hebrews. Not all of them, however, were real letters—real in the sense of placing both writer and recipients in a friendly or perhaps loving relation.[4] Pseudonymous letters, in contrast, make a special point of asserting their authors' authority. They neither reveal their writers' emotions nor stir emotions in readers, with the possible exception of anger and fear. Thus while the pseudonymous letters of the New Testament adopt the literary form of a letter, they are more interested in teaching theological principles and enforcing hierarchical organization than expressing and eliciting emotion. In short, real letters host events of hospitality, while pseudonymous letters take charge.

The ancient dispute between poets and philosophers over emotion will help us understand the difference between the letters Paul wrote and the ones claiming to have been written by him. Paul sides with the poets' embrace of feelings, while the unknown author of Colossians and Ephesians, two letters also examined in this chapter, appeals instead to cosmic order, political structure, household management, and the discipline of the self. To secure order in the cosmos, government, family, and the reader's soul, the pseudonymous Paul rids Paul of his emotions and turns him into a philosopher. To illustrate this transformation, I will first explore the motif of Christ as a slave in Philippians. Then in Colossians and Ephesians, I will examine the headship of Christ, an opposing motif related to the control of emotions and the promotion of hierarchy within the household. Christ the head in the pseudonymous letters replaces Christ the slave in the genuine ones; similarly, the disciplining and self-disciplined Paul of Colossians and Ephesians replaces the emotional Paul of Philippians. The Letter to the Philippians is Paul's confession of longing desire, not an instrument of control. In contrast, the author of Ephesians and Colossians had order in mind and wrote to instill it in readers.

Epictetus and Penelope

We turn first to the ancient conflict between philosophers—chiefly the Stoics—and poets over emotion. My proposal is this: while Paul and poets paradoxically welcomed and feared passion, Colossians and Ephesians rejected it and reiterated the Stoic understanding of emotion as an erroneous judgment.

As early as the seventh century BCE, poets (and doctors a little later) imagined emotions as events occurring in the body's internal organs (*ta splagxna*). The *innards*, as a prominent classicist has translated *ta splagxna*, extend from the diaphragm to the collarbone and include the heart, spleen, lungs, and connective tissue.[5] For these poets and medical writers, an emotion is not, as the Stoics would later assert, the mind's rash judgment about an external condition or event. Rather, passion is the innards heating up, liquefying, and draining away. To have strong emotion was to experience oneself emptied of one's materiality. To grieve, to fall in love, to grow angry, to envy, or to long for a departed friend or loved one—all these events that we call psycho*logical* (and in naming them in this way, we reproduce the ancient philosophic notion of emotion as the soul's bad *logic*)—poets thought of as liquefaction of the body and the emptying of melted flesh.[6] Homer's tender description of Penelope's longing for her husband illustrates *kenosis* (emptying). In this famous passage, she responds to a beggar, none other than the disguised Odysseus himself telling tales of her husband's exploits: "Her tears flowed and her face melted." Then Homer lends nature's grandeur to her longing: "As the snow melts on the lofty mountains, the snow which the East Wind thaws when the West Wind has poured it down, and as it melts the streams of the rivers flow full: so her lovely cheeks melted as she wept and mourned for her husband, who even then was sitting by her side."[7] Penelope's tears began love's literary history of dissolving the self. Indeed, love as a consuming fire was one of the most frequently employed erotic motifs in ancient writings.[8]

So why is it important for twenty-first-century readers of the New Testament to know how poets thought of emotion? For this reason: we readers have been far too impressed by ancient philosophers and their cerebral approach to human experience. We need to know that there was (and is) an alternative to the Stoic view. This alternative is difficult to detect in the early Christian writings, however, since once the idea of self-control got a foothold in the letters falsely written in Paul's (and Peter's) name, the philosophic construction of emotion entered Christian theology and profoundly shaped the practice of reading all New Testament texts, even the ones like Philippians that resisted philosophy's rationalism. Self-control, which presupposes a monitor of the body located in the heart or head, has to this day influenced what we understand as the *self*, with the result that we read all of the writings of the New Testament through the ancient philosophers' disdain for Penelope's tears.

How did the Stoics explain emotion? In their view, emotion was quite literally a *rush* (*hormē*) to judgment, a rash and faulty conclusion about the badness of an event or a state of affairs based on sense perception.[9] Consider the favorite word of the Greek Stoics for emotion, *pathos*. This term was derived from *paschein*, which means "to suffer"—that is, "to be acted upon." The Stoics drew a line down the middle of human experience and claimed that individuals acted on (*poieō*) the world or were acted upon (*paschō*) by the world. Activity and passivity were the only two ways for a person—in fact, for any entity, from dirt to deity—to exist. The division between active and passive was not the Stoics' idea alone, since elite males holding various philosophic views, or with no interest in philosophy at all, were nevertheless keen to construe the world as a place where one acts like a hammer or like a nail, like a cobbler having the idea of a shoe or a scrap of leather destined to become a shoe. The list of binary pairs could go on: you are either male or female, master or slave, rich or poor, urban or rural. In the minds of the elite, there was no question that it was morally better, more dignified, and more consistent with human and divine nature to be the one who acts and never the one acted upon. Better to be a *doer* than a *done-to-er*.

Yet the Stoics also knew that strictly speaking, it was not possible for a human to act on the world. The Stoic philosopher Epictetus taught there was nothing external to the self that the self could control. One must instead follow God, the maker of all things. One must will what God wills. God (or Fate, Zeus, Nature, Destiny—it does not matter, since the terms were interchangeable for the Stoics) controls the world. God causes the shipwrecks and the tumors and assigns each individual to a social role, such as master, slave, wife, uncle, aunt, emperor, and so on. The one thing, however, God leaves to individual agency is the choice to agree with divine acts. You cannot keep the tree limb from falling on your head, but you can accept the injury as God's providence or consider it an evil and in so doing reject God's will. A *pathos* arises when in a rush to judgment and in ignorance of what cannot be controlled (the external world), an individual forgets what they can control (one's attachment to the external world). To act rationally is to accept events and one's assigned social role. Emotion is fighting back against God. Emotions come from believing that one was dealt a bad hand and reality should be other than it is.[10]

Imagine what Penelope might have thought of the Stoic theory of emotion: a cold abstraction, the kind bereaved persons encounter when well-intentioned but ill-advised friends try to talk them out of grief. Had Epictetus been in Ithaca to comfort Penelope, he would have advised her to go into her soul, where her identity dwells, and rekindle the God-given power to detach herself from her husband's memory and resign herself to his absence.[11] Then she should just move on.[12]

The philosophical *self* thus stands in stark contrast to Penelope's *self*, which is her melting flesh, and by "her," I do not mean to imply that she is other than her melting flesh. She—the body that she was—longed for Odysseus, and that emotion, which no one could have talked her out of, emptied itself as her face turning to tears ran down her hollowed-out cheeks. In this imaginary scene, as Epictetus attempts to help Penelope get a grip on her emotions, we witness the Western invention of the *self*. That *self* attempts to take the place of Penelope's soul when the philosopher exhorts her to identify herself with the alleged power within her to stand above her circumstances. The point is this: the Western, philosophic *self* found a home in Colossians and Ephesians, letters written in Paul's name while betraying his thought and walking over his and Penelope's emotions. Evidence for this charge against Colossians and Ephesians will be provided below.

Rediscovering Emotions

But first, I must own up to the fact that an antiauthoritarian, pro-emotion interpretation of Paul's letters is quite a leap. Part of the problem, of course, is the confusion between the genuine letters and the pseudonymous ones. Yet even when that distinction is acknowledged, the genuine Paul often comes off bossy and egotistical. Once again, however, I will come to Paul's defense. Modern translations are often the culprits here, since even competent ones routinely replace the apostle's emotional language with claims of authority. Take, for example, the NRSV's translation of Philippians 2:12–13:

> Therefore, my beloved, just as you have always obeyed me, not only in my presence, but much more now in my absence, work out your own salvation with fear and trembling; for it is God who is at work in you, enabling you both to will and to work for his good pleasure.

The NRSV inserts "me" after "obeyed" and "his" before "good pleasure," making it look as if Paul is praising the Philippians for their obedience to him and as if God looks down on humans as he awaits behavior that will please him. "Me" and "his" turn Paul and God into authorities. Yet nothing in the Greek text supports "me" or "his."[13]

Reading Philippians 2:12–13 with "me" and "his" crossed out raises interesting questions. First, if not to Paul, then to whom does the community give obedience? My suggestion is the Philippians have obeyed one another, and for that reason, Paul praises them. This fits well with Paul's call in Galatians for individuals to think of their relationships with one another as mutual slavery: "For you were called to freedom, brothers and sisters; only do not use your freedom as an opportunity for self-indulgence [better, 'the flesh'] but through love become slaves to one another" (Gal 5:13). Moreover, the church as a gathering of persons enslaved to one another matches up with Christ's enslavement to humanity narrated in Philippians 2:5–11. I will have more to say in a moment on the emotional dimension of the slavery motif in Paul.

So much for the misleading "me" of Philippians 2:12. How might we read verse 13 once "his" has been removed? Here it helps to know that "good pleasure" is not the only possible translation of *eudokia*; this term might refer to the mutual respect and love that Paul had written about in 2:1–4. If this is the case, then 2:13 is about not God's pleasure but the emotional attachments that Paul seeks to foster in the community. In 2:13, then, Paul does not paint a picture of a transcendent God observing the Philippians' behavior. In a radical move, Paul redefines the word *theos* (God; or, better, "god," since the word is not a proper noun). Here is a paraphrase of his definition: theos is the one working in you to will and work for mutual high regard. *What is a god?* That is the question Paul asks his readers to think about in this portion of the letter. And in 2:13, he answers his own question: theos is not external to the community but on the inside of the Philippians' wishing and working for their own salvation. *Salvation* here has a political connotation, since it refers not to the preservation of the individual soul past death but to the preservation of the Philippian community. It is a salvation worked through mutual slavery or, as Paul says in Romans, through members of the community bearing one another's weaknesses, as I will discuss in the next chapter. In other words, Paul is *not* claiming in 2:13 that some superentity named *God* causes the Philippians' wishing and working. It is even doubtful whether the verb "is" in the phrase "God is the one who" does justice to the event that happens in writing or saying *theos*. John D. Caputo makes a similar move when he distinguishes between the *existence* of God and the *insistence* of God:

> The proper way to speak of God is to say not that God exists, but that God insists, while we are called upon to make up the difference. We are asked to pick up where God leaves off, to fill up the existence that is lacking in the insistence of God. God insists, but the weight of God's existence falls on us. The easy yoke and incredible lightness of God's insistence implies that the gravity of existence is our responsibility, that the burden of existence falls on our shoulders. As the mystics say, God needs us.[14]

God insists, existing within the Philippians' wishing and their energy for loving and respecting one another. In other words, *theos* is the word Paul sets aside to mark the event of *eudokia* in the community.

The point I want to bring out here is that Paul associates the word *God* with emotion—in this case, a passion that binds people together in shared suffering.[15] That was a distinctly unphilosophical move in the first century, when *theos* in the mouths of philosophers meant the origin, cause, and goal of all things. Now, to say that God energizes emotions is a very broad statement, since passions differ from one another, but we can narrow down the field by paying attention to the phrase "fear and trembling" in Philippians 2:12. In 1 Corinthians 2:3 NIV, the phrase "fear and trembling" is paired with "weakness" (*astheneia*), the feeling of coming undone as one bears the coming undone of others. These are feelings that the philosophers had a scant vocabulary to express even if they had wanted to, which they most certainly did not. Ancient philosophy, then, with its emphasis on reason and self-control, is not the way into reading the genuine Pauline Epistles. Rather, the way in is a poetic imagination like Homer's that gave Penelope's tears to the world.

The Double Effect

In Philippians 2:1 NIV, Paul writes, "Therefore if you have any encouragement from being united with Christ, if any comfort from his love [or 'comfort of love,' *paramythion agapēs*]." Here the NIV has inserted "his" into the translation where there is no grammatical reason to do so; the NRSV, to its credit, does not make this mistake. A better translation is simply "if there is such a thing as comfort of love." The only trouble (yet I think this is actually the genius of the phrase) is that "comfort of love" leaves the reader, just as love leaves lovers, with an ambiguity that cannot be resolved. This ambiguity gives rise to powerful emotions.[16] Does the phrase mean "comfort that love gives," or does it mean "comfort that loving makes necessary"? In other words, is love the cure of suffering, or is love suffering's cause? The answer is yes to both cure and cause, since *paramythion agapēs* means both.[17] This means that our reading of a genuine Pauline letter must take place in the unresolved tension of presence and absence in the phrase "comfort of love."

Poets embraced the doubleness of love, and Latin literature had a name for it: *consolatio amoris* (the consolation of love), which is an exact translation of Paul's *paramythion agapēs*.[18] Indeed, the idea that propelled a great deal of erotic literary expression—in both Greek and Latin, from antiquity through the Middle Ages and beyond—is both simple and alarming: when you love someone, you open yourself or, more accurately, you find yourself opened to suffering. For the poets, love is a sickness for which there is no cure.[19] In fact, to love another is not even to want healing, as Gilbert of Hoyland in the twelfth century observed in one of his homilies on Song of Songs: "Love seeks no cure for the impossible."[20] Love leads to a low—not lowly as in humility—mind; in other words, love leads to a kind of melancholy.[21] Love is a desire for the other mixed with grief over the other's possible (inevitable, really) absence. The only comfort in these sufferings is the other's love that calls forth love, and that call is of course what got the suffering started in the first place. Lovers know this paradox all too well.

Might readers know it too? Some forms of literature, like poems and epistles, by their very nature bear the marks of *consolatio amoris*. In the case of an epistle, the *consolation of love* names the phenomenon of the beloved's illusory presence that soothes pain even as it reignites it.[22] A love letter is like love itself, since it has the power to comfort *and* to afflict, its illusion of presence a painful reminder of absence.[23] Ancient epistolary theory, however, was blind to this double effect, focusing instead on the illusion of presence while ignoring the perception of absence.[24] The ancient theory of letter writing claimed that a letter substitutes for the writer's body and overcomes the distance between the sender and recipient.[25] Synesius (ca. 373–ca. 414), the Christian bishop of Ptolemais, expresses what in his day had become a six-hundred-year-old consensus about the miraculous power of writing:

> I once heard one of our brilliant speakers praising the practice of letter-writing. . . . He hymned an encomium on it for various reasons, but particularly because of the letter's power to be a solace for unhappy loves affording as it does in bodily absence the illusion of actual presence, for this missive seems itself to converse, thus fulfilling the soul's desire. In this way he celebrated the inventor of letters, and came to the conclusion that they were not a gift from any man but one from God to men. For my part I enjoy this sacred gift of god, and to whomsoever I needs must talk, if I cannot speak to him, at all events I can write, and this I often long to do. I then rejoice in those I love and am present with them to the best of my power.[26]

Sometimes, however, the illusion does not hold, as Synesius himself admits in another letter:

> When I came back from Egypt to my own city, and when I read all your letters of the two last years, I watered them with my tears. For I got no pleasure from the letters, out of the joy I always take in you, but

rather sadness, recalling in them your living fellowship, and thinking of what a friend and father alike I am bereaved, although one who is in reality living.[27]

Letters indeed have the power to make the sender present to the recipient, but they are also painful reminders of the sender's absence.[28] This is their double effect. Thus in spite of epistolary theory's confidence that letters deliver the presence of the author, letters of friendship often conveyed the bittersweet paradox of the *consolatio amoris.*

It is worthwhile to spend a moment thinking about how a letter gave a reader the sense of the writer's presence. Epistolary theory gave several answers. Word choice mattered, and that is why theorists insisted letters imitated friendly conversation. They permitted no flights of embellished rhetoric, since only the sincerity of everyday speech sustained the illusion the writer was speaking then and there as the reader read.[29] Another factor simulating presence was the epistle's very physicality, as the following letter of Seneca to Lucilius illustrates:

I thank you for writing to me so often; for you are revealing your real self to me in the only way you can. I never receive a letter from you without being in your company forthwith. If the pictures of our absent friends are pleasing to us, though they only refresh the memory and lighten our longing by a solace that is unreal and unsubstantial how much more pleasant is a letter, which brings us real traces, real evidences, of an absent friend! For that which is sweetest when we meet face to face is afforded by the impress of a friend's hand upon his letter,—recognition.[30]

Here the sense of touch connects sender to recipient, not hearing as one might expect. Reading, as we saw in the introduction and will explore further in the following chapters, was thought of as an auditory event, and a written surface was a technological device for replaying the author's voice as the reader vocalized the phonetic symbols. Seneca, a Stoic who took the side of reason in nearly all matters, in this passage opens the door to emotion just a crack. He did not just read the epistle and say, *Yes, that sounds like the person I know.* Rather, he touched the same surface the writer had, and in that moment, he mused they were united, or in Synesius's honest words, he enjoyed the *illusion* of communion.

A letter substitutes for the writer's presence.[31] That is the foundation of epistolary theory. As we will see in a moment, the author of Colossians and Ephesians turned this power of making himself present to his own advantage as he injected a theology of hierarchical control into the Pauline tradition. Yet the wife of Pliny the Younger, Calpurnia, reveals how much we miss if we think of a letter *only* as an instrument for the communication of an author's thoughts and the instrument of their designs upon the recipient. Pliny responds to a letter he had received from Calpurnia:

> You write that my being absent from you causes you no little sadness, and that your one consolation is to grasp my writings as a substitute for my person, and that you often place them where I lie next to you. I am happy that you are missing me, and that my books console you as you rest.[32]

Separated lovers in antiquity had remedies for grief: they treasured small portraits, figurines, lockets of hair, and other objects as reminders of absent loved ones. Calpurnia's remedy, however, was an extraordinary extension of these strategies. Pliny's wrinkled sheets already substituted for his physical presence, but Calpurnia magnified the bedclothes' effect by placing his letters within their folds. Yet did they only console? Might they not have also increased her grief by their very power to console?[33]

Pliny hints they did, and our recognition of that power is crucial for understanding what it meant to receive and read a Pauline epistle. As Synesius reported, letters simultaneously comforted and afflicted those who received them. The object that simulates presence also reminds the reader of absence. And so Pliny continues in the same letter to Calpurnia:

I in turn keep reading your letters, repeatedly fingering them as if they had newly arrived. But this fires my longing all the more, for when someone's letter contains such charm, what sweetness there is in conversing face to face! Be sure to write as often as you can, even though the delight your letters give me causes me such torture.[34]

Years later, in unknowing sympathy with Pliny, a tortured Saint Augustine writes to a friend:

When these letters present you to us so that you are almost seen, how they rouse us to seek you! For they make you clearly visible and desirable, and the more they show your presence among us, in some sort, they make it impossible for us to bear your absence.[35]

Slave of Love

Keep the tortured Augustine in mind in what comes next. A confident Augustine is about to take his place.

It is widely agreed that Philippians 2:7 is one of two pillars of the Christian doctrine of the incarnation. The other is John 1:14, which Augustine interpreted with the help of an ancient theory of language in order to protect the eternity (i.e., the everlasting presence) of the divine from the temporality (i.e., the inevitable absence) of flesh. Philippians 2:7 suffered a similar fate at the hands of its many commentators. As in the case of "became" in John 1:14, the "emptied" of Philippians 2:7 was and still is explained with the help of metaphysical assumptions. Interpreters think the Son of God must have emptied himself *of something*; otherwise, he would have diminished his divine self, and that is unthinkable, like the Word *becoming* flesh in John 1:14 is unthinkable. Few commentators have taken the poetic path and ventured the interpretation that emptying in Philippians has to do with an emotion like the one that overwhelmed Penelope. Aside from some readers in the medieval period who came close to this view, few interpreters think that the one who in the discourse of Christian theology would become the

Second Person of the Trinity was overcome by a love filled with desire and the sense of loss that the ancient Greeks called longing (*pothos*).

So what do these observations have to do with the act of reading Philippians today? They help us see that the traditional interpretation of 2:7 is freighted with unexamined philosophic assumptions that make Philippians look like an instrument of apostolic authority.[36] According to the vast majority of interpreters over the centuries, Philippians 2:5–11 tells of the pre-incarnate Word who did not hold on to divine attributes, such as omnipresence and omniscience. Yet what exactly did the word of God do with them? On this point, there has been little agreement. Did the Word hide his divine omnipotence so he might convincingly present himself as human? Or did the Word keep the attributes of God in reserve, bringing them out on occasion to work miracles and read his disciples' minds or detect his opponents' secret plots? If, however, he hid or retained divine properties, how does that square with 2:7, which proponents of the traditional interpretation insist is proof he emptied himself of them?

There is another way to interpret Philippians 2:7, one in which "he emptied himself" (CSB) has a physical-emotional meaning rather than a metaphysical-ethical one. What if we thought of Jesus in the Christ hymn to be like Penelope as her face melts into tears in longing for her absent husband? To make this interpretation plausible, there needs to be a slow reading of 2:5–11, all the while suspecting that the influence of Greek metaphysics, which tends to hide emotions, shapes modern translations. The NRSV is no exception to the emotion-masking slant of metaphysics:

> Let the same mind be in you that was in Christ Jesus,
>> who, though he was in the form of God,
>>> did not regard equality with God
>>> as something to be exploited,
>> but emptied himself,
>>> taking the form of a slave,
>>> being born in human likeness.

And being found in human form,
    he humbled himself
    and became obedient to the point of death—
    even death on a cross.

Therefore God also highly exalted him
    and gave him the name
    that is above every name,
so that at the name of Jesus
    every knee should bend,
    in heaven and on earth and under the earth,
and every tongue should confess
    that Jesus Christ is Lord,
    to the glory of God the Father.

In this translation, the hymn concludes with "God the Father." Yet there is no "the" in the Greek text; the translation should be "to the glory of theos, father." Admittedly, even with this correction, the hymn has a patriarchal ring to it, but the events between verses 6 and 11 actually lead to a powerful critique of patriarchy. More on that in a moment.

We return to the hymn's beginning: Christ Jesus was in the "form of God."[37] The metaphysical interpretation of the emptying leads to a dilemma, as I pointed out above: Did Jesus hide his divine powers, or did he give them up (only, of course, to get them back again at his exaltation)? Interpreters have not considered what "form of God" might have meant to the Philippians themselves, whose language and concepts were not limited by Greek philosophical thought. If literature and art serve as guides, the phrase "form of God" referred to divine beauty.[38] Gods and goddesses in the ancient imagination were drop-dead gorgeous. What made them so? It was the fact that they never grew old but remained forever young.[39] This explanation of "form" is strange to twenty-first-century readers, but ancient ones were accustomed to stories of divinities interacting with humans.

"Interacting" is too mild a word, however. A common story line in ancient mythology told of Zeus, for example, looking down on a mortal's beauty; changing his form into a swan, a bull, lightning, or the like; and then abducting the powerless victim.[40] As a prominent classicist once remarked, "To take Greek myth at face value . . . is to learn that the gods have only two easy ways of communicating with men: by killing them or raping them."[41] Zeus, for example, kidnapped Ganymede, Europa, and a host of other mortals. Eos, goddess of the dawn, seized the young man Tithonus. Bitter words inscribed on gravestones vilify Hades for abducting humans; often, these inscriptions tell of a daughter too young for marriage taken by Hades to be his bride.[42] What this backdrop of sexual violence means is that the word *theos* likely stirred deep emotions in Paul's first readers. Unlike today's word *God*, a term defined by metaphysical properties like omniscience and omnipresence and at home in the rationalism of the West, for the ancients, with the exception of the philosophers, the word *theos* called out apprehension and feelings of helplessness in the face of overwhelming forces.

Thus although "form of God" was a disquieting phrase hinting at abduction, its appearance would not have surprised Paul's readers, who were accustomed to the praise of divinities' exploits of sexual violence. Paul goes on, however, to write something utterly out of the ordinary. This unexpected turn is only available in the Greek text, but here is the NRSV's translation of 2:6 to get us started: "[He] did not regard equality with God as something to be exploited." The Greek word standing behind "something to be exploited" is *harpagmos*, which in Paul's day meant "erotic abduction" like the kidnappings described in the previous paragraphs.[43] Only now—and this would have been the surprising turn—the one in the form of theos, Christ Jesus, utterly rejects such violence. He refuses to act like a theos in the way gods were understood to act: *he did not regard erotic abduction as equal to a theos.* Christ Jesus repudiates the image of being a theos that the word *theos* painted in the minds of Paul's readers.

Instead, the Christ Jesus of Philippians empties himself, but not in the metaphysical sense of emptying himself of omniscience and omnipresence. Rather, he finds himself emptying out as Penelope does, draining

away in grief, sick at heart over the absence of her husband.[44] As Homer's
Penelope longs for Odysseus, so Paul's Christ Jesus longs for humanity (i.e.,
as long as *humanity* is not allowed to subsume the individual into a universal
category). If this interpretation seems far-fetched, what Paul writes earlier
in the letter about his emotional attachment to the readers makes it more
plausible: "For God is my witness, how I long for [*epipothō*] all of you in
the innards [*splagxnois*] of Christ Jesus" (1:8; translation modified). That
verse is a powerful witness to the antiauthoritarianism of Paul's Letter to
the Philippians, since the letter, as a confession of longing, itself becomes
proof of his desire for the church and not simply the disclosure of his mind.

Someone might object: What about the reference to *slavery* in 2:7? And
the phrase "humbled himself in obedience" in 2:8 NLT? Don't these terms
point away from the emotion of longing and portray Jesus as a humble
servant of God, a model for humanity? Fair questions, but if the historical-
critical principle of reading from the perspective of first readers is observed,
and of course determining that perspective with certainty is not possible,
then other meanings arise. For example, note the text does not explicitly
say Jesus becomes the slave of God, nor does it say he directs his obedience toward God. What if, as Martin Luther claims, the slavery and the
obedience depicted in the hymn are instead offered to humanity?[45] Before
this idea occurred to Luther, it had entered the mind of Guerric of Igny
(1080–1157). Note how Guerric first starts down the path of the traditional,
metaphysical interpretation only to veer off (starting with "But reckon it
too little") into an extraordinary interpretation of the incarnate Word's
slavery to humans:

> Christ was by nature God; equal to God not through robbery but
> by birth because he shared omnipotence, eternity, and divinity. He
> nevertheless dispossessed himself and not only took the nature of a
> slave, fashioned in the likeness of men, but also carried out the ministry
> of a slave, lowering his own dignity and accepting an obedience to the
> Father which brought him death, death on a cross. But reckon it too
> little for him to have served the Father as a slave although his Son and

co-equal unless he also served his own slave as more than a slave. . . . "I will not serve," man says to his Creator. "Then I will serve you," his Creator says to man. "You sit down. I will minister, I will wash your feet. You rest; I will bear your weariness, your infirmities. Use me as you like in all your needs, not only as your slave but also as your beast of burden and as your property."[46]

Neither did Guerric's bold reversal come out of the blue. In ancient love poetry and the erotic novel, anyone who fell in love was called the *slave of love*.[47] The vulnerability to which love opened the lover brought about the lover's low mind, in the sense of melancholy and degradation of social power. Loving another—at least in the imagination of the elite slave-owning class, who wrote and read love poetry and novels—mirrored a slave's experience of being owned and commanded by another.[48]

To sum up, Paul's Letter to the Philippians is not an instrument of authority. It is a tale of longing that has overtaken both the divinity (2:6–8) and Paul (1:8). It opens readers to thoughts of shared existence not governed by hierarchical control and, in fact, not governed by anything except all hanging on together by a thread of desire for one another and grief over the absence hidden in the presence of every other. In a word, longing.

Christ as Head

In contrast, Colossians and Ephesians remove longing from the person of Christ, and neither letter exhibits the double effect, the *consolatio amoris*, Philippians might have had on its first readers. In fact, both Colossians and Ephesians pride themselves on being tools of authority. Note, for example, how the author of Colossians employs the epistolary cliché *absent in body / present in spirit* not to set the scene for the confession of longing as Paul did but to undergird the pseudonymous Paul's authority:

For I want you to know how much I am struggling for you, and for those in Laodicea, and for all who have not seen me face to face. I want their hearts to be encouraged and united in love, so that they may have all the riches of assured understanding and have the knowledge of God's mystery, that is, Christ himself, in whom are hidden all the treasures of wisdom and knowledge. I am saying this so that no one may deceive you with plausible arguments. For though I am absent in body, yet I am with you in spirit, and I rejoice to see your morale and the firmness of your faith in Christ. (Col 2:1–5)[49]

Ephesians 3:2–4 likewise directs readers to think of the letter in terms of standard epistolary theory. That is, the letter they have received is a substitute for the presence of the author and nothing more complicated than that. To read Ephesians, according to Ephesians, is to know the mind of its author:

For surely you have already heard of the commission of God's grace that was given me for you, and how the mystery was made known to me by revelation, as I wrote above in a few words, a reading [*anaginōskontes*] of which will enable you to perceive my understanding of the mystery of Christ.

The letter displays an "understanding of the mystery of Christ" to secure readers' assent to the author's teachings. Thus while the Paul of Ephesians refuses to dwell on the separation from the recipients of the letter, the Paul of the genuine Epistles made that absence the space in which the writing and reading of theology happen. The pseudonymous Paul rejects longing as an emotion befitting an apostle and instead trumps up his authoritative presence. The letter delivers the mind of the author to the readers.

Not only do Colossians and Ephesians share a reading theory that departs from the *consolatio amoris* of Philippians; they share a Christology that rejects Philippians 2:5–11. Colossians 1:15–20 presents the doctrine of Christ's headship, a doctrine that replaces the *servitium amoris* motif in the Christ hymn and supports a church dependent on authoritarian leadership:

He is the image of the invisible God,
  the firstborn of all creation;
  for in him all things in heaven and on earth were created,
  things visible and invisible,
  whether thrones or dominions or rulers or powers—
  all things have been created through him and for him.
He himself is before all things,
  and in him all things hold together.
He is the head of the body, the church;
he is the beginning,
  the firstborn from the dead,
  so that he might come to have first place in everything.
  For in him all the fullness of God was pleased to dwell,
  and through him God was pleased to reconcile to himself all
    things,
  whether on earth or in heaven, by making peace through the
    blood of his cross.

It is tempting to think, though not possible to prove, that the author of Colossians intended this hymn to correct Christ's disastrous giving into emotion in Philippians 2:5–11. For one thing, it is striking that divine visibility is the first thing the author of Colossians denies. Visibility, however, is built into "form of God" in Philippians 2:6, which begins with the story of a body and what happens to that body's innards (*ta splagxna*) when it longs for others. Moreover, in Philippians, the one who longs for others will be confessed as Lord by all manner of beings, and indeed God was the first to do so (2:9–11). In contrast, Colossians 1:15 eliminates God's response to Christ Jesus's emptying—that is, the dissipation of his body in longing for the world. In place of emptying, Colossians 1:15 asserts the Son of God is "the image [*eikōn*] of the invisible God." The idea behind "image" is that of representation; the Son models an unchanging God and God's fullness filling the world: "For in him all the fullness of God was pleased to dwell" (Col 1:19).[50] It seems that Paul's critique of God's sovereign rule over humanity was too much for the author of Colossians and Ephesians to take, although the God of Philippians 2:9 seems to have been quite pleased to step away from lordship, since he gave it to the longing one: "Therefore God also highly exalted him and gave him the name that is above every name." Thus Colossians and Ephesians replace a God who both exalts the longing one and calls him Lord with a God who endlessly repeats his fullness and self-sufficiency.

Colossians and Ephesians also replace the *servitium amoris* motif in Philippians with the image of the head: "He [Christ] is the head of the body, the church" (Col 1:18; see also 2:10, 19).[51] The most extensive treatment of this motif is in Ephesians:

> In him we have redemption through his blood, the forgiveness of our trespasses, according to the riches of his grace that he lavished on us. With all wisdom and insight he has made known to us the mystery of his will, according to his good pleasure that he set forth in Christ, as a plan [*oikonomia*] for the fullness of time, to gather up [better, "head up," *anakephalaiōsasthai*] all things in him, things in heaven and things on earth. (Eph 1:7–10)

The cosmos is guided by a "plan," an inadequate translation of *oikonomia*, a word made up of *oikos* (household) and *nomos* (law). Christ *heads up* the universe just as elite males head up their households by ruling wives, children, and slaves (see Eph 5:21–6:9 and Col 3:18–4:1). Ephesians 1:22 reiterates the idea that Christ is the head of the cosmos:

> God put this power to work in Christ when he raised him from the dead and seated him at his right hand in the heavenly places, *far above all rule [*pasēs archēs*] and authority [*exousias*] and power [*dynameōs*] and dominion, and above every name that is named, not only in this age but also in the age to come.* And he has put all things under his feet and

has made him the head [*kephalēn*] over all things for the church, which
is his body, the fullness of him who fills all in all. (Eph 1:20–23; my
emphasis; see Col 2:10)

A comparison of Ephesians 1:22 ("far above all rule") with 1 Corinthians
15:24 reveals the radical transformation the author of Ephesians worked
on Paul's antipathy toward authority. Here is 1 Corinthians 15:24: "Then
comes the end, when he [Christ] hands over the kingdom to God the
Father, when he has nullified all rule [*pasan archēn*], all authority [*pasan
exousian*], and power [*dynamin*]" (my translation). It is one thing to render
all rule, all authority, and power null and void as Paul imagined Christ
doing and another matter entirely for Christ to exist as head *beyond* all rule,
all authority, and power as the author of Ephesians thought. In 1 Corinthians 15:24, Christ in the present moment and until the end of time
contests authority's self-proclaimed right to order the self, communities,
and the cosmos. Christ as the Messiah who is always yet to come is *right
now* deconstructing authority, which always wants to have its way by saying,
Well, that is just how it is. Indeed, the Greek word for authority is *exousia*,
which literally means "from being." In Paul's imagination, the kingdom
(or, better, reign or ruling activity) that the Son hands over to the Father
in the end will paradoxically have been purged of all rule, all authority,
and power. The author of Ephesians, however, spares the Father (and all
male heads of households everywhere and indeed even into the next age) a
crisis: the Father will never have to decide whether to accept the Son's way
of ruling without rule. Never, according to Ephesians, will the Father be
confronted with the Son's lordship—a sovereignty that in Philippians 2:5–11
was a matter of longing for communion. The Christ of Ephesians hands
nothing transformed to the Father but remains head of the universe as if the
universe were a household "not only in this age but also in the age to come."

Furthermore, in Ephesians and Colossians, not only is Christ, the
head, very male and authoritative; he is also very moral, if by "moral"
one means what ancient philosophers took it to mean: self-controlled.[52] In
the following passage, Christ is called the *perfect* or *mature male* (*anēr teleios*),

although the gender specificity of this phrase has been obscured by the NRSV's translation "to maturity":

> The gifts he gave were that some would be apostles, some prophets, some evangelists, some pastors and teachers, to equip the saints for the work of ministry, for building up the body of Christ, until all of us come to the unity of the faith and of the knowledge of the Son of God, to maturity ["into the perfect male," *eis andra teleion*], to the measure of the full stature of Christ. We must no longer be children, tossed to and fro and blown about by every wind of doctrine, by people's trickery, by their craftiness in deceitful scheming. But speaking the truth in love, we must grow up in every way into him who is the head [*kephalē*], into Christ, from whom the whole body, joined and knit together by every ligament with which it is equipped, as each part is working properly, promotes the body's growth in building itself up in love. (Eph 4:11–16)[53]

The *perfect male* was a philosophic term of art.[54] He is perfect in virtue and the model for all who strive to live lives of self-control.[55] An individual aspiring to virtue grew into the *perfect male* by imitating his manner of life, as Plutarch writes:

> The man who is truly making progress, comparing himself with the deeds and conduct of a good and perfect man [*andros agathou kai teleiou*], and being pricked by the consciousness of his own shortcomings, yet at the same time rejoicing because of his hope and yearning, and being filled with an urging that is never still, is ready in the words of Simonides "To run like weanling colt beside its dam," so great is his craving all but to *merge his own identity in that of the good man.*[56]

The individual making progress disappears into the perfect male—growing into the head, as it were. This philosophic concept of imitation reappears in Ephesians 5:28–29, as I will point out below.

The motif of the head occurs again in Ephesians 5:21–33. These verses have profoundly influenced the Christian church's hierarchical views of marriage and ecclesiastical authority. They have also soured many readers on the genuine letters of Paul. This is unfortunate, since the following contrast could not be greater: on the one hand, there is the Christ of Philippians 2:6–11, who is a slave of love, the longing Lord whose grief over the beloved's separation melts and empties his body, and on the other hand, there is the Christ of Colossians 1:15–20, the Son of God, "the head of the body, the church." After Paul's death, Colossians and Ephesians pitted hierarchical control against longing, and longing lost.

The defeat of Pauline theology is apparent in Ephesians 5:21–33, where the pseudonymous Paul puts forward three analogous relations of power: the husband rules his wife as a head (*kephalē*) rules its body and as Christ rules the church. In each relation, the appropriate response to being ruled is subordination:

> Be subject [better, "be subordinate," *hypotassomenoi*] to one another out of reverence [better, "fear," *phobō*] for Christ. Wives, be subject to your husbands as you are to the Lord. For the husband is the head [*kephalē*] of the wife just as Christ is the head [*kephalē*] of the church, the body of which he is the Savior [*sōtēr*]. Just as the church is subject [*hypotassetai*] to Christ, so also wives ought to be, in everything, to their husbands. (5:21–24)

Subordination is not just the wife's acceptance of the husband's rule. There is a more sinister demand placed on her: as Diane Enns observes, subordination requires that the wife allow herself to be erased: "In Paul's version of conjugal love, husband and wife do not become one flesh but one self, and it is the husband's self that the two become. This relation does not sustain her; it sustains him. He feeds on his wife's devotion; as her self diminishes, his engorges."[57] The wife is not an other to the husband. She is an extension of his body. He regards her as if she *were* his own body. Control of his body / his wife serves his interests: "He who loves his wife loves himself. For no one ever hates his own body, but he nourishes and tenderly cares for it, just as Christ does for the church, because we are members of his body" (Eph 5:28–30).[58] In gratitude for her head's love—"love" understood here as benevolent supervision—the good wife disappears into her husband.

Conclusion: Consolation of Love, Messiah, and Hope

I had three aims in this chapter. First, with respect to Paul's alleged authoritarianism, I sought to rescue him from his critics—and even more from his admirers—and to shift the charge that his letters should be considered among the master narratives of the West to where that accusation properly belongs. I sought to lay it against the author of Colossians and Ephesians. Second, I wanted to read an undisputed Pauline epistle—in this case, Philippians—in light of ancient epistolary theory's claim that a letter delivers the presence of the writer to the reader. The idea that writing is a technology for the reproduction of the author's voice bears a striking resemblance to phonocentrism and its relation to hierarchical control, a topic addressed at greater length in the next chapter. In Philippians, Paul steps away from epistolary theory's confidence that a letter delivers the writer's presence. Instead, the letter paradoxically reiterates the absence of the writer to the reader by the very means through which it delivers the illusion of presence. Third, I wanted to correlate the uncontested acceptance of epistolary theory in Ephesians and Colossians with the repressive hierarchical structure of church, family, state, and the self found in these letters. Reading theory and social/political/personal life also intersect in Philippians but in a radically different way. Paul's emphasis in the letter on the emotion of longing calls attention to the absence, the gap, the internalized emptiness in desire mixed with grief that resides between friends and lovers and generates an anti-hierarchical politics of respect, desire for communion, and the inescapable mourning of its impossibility.

And now a brief note about how I came to write this book. Just after I finished a manuscript on the motif of longing in ancient erotic poetry and in Paul's Letter to the Philippians (that book's influence runs throughout the present chapter), I picked up John D. Caputo's *The Prayers and Tears of Jacques Derrida: Religion without Religion*. I read it several times (OK, five or six times) in the next few years hoping to understand more each time, and by "understand," I mean both "comprehend" and "fall prey to fascination." One section of the book among several that still intrigues me is entitled "The Messianic," and by "intrigues me," I mean "just when I think I have it, I realize I don't, but that just whets my appetite to understand." Caputo raises up to prominence a definition of the Messiah that I had been familiar with but had not thought much about: the Messiah is the one who is to come. Nor had I any idea of how important the figure of the Messiah as the coming one was for twentieth-century thinkers Walter Benjamin, Emmanuel Levinas, Maurice Blanchot, and Jacques Derrida and, now into the twenty-first century, for Caputo and a growing number of others. Baldly stated, the logic of the Messiah that has garnered so much attention is this: if the Messiah is the one who is to come, then if the Messiah shows up, he is not the Messiah; in other words, the condition for the possibility of the Messiah is also the reason for the impossibility of the Messiah. The Messiah can't come and still be the Messiah. Caputo writes about the significance of this reasoning:

> But this non-arrival of what is to come is also, and this is what inter-
> ests me here, a way of safeguarding the indeterminacy, chance, and
> lightness of what is to-come—which is its messianic side. That can be
> expressed by saying that the Messiah never comes, that the very idea
> of the Messiah would be destroyed were the Messiah, to everyone's
> embarrassment and consternation, to have the indiscretion to show
> up and actually become present. The very idea of the Messiah is that
> he is *to come, à venir*, someone coming, not that he would ever actually
> arrive. . . . The messianic idea turns on a certain structural openness,
> undecidability, unaccomplishment, non-occurrence, non-eventuality,
> which sees to it that, in contrast to the way things transpire in ordinary
> time, things are never finished, that the last word is never spoken. Were

the Messiah ever to show up, that indiscretion would ruin the whole idea of the messianic.[59]

When I read this paragraph (perhaps not the first time), I saw a connection between the *consolatio amoris* in Philippians and what Caputo calls "the very idea of the Messiah." In other words, Paul gave a messianic twist to epistolary theory in Philippians: the condition for the possibility of the absent writer's presence, the letter itself, is also a reminder of the writer's absence. I also saw a connection between longing and what it means to believe in the Messiah. The rest of this book returns again and again to the idea of the Messiah—how in the Gospel of Mark and the letters of Paul, the Messiah's "non-arrival" structures reading, faith, grace, justice, and in the following chapter, hope.

CHAPTER 3

Reading for Hope, Reading for Discipline

ROMANS 12–15 IS a chaotic scene, nothing like the well-ordered universe the Paul of Luke–Acts, second-ranking master of hermeneutics, read like a book in Athens at the Areopagus to please Stoic ears. In Rome, an emperor brandishes a sword while vegetarians judge meat eaters and meat eaters look down their noses at vegetarians as both factions read about the Messiah, the anointed one, the one who is always yet to come, who in an impossible inversion of human appearing and disappearing first dies and then lives. Barely noticeable in this hubbub lies a revolutionary theory about reading the Bible. Revolutionary because instead of regulating the political/ dietary/death-life jumble that surrounded him and infiltrated his mind, Paul gave to the disorder another spin by stating in a single verse what Scripture is good for: "For whatever was written in former days was written for our instruction, so that by steadfastness and by the encouragement of the scriptures we might have hope" (Rom 15:4). While it is true that the first three results of reading—"instruction," "steadfastness," and "encouragement"— are good things, especially in chaotic times, nevertheless, these benefits do not reach all the way to revolution. Revolution comes with hope, for hope takes the risk of desiring the world to be other, impossibly other, than it is.

But the revolution died with Paul. The Pastoral Epistles (1 and 2 Timothy and Titus) killed it. If Paul read his Bible because he desired the impossible—that is, if he read for hope—then the unknown author of the Pastoral Epistles, deceitfully calling himself *Paul*, read the same Scriptures Paul read but for a radically different reason: to make something of himself. In

this respect, the author of the Pastoral Epistles imitated the ancient philosophers for whom the fashioning of the self was the only reason a sober,
elite male ought to spend time in the company of a book.[1]

In this chapter, I will describe how the author of the Pastoral Epistles
set aside Paul's theory of reading for hope and, in line with ancient philosophers, narrowed the point of reading to self-formation. To this end, I
will focus on 2 Timothy 3:14–16, a famous passage that has overshadowed
Romans 15:4 in the history of Christian hermeneutics:

> But as for you, continue in what you have learned and firmly believed,
> knowing from whom you learned it, and how from childhood you
> have known the sacred writings that are able to instruct [*sophisai*]
> you for salvation through faith in Christ Jesus. All scripture [*graphē*]
> is inspired by God and is useful for teaching [*didaskalian*], for reproof,
> for correction, and for training [*paideian*] in righteousness [*dikaiosynē*].

What makes these letters sacred? They have the power to "*sophisai* you for
salvation through faith in Christ Jesus."[2] According to the Pastoral Epistles'
theory of reading, Scripture is sacred because its words make the reader
wise in the matter of self-discipline, which in turn leads to salvation.[3] If
you ignore the call to self-discipline, whether it is the moral philosophers
or the author of the Pastoral Epistles who issues the call, you bring disaster
upon yourself.[4]

Twenty-first-century proponents of 2 Timothy 3:14–17 are not fazed by
the absurdity that the author of the Pastoral Epistles, who was not the self
he claims to be, exhorts his children, Timothy and Titus—also fictions—to
make something of themselves.[5] Putting aside the double deception, however, we will explore how the author of the Pastoral Epistles took advantage
of the apostle's death to appropriate his reputation for establishing and
guiding churches and how he sought to domesticate his theology.[6] This
pseudonymous Paul opted out of hope's revolution by putting an end to
readers' desire for things to be other than they are. Instead of hope for a new
world—that is, hope for a *new* something more just than can be imagined

in all spheres of life—in the Pastoral Epistles, moral discipline of the *self* prevails and does so with repressive consequences for social, political, and personal life.[7] In the world imagined by the Pastoral Epistles, self-control reigns. Gone are the emotional instability and the social class upheaval that would surely come if others share the real Paul's belief that the powerful have an infinite obligation to bear the weaknesses of those without power.[8]

Under the Influence of Hope

In Paul's Letter to the Romans, hope works by the same *logic of impossibility* that enlivens John D. Caputo's reimagining of religion.[9] For Caputo, hope differs from optimism, which is a positive expectation of future possibilities. What distinguishes hope is its yearning for the impossible.[10] Caputo writes that "hope means that a great 'perhaps' hovers over the world, that what holds sway over the world is not the Almighty but a might-be. But 'perhaps' does not signify an attitude of lassitude or indifference. 'Perhaps' is risky business, a resolute staying open to a future that is otherwise considered closed."[11] Very few ancient authors embraced this paradox of hope Caputo finds in Romans 4:18: "Hoping against hope, he [Abraham] believed that he would become 'the father of many nations,' according to what was said, 'So numerous shall your descendants be.'" Paul's Abraham illustrates that hope kicks in, if it ever does, when no reason to hope presents itself.[12] Hope is an example of *the logic of impossibility*.

Ancient philosophers, however, valued hope quite differently than Paul and Caputo. For philosophers, hope was a moral disease, a weakness standing in the way of inner peace. They would not have shared Paul's admiration for the decrepit Abraham in Romans 4, who exemplifies a hope that lives without reason for hoping. How could hope live, reason asks, since Abraham's next-to-dead body together with Sarah's advanced age says a flat-out no to their desire for children? Yet not only does hope get going in hopelessness, if it gets going at all, but Paul also asserts that salvation itself depends on hope—in the sense not that hope earns salvation but that salvation happens when hope happens: "For by hope we were saved. Now hope that is seen is not hope. For who hopes for what is seen? But if we hope for what we do not see, we await eagerly with endurance" (Rom 8:24–25; my translation). Clearly, the salvation Paul has in mind does not look like the later Christian doctrine of salvation as the eternal preservation of the soul or like that doctrine's precursor in the teachings of the philosophers, salvation as the inner tranquility of the self-disciplined soul.[13] In fact, hope does not *look* like anything, since one hopes for the unseen.

"Hope that is seen is not hope." That paradox drives Paul's theory of Scripture in Romans 15:4. Hope depends on the *nonappearance* of what is hoped for. Hope is therefore very similar to the Messiah, who, if he/she/it/they ever show(s) up, would not be the Messiah, since the Messiah is the one (or more than one) always yet to come. Hope is also like faith. When faith turns into knowledge, it ceases to be faith, as Paul wrote elsewhere: "For we walk by faith, not by sight" (2 Cor 5:7). There is something always yet to come in hope. That is why hope differs from optimism and makes it more like insatiable desire. The kind of hope Paul speaks about requires whatever is hoped for to *not* appear and *not* be seen. The moment the hoped-for thing arrives, hope evaporates.

Judging, then, by what ancient philosophers said about hope and in light of hope's logic of impossibility, it is easy to imagine that elite readers of Romans, who were accustomed to hearing public figures speak on philosophical topics, would have found Romans 15:4 perplexing, frustrating, and even absurd.[14] As much as philosophers despised hope, they loved self-discipline, and this attitude likely was shared by at least some of Paul's readers. The Stoics especially, whose influence on the writings of the New Testament and its readers scholars increasingly recognize was quite significant, taught that self-control was the only rational approach to life. Only achieving reason's goal of inner tranquility justifies the risk of reading, which carries with it the stimulation of emotion. Thus it is reasonable to think that Paul's theory of reading for hope, reading to spark desire for the infinite otherwise, landed with a thud for his first readers in Rome. Convinced of the Stoic claim that happiness depends on detachment from worldly values such as money and glory but also from spouses, children, and even the fate of one's body, Paul's readers in Rome might have dismissed his turn to hope. Not hope but wisdom is the goal of reading; one must turn inward to the soul and accept whatever happens as the will of God. To wish that things might be otherwise than they are—that is, to hope for the new and unexpected—was the raving of a fool and an insult to God, the author of creation, who is both master and manager of the universe. Hope is, therefore, a shortcut to misery, as a poem attributed to Seneca, a Stoic philosopher of the first century and advisor to the emperor Nero, warns:

> Hope the deceiver, Hope the sweet evil, Hope the sum of all evils,
>   Solace for the wretched whithersoever their destinies drag them,
> Credulous being whom no misfortune can put to flight,
>   Hope stands by her duty in time of ultimate evil.
> Hope forbids one to find peace within the everlasting gates of Death
>   And with the sword to cut short anxious cares.[15]

The poem goes on to list the foolish and disastrous actions taken by hopeful sailors, prisoners, criminals, gladiators, and others who would be better off to resign themselves to fate and just die. Hope only makes matters worse.[16] Only a fool would read for hope.

Reading for Discipline

For a moment, turn your backs on Paul and heed the warning of the philosophers. Look away from Romans 15:4 and reject hope as the reason for reading Scripture. Instead, submit to the authoritative voice in 2 Timothy 3:16–17 that tells us to read in order to increase our capacity for self-discipline. This turn has implications greater than the ordering of the inner life. From self-control come social and political order as well. I make this point because the reading theory that the Pastoral Epistles and the philosophers shared might seem oriented to individuals and to lack social and political significance, but that was not the case. The self's ordering of

the self was not a stand-alone topic in ancient philosophy, nor was it in the
Pastoral Epistles and the later writings of the New Testament. Philosophers
and the early Christians who accepted their conceptual framework sought
to gather physics, politics, household management, and self-formation
under a single structure or order (*taxis*). The *household* (*oikia*) is one name for
this structure.[17] This was not a radical move, since the *law of the household*
(*oikonomia*) had been the paradigm for politics, theology, and the organization of the self from classical antiquity to imperial Rome and would
continue in this role for centuries to come.[18] Just as God orders (*tassō*) the
universe, just as the emperor rules his subjects, just as the individual's ruling
principle (soul, self, etc.) governs the body and its passions, so also the
head of the household orders persons under his authority (wife, slaves, and
children). I am by no means the first to point out these structural parallels
among ancient theology, politics, psychology, and family life.[19]

The point I want to emphasize is that the reach of *oikonomia* extended
also to reading. The writer's intention rules over the text as the soul rules
over the body, as the husband rules the wife, and so on. Thus the Pastoral
Epistles do not simply exhort elite males to search Scripture for models of
subordination in personal, political, and cosmic settings. That is certainly
a feature of these letters, but I want to go further to claim that the pseudonymous Paul, like his philosophic precursors, built subordination into the
act of reading itself. He adopted the traditional, phonocentric idea that
the author writes to encode his voice in ink figures; to read is to decode the
letters—that is, to revocalize the author's voice, which is a reflection of
his (always *his* in the ancient form of this theory) mind.[20] Reading makes
it possible for the author's voice to live again in the reader's mind and
rule the reader's body. But I am getting ahead of myself. We need to take
a step back and review the ideology of the ancient Greek household, the
birthplace of *oikonomia*, to understand its influence on the Pastoral Epistles'
theory of reading.[21]

To understand *oikonomia*, we need to think of the ancient household
(*oikos*) as a social structure. According to Aristotle, three asymmetrical

relationships define the *oikos*. That is, three streams of ruling or ordering power emanate from the male head to the other members of the household. As father, the head of the household rules the children for the children's benefit. As husband, he rules the wife for their common benefit. As master, he rules slaves for his own benefit. Wives, children, and slaves have one proper response to the control imposed on them: subordination (*hypotagē*), a crucial term in the Pastoral Epistles as well as Colossians, Ephesians, and 1 and 2 Peter. The root (*tag*) points to the order (*taxis*) these authors are so eager to impose. Order guarantees harmony within the household, as it does also within the cosmos, which Stoic philosophers and the Pastoral Epistles imagined to be the Greek household writ large. God manages the universe as a father manages his household.[22] Accordingly, the God of the Stoics was called "he that ordains" (*ho diatassōn*). Epictetus writes,

> But instruction consists precisely in learning to desire each thing exactly as it happens. And how do they happen? As he that ordains [*ho diatassōn*] them has ordained [*dietaxen*] And he has ordained [*dietaxe*] that there be summer and winter, and abundance and dearth, and virtue and vice, and all such opposites, for the harmony of the whole, and he has given each of us a body, and members of the body, and property and companions.[23]

To live wisely is to subordinate one's will to the governing power.[24]

The significance of the *oikos* for understanding writing and reading appears more distinctly when we compare it to another major social institution in the ancient world, the assembly (*ekklēsia*). Beginning in the sixth century BCE, the assembly was the regular public gathering of male citizens whose conversation, deliberation, and voting governed the city.[25] Not only were the members of the *ekklēsia* male and freeborn citizens, but they were also masters, since each participant in the assembly was required to own at least one slave. Evidence from the genuine Pauline Epistles suggests the earliest gatherings of the urban followers of Jesus adopted the name

ekklēsia (consistently translated as "church" throughout the New Testament) and the assembly's democratic practices of free speech, conversation,
and deliberation.[26] Significantly, this new assembly in the time of Paul
rejected the traditional limitation of membership to slave-owning, male
citizens. The Pastoral Epistles, however, departed from these democratic
practices and modeled their groups after the Greek *oikos* rather than the
ekklēsia even though the latter term remained in use. This redefinition of
church as household received the blessing of the author who falsely called
himself *Paul*:

> I hope to come to you soon, but I am writing these instructions to
> you so that, if I am delayed, you may know how one ought to behave
> [*anastrephesthai*] in the household [*oikō*] of God, which is the church
> [*ekklēsia*] of the living God, the pillar and bulwark of the truth.
> (1 Tim 3:14–15)

Note in this passage the connection among reading, writing, and the control
of behavior. The linkage among them will be important in a moment when
we dig deeper into the reading theory of the Pastoral Epistles.[27]

First Timothy 3:1–7 provides further evidence of the household's
displacement of the assembly. Here are the qualifications of an *episkopos*
(bishop, although this is an anachronistic term). Again, note the key term
"subordination" (*hypotagē*; see 2:11–12): "standing first in a good way over
his own household [*oikou*], having children in subordination [*hypotagē*] with
all possible reverence. If someone does not know how to stand first over his
own household [*oikou*] how will he care for the church [*ekklēsias*] of God?"
(my translation). Translation of the term *episkopos* (perhaps "overseer") is
less important than the way power relations of the Greek household defined
his role in the church (which is really an *oikos*): *he knows how to stand first*.
The term *subordination* is a sign of the sexism and male dominance present throughout the Pastoral Epistles and, for that matter, in Colossians,
Ephesians, and 1 and 2 Peter as well. To sum up, the writers of these

pseudonymous letters transformed the democratic social relations of the Pauline church or assembly (*ekklēsia*) into the hierarchical social relations of the ancient household.[28] The related point I want to emphasize is this: in addition to silencing women and slaves, this transformation required a theory of reading that reinforced hierarchical structure. Second Timothy 3:16–17 claims that the holy writings promote self-ordering. In this respect, they mirror the subordinating power belonging to the head of the household, to God (the master of the universe), and to the emperor (head/father of the inhabited world, or *oikoumenē*).[29]

Philosophers and the author of the Pastoral Epistles define the relation between men and women in terms of subordination. Although some ancient philosophers thought women were capable of moral virtue, these intellectuals were not protofeminists.[30] Far from it. Since they thought women were more susceptible to desire than men, a prejudice reflected in 1 Timothy 2:14, the only virtue women needed was self-control (*sōphrosynē*). *Sōphrosynē* stands behind "modestly" in 1 Timothy 2:9 and "modesty" in 2:15. So how does a woman exercise self-control? By setting aside her own emotions. And how does she do that? By disappearing into her husband. Plutarch explains, "Just as lines and surfaces, in mathematical parlance, have no motion of their own but only in conjunction with the bodies to which they belong, so the wife ought to have no feeling of her own, but she should join with her husband in seriousness and sportiveness and in soberness and laughter." Wives ought to disappear from their own self-consciousness by subordinating themselves to their husbands. Plutarch is similarly oblivious to these murderous thoughts as he praises the husband's gentle eradication of the wife's otherness:

> If they subordinate themselves [*hypotattousai*] they are commended,
> but if they want to have control, they cut a sorrier figure than
> the subjects of their control. And control ought to be exercised
> by the man over the woman, not as the owner has control of a piece
> of property, but, as the soul controls the body, by entering into her

feelings and being knit to her through goodwill. As, therefore, it is possible to exercise care over the body without being a slave to its pleasures and desires, so it is possible to govern a wife, and at the same time to delight and gratify her.[31]

Thus the ideal husband colonizes his wife as the emperor colonizes foreign nations.[32] Imitating the colonizer's pretense of good intentions, a husband occupies his wife's feelings and never bothers to ask where she has gone in order to make room for him. Plutarch's words about the good wife's disappearance suggest that the translation "full submission" in 1 Timothy 2:11 does not adequately convey the depth of the author's misogyny. Like Plutarch, the author of the Pastoral Epistles thinks a wife not only ought to be obedient to her husband, and cheerfully so, but she must also recognize that her being comes from her husband. And since he is the source of her life, she owes him silent obedience and puts her self-control into practice by dressing in a way that advertises her invisibility and subordination to her husband.[33]

What do these social and political facets of subordination and household management mean for the Pastoral Epistles' theory of reading Scripture? Many readers regard 2 Timothy 3:16–17 as the definitive statement about Christian hermeneutics, but they might consider whether they also embrace the author's quietism in the face of empire, hierarchical control in family life, the male self's preoccupation with itself, and the subordination of women to men. The theory of reading in the Pastoral Epistles is in league with these ills.

God-Breathed: The Phonocentrism of 2 Timothy 3:16

The theory of reading in the Pastoral Epistles has another name: phonocentrism, a word invented by Jacques Derrida that stands for a set of ideas and social practices related to the spoken word's alleged superiority over writing. Derrida discussed Plato's *Phaedrus* to get at phonocentrism and its involvement with patriarchy. I will turn to the historian and politician Arrian, a student of the Stoic philosopher Epictetus. Arrian vigorously denies having written anything at all in a letter that serves as a preface to the eight books he did in fact write, only four of which survive, recording Epictetus's lectures.[34] In this brief letter introducing his teacher's *Discourses*, Arrian makes clear that the text of the *Discourses* should not be read as literature.[35] It is instructive how it chafes Arrian to think readers might mistakenly regard him as a writer. This was not a matter of modesty. The writing they have in their hands, according to Arrian and the tenets of phonocentrism, is not a text that he has composed but the voice of Epictetus speaking his mind:

> Arrian to Lucius Gellius, greeting: I have not composed [*synegrapse*] these Words of Epictetus as one might be said to "compose" [*syggrapseie*] books of this kind, nor have I of my own act published them to the world; indeed, I acknowledge that I have not "composed" [*suggrapsai*] them at all. But whatever I heard him say I used to write down [*grapsamenos*], word for word, as best I could, endeavouring to preserve it as a memorial, for my own future use, of his way of thinking and the frankness of his speech. They are, accordingly, as you might expect, such remarks as one man might make off-hand to another, not such as he would compose [*suggraphoi*] for men to read in after time. This being their character, they have fallen, I know not how, without my will or knowledge, into the hands of men. Yet to me it is a matter of small concern if I shall be thought incapable of "composing" [*suggraphein*] a work, and to Epictetus of no concern at all if anyone shall despise his words, seeing that even when he uttered them he was clearly aiming at nothing else but to incite the minds of his hearers to the best things. If, now, these words of his should produce that same effect, they would have, I think, just that success which the words of the philosophers ought to have; but if not, let those who read them be assured of this, that when Epictetus himself spoke them, the hearer could not help but feel exactly what Epictetus wanted him to feel.[36]

Epictetus's "way of thinking and the frankness of his speech" require preservation so that others might have Arrian's experience of his teacher's ability to incite students' minds "to the best things."[37] Hearing the living voice of Epictetus is the only way this can happen.[38] Thus if Arrian's written words are to have any value, they must be conceived by the reader as Epictetus's voice.[39] For this reason, Arrian calls his writing "memorials" (*hypomnēmata*) that preserve Epictetus's mind. My point is this: Arrian's confusion of voice and text is the same confusion at the heart of 2 Timothy 3:16, where the Scriptures (*graphai*, "writings") are claimed to be "God-breathed" (NIV), which is another way of saying "God's voice." The same confusion stands at the center of phonocentrism and at the center of the theory of reading in the Pastoral Epistles: text is mistaken for voice.

Why would Arrian and the author of the Pastoral Epistles confuse an inscribed surface with articulated breath? For one reason, the inherent deficiencies of writing disturbed these two first-century authors just as they had disturbed thinkers from Plato to today's interpreters.[40] What are these shortcomings? The phonetic alphabet, it will be recalled from the introduction, was conceptualized and gratefully received in antiquity as a technology that recorded the writer's voice for later retrieval. And yet the technology was not perfect. The written word has a severe drawback: it cannot stabilize the meaning it transmits. Once a writing has been separated from its author, direct inquiries to the author about intended meanings are no longer possible. Texts are therefore subject to questions they cannot answer because they do not in fact speak. Guesses can be made, of course, and they can be more or less educated, but no certainty about the original thoughts (if indeed there ever was certainty about the thoughts) can be achieved no matter how informed the guesses. This uncertainty obstructs the philosophic project of self-formation adopted by the Pastoral Epistles. The task of self-fashioning that these letters set for themselves requires both certainty about the goal of self-discipline and clarity about the methods to achieve it. In other words, a student requires the teacher's mind and the ideas contained within it. Now we can understand why Arrian and the author of the Pastoral Epistles were forced by their own logic to misconceive text as voice; only if they ignored this confusion could the clarity of the teacher's mind guide the student's self-formation.

Phonocentrism is the false confidence that the living voice does not share in writing's drawbacks. Voice (*phonē*) supposedly transports an idea in its purity from the teacher's mind to the student's mind.[41] The teacher's voice as a reflection of his mind motivates and guides the student to form himself (the gender specificity of teacher and student in the ancient world was a given) into a self, the perfect male (*anēr teleios*; see Eph 4:13). When teacher and student are separated in space (the fictive occasion of the Pastoral Epistles) or in time (the problem every new generation faces in response to its tradition), writing becomes the necessary but regrettable substitute for the voice.[42] The absent teacher writes to remind students of what was once said (see 2 Tim 2:14; 2 Pet 3:1–3), and students read to remember the teacher's words that once had moved them, or motivated their forebears, to actualize the power for self-control implanted within them by God. Written words are at best only an aid to memory, notes to assist the readers' rekindling of already existing moral capacities.[43] To provide this assistance, writing *must* be mistaken for voice, which was (and widely still is) taken to be an illumination of the speaker's mind.[44]

There is another defect of writing, according to ancient philosophers: writing spawns more writing. That is, if an author or first readers are no longer available to answer questions about the written words, later interpreters are left on their own to puzzle out a dead or absent author's meaning and then broadcast their findings by writing more words, which, of course, will need to be interpreted and written about. And so it goes without an end in sight. Writings piled upon writings stray further from the original, intended meaning. The author of the Pastoral Epistles worries with the philosophers about the proliferation of words. Second Timothy 2:14 is an exhortation to preach against disputants who quarrel about words (*logomachein*), a catchy term used since the time of Plato to describe the verbal battle of sophists.[45] Moreover, in contrast to those who, like women, waste time with many words and detract from the simplicity of authoritative teaching, Timothy is told he must "rightly cut [*orthotomounta*] the word of truth" (2 Tim 2:15; my translation).[46]

To cut discourse meant to shorten it, to keep it to its essentials so the minds of the hearers would not wander off.[47] Cut speech is clear, male, powerful, and useful for moral education. And most of all, it is *speech* and not text.[48]

Back to Hope

Here is this chapter's argument so far. The Paul of the undisputed letters, who desired the world to be impossibly other than it is, read Scripture for the hope one day it might be. The Paul of the Pastoral Epistles shut down hoping against hope and consigned reading to moral formation. For the fictive Paul, reading is useful when it is put under the control of God, the emperor, the father, the teacher, and the ideal self. In the Pastoral Epistles, one reads not to hope but to subordinate oneself to the way authoritative voices say (in writing) things are.

This conflict between hope and discipline reflected in the antagonism between Romans 15:4 and 2 Timothy 3:16–17 has gone largely unnoticed in the history of Christian thinking about reading the Bible. Taking their cues from 2 Timothy 3:16–17, interpreters of Romans 15:4 from the second century onward have latched on to the word "instruction" (*didaskalia*), which the two passages do indeed have in common. *Didaskalia* was a philosophic term referring to the body of knowledge ancient teachers of wisdom transmitted to students. Their aim was to instill certitude, self-control (*egkrateia*), and moral virtue (*aretē*) in their students.[49] This is exactly the way Clement of Alexandria interprets *didaskalia* in Romans 15:4:

> Fit objects for admiration are the Stoics, who say that the soul is not affected by the body, either to vice by disease or to virtue by health; but both these things, they say, are indifferent. And indeed Job, through exceeding continence [*egkrateia*] is depicted as a good example . . . teaching that it is possible for the gnostic to make an excellent use of all circumstances. And that ancient achievements are proposed as

images for our correction, the apostle shows. . . . "For what things the Scripture speaks were written for our instruction [*didaskalia*] that we, through patience and the consolation of the Scriptures, might have the hope of consolation."[50]

Clement transforms Paul's words about reading for hope into reading for virtue.[51]

So how did a code word like "instruction," which for ancient readers signified self-formation through self-discipline, find its way into the same verse (Rom 15:4) as "hope"? This question does not even arise for Clement, since in admiration for a Stoic-like Job, he downplays the importance of hope and goes all in for self-control. But what if Paul brought *didaskalia* on board in Romans 15:4 in order to release a meaning from the word other than self-discipline? In what follows, I will suggest that Paul lets *didaskalia* be dispersed into life's flux and transformed by the unpredictable flow of experience. But that states the matter too abstractly. So imagine emperors with swords, arrogant vegetarians, condescending meat eaters, and other troubles so severe that one does not know whether one is alive or dead, and birth feels like the point of entry to death. These conditions make hope (as optimism) impossible, but they are the right conditions for a hope that defies hope, a hope that blossoms when there is no reason to hope. "Instruction" in Romans 15:4 opens itself to my hopelessness when I encounter the universe's disregard for me and my projects of self-formation. Instead of "instruction" leading to the inner strength of the individual as it did with Clement and the philosophers, for Paul, "instruction" leads to weakness, a coming undone of the self that, in an act of radical hospitality, shares in the coming undone of the other. Paul's "instruction" turns the "self" outward to welcome what the flux brings—the new, the unforeseen, which often is written on the face of the other.[52] In Paul's reformulation of "instruction" (might we call it the *deconstruction* or, as the Lutheran in me wants to call it, the *reformation* of *instruction*?), what counts as learning is *endurance* (*hypomonē*), indeed, but also the *call* (*paraklēsis*) of the other and, most of all, hope. In other words, Paul invents a new *didaskalia* by pairing it with hoping against hope, the very openness to the other that ancient philosophy tried to exclude through instruction in virtue.[53]

Romans 15:1–4, the immediate literary context of Paul's one-verse theory of reading, is a good example of his inventiveness with texts, or as I will speak of it, his playfulness:

> We have a debt, we the powerful, to carry the weaknesses of those without power, and not to please ourselves. Let each please the neighbor for the good, for building up. Indeed, the anointed one did not please himself, but just as it stands written: "The reproaches of the ones reproaching you fell upon me." For whatever was written before was written for our instruction, in order that through the endurance and through the exhortation of the writings we might have hope. (My translation)

This passage is loaded with philosophic, poetic, and biblical words repeated by a multitude of writers before Paul ever came on the scene. Paul's method is to repeat what had been written before, but he does so with a twist, creating opportunities for readers to change how they think, feel, and act. In short, Paul works from the inside out. He does not throw aside philosophic and religious traditions but repeats them and teases out new meanings from them.[54]

Romans 15:3 is a prime example of Paul's subtle maneuvering or playfulness: "The insults of those who insult you have fallen on me."[55] Here he quotes a small portion of Psalm 69. It is not that Paul adds, changes, or leaves out any words. Still, his version seems to differ from the original. What is going on? The meaning of Psalm 69 taken as a whole does not seem to be Paul's concern. He is interested only in the words he quotes. He copies eleven words (eight in Greek) from the Psalm and places them into his own discourse. Now in their new context, the pronouns "you" and "me" throw out their lines to different referents. In Psalm 69, the word

"you" refers to God and "me" refers to the writer of the Psalm, traditionally understood to be David. But now in the setting of Romans 15:3, the
"me" is no longer David but the Christ, the anointed one, and the "you"
refers to anyone who has suffered insult or reproach. Thus by placing these
words borrowed from Psalm 69 in a different context, Paul opens them to
a different meaning. That is one way Paul repeats tradition with a twist.
There are others, as I will discuss below.

These twists are barely noticeable and rarely commented on, and
yet they undermine the view of authority in 2 Timothy 3:16–17 that many
readers bring to the Bible. It must be admitted, however, Paul's playfulness also challenges the historical-critical method itself, which looks to
the original context of a writing and the first readers' reception to deter-
mine the author's intention—the method I primarily employ in this book.
Unlike many conservative *and* liberal readers, Paul does not feel bound
by the intention of the author (whether it was King David or God), who
clearly had other ideas about those pronouns in Psalm 69. Simply put,
Paul was not impressed with *authorial intention*, the gold standard of literary interpretation that held sway until the middle of the twentieth century
and for many readers still is in effect. And so we have come to a perplexing
problem, perhaps even embarrassing, for liberals and conservatives alike.
Paul, a recognized biblical authority, a model interpreter, and a guide
to proper hermeneutical method, disregards the plain sense of a verse taken
from his own Bible, the Septuagint, and generates a new meaning not even
hinted at in the author's (and for the vast majority of Christian readers
in the last two millennia, this would be God's) original, intended meaning.
And he called himself an apostle!

Here is the point I think matters for reading the Pauline Epistles in the
twenty-first century. Paul is quite adept at repeating what had been written
in Scripture and in the literary and philosophical traditions of his day, but
he does not *merely* repeat tradition as Clement thinks he does. He repeats
and tweaks patterned phrases and accepted ideas as he lets the traditional
train of thought flow in new directions. To read Paul's act of reading the

Bible requires that we follow the twists he makes with traditional texts and the turns he takes with commonplace philosophic ideas on the way to something new.

Playing Seriously

If I have given the impression the apostle was a rambunctious child—thumbing his nose at authors and authority, cutting out strings of words from one old book, the Septuagint, and pasting them haphazardly into another piece of writing that generations later would be called holy—then I have not said what I want to say. There is a serious side to Romans 15:1–6, and the trick to reading Paul's writings is to detect how his play serves a moral purpose. Now, everything I admire about Paul's theory of reading and want to commend to today's readers rests on (1) what "moral" means in the phrase "moral purpose" and (2) what "play" is. For Clement of Alexandria, morality meant moral virtue, and moral virtue presupposed the power of an elite male who, because he owned slaves, had the leisure to dissipate his life or, if he heeded the exhortations of the philosophers, to come to his senses, reject desire, and form himself into a self-controlled individual. With respect to Paul's way of reading, as I will now attempt to show, *moral* has a different meaning than it had for Clement. For Paul, morality does not start with personal freedom, which could go in the direction of dissipation or in the direction of self-control. *Moral* in the Pauline vocabulary means responsibility—or, better, a responsiveness—to the vulnerability and otherness of others; it means to offer hospitality to familiar persons, of course, but more importantly to welcome the unfamiliar, the excluded, and the despised. And to do so out of one's own weakness and in a way that does not turn the strange into the familiar. *Play* for Paul is a matter of putting pressure on words, bending them, squeezing unintended meanings out of them, and relying on his readers to do the same, all for the sake of reaching out to the isolated and to those who count as nothings. Paul plays, therefore, so that he might be moral.[56]

For this reason, Paul chooses his words very carefully. His playthings are words with philosophic resonance ripe for tweaking. Nevertheless, he does more than repeat words preloaded with significance; he further loads them with diverse and sometimes incompatible connotations. As I discuss below, Paul plays with words to allow concepts to deconstruct themselves, concepts that his readers might have supposed had dropped from heaven or sprouted from the head of a sage attuned to the heavens. Paul indicates that concepts, words, and institutions are created things and therefore exposed to re-creation and, for the playfully minded, recreation too. In the case of Romans 15:1–3, Paul plays for this moral aim: to open up the philosophic tradition's concept of moral virtue as perfection of the self to something far less narcissistic. Rather than the virtue of self-control, Paul promotes the morality of welcoming the other and bearing others' weaknesses.[57] It hardly needs saying, but the author of the Pastoral Epistles had no time for such sentimentality, as he would have regarded Paul's other-oriented morality.

As a further example of Pauline playfulness, observe the way he toys with the first three letters of the word "please" (*areskō*) in Romans 15:1–3. *Please* (*areskō*) starts with the same three letters as *virtue* (*aretē*), one of the weightiest terms in ancient philosophy: "We, we the powerful have a debt to carry the weaknesses of those without power and not to please [*areskein*] ourselves. Let each please [*aresketō*] the neighbor for the good, for building up. Indeed, the anointed one did not please [*ēresen*, the past tense of *areskō*] *himself*" (my translation). I suggest Paul repeats the word "please" (*areskō*) to allude to moral virtue (*aretē*) and then to criticize it. In this way, he distances himself (and makes it possible for his readers to do so) from the philosophic preoccupation (see 2 Pet 1:3–4) with happiness acquired through the virtue of self-control.

To make this interpretation plausible, I need assistance from ancient experts on language, grammarians, whose speculations about definitions relied on words alluding to other words. Clearly, Paul was not the only one who loved language's openness to play. For example, Orion, who lived in the fifth century CE, notices what I have pointed out (not in connection with Paul, however)—that the word *aretē* looks like *areskō*. Orion takes his play a step further than I would. He claims *aretē* came from *areskō*. Why does he think this? "It is called virtue [*aretē*]," he writes, "because it pleases [*areskei*] the truth; virtue comes from the word to please."[58] Here Orion might also have been thinking of flattery, the insincere pleasing of another person.[59] To please another is to conform oneself to them, to praise them to the skies, to agree with them always, to say yes when they say yes and say no when they say no.[60] Flattery in turn leads to a further association: slavery. Flatterers were often called slaves, who stereotypically pleased their masters by expressing no contrary opinions.[61] Putting these associations together, we can see how Paul cleverly redirects reading away from virtue to hospitality. He writes the letters *a-r-e*, and in the split second it takes to read them, our minds (if we were thinking in Greek) are taken to Greek equivalents of *virtue, flattery*, and *slavery* before we go on to pronounce *s-k-ō* and arrive at *please*.

Paul builds one more bit of playfulness into *areskō* for Greek readers. It is contained in the phrase "please himself" (*heautō ēresen*) in verse 3. This phrase has at least two meanings. It could have designated persons who were virtuous, since their bodies served or pleased their minds—that is, they kept their passions obedient to reason. Or the phrase could have signified arrogant behavior—that is, putting oneself first and overriding the interests of others by self-indulgence.[62] And one more association with *a-r-e* might be noted: the Greek god of war was Ares. Now all of these allusions—virtue, flattery, slavery, pleasing, and arrogance, and perhaps even Ares—need to be brought to bear on Romans 15:3: "Christ did not please himself."

Here is the point I hope is becoming clear. Reading is chaotic. Reading a Pauline letter especially so. A flurry of words alluding to other words passes in and out of the reader's mind, setting a wild scene not unlike the opening of this chapter, where vegetarians shout at condescending meat eaters and the emperor spews forth threats backed by the sword. In the middle of such a melee, questions arise. What was it that Christ, the anointed one, did? Did he renounce arrogance? Did he renounce moral virtue—that is, morality as virtue? Or did he renounce both arrogance and virtue?

The point I set out to make about 15:1–3 is that Paul refuses to play along with ancient philosophy's reduction of reading to its usefulness for moral (in the ancient philosophic sense) improvement. He refuses to grant that Scripture's purpose is to supply examples of virtue (*aretē*). Yet he does not contest the Greek word *aretē* directly. Like a basketball player giving a head fake, Paul *almost* writes the Greek word for virtue three times, only to veer away each time at the last moment. Paul simultaneously hints at virtue and at arrogance. Is Paul suggesting that virtue is the same as arrogance? Quite possibly. Perhaps he is saying the anointed one had no truck with arrogance or with virtue, or with the arrogance of virtue. Where was Paul taking his first readers? Those who were philosophically minded and unwilling to read playfully might have thought he was encouraging them to become slavish flatterers ("Let each please the neighbor").[63] Perhaps, in a sense, he was, although he insisted on calling pleasing others by another name, *love*.

Coming Undone

Love is crucial for Paul's theory of reading Scripture, as important as hope. But love is just as difficult to pin down as hope, so we should be grateful that interpreters agree on one thing, that Paul defines love in 15:1: to love is "to carry [*bastazein*] the weaknesses of those without power." That is my translation. I offer it because there is an air of condescension in the NRSV's translation of *bastazein* that confuses Paul's view of love with the magnanimous act of superior persons toward inept or morally corrupt inferiors: "We who are strong ought to put up with the failings of the weak, and not to please ourselves."[64] Against the translation "to put up with," it might be observed that in ancient literature, *bastazein* was associated with carrying the corpse of a loved one to its burial site.[65] This image of the living bearing the dead suggests that something more profound is going on than morally and socially superior persons *putting up with* or tolerating the missteps of persons perceived to be inferior.[66]

Consider also the NRSV's phrase "the failings of the weak," for which I did not provide an alternative translation, although there is the need for one. "Failings" implies that the strong are much better at managing their lives than the weak. The translation "weaknesses of those without power" is better, yet this alternative still misses something significant about *asthenēmata*, which more accurately is translated as "weak things." Judging from the frequency of its occurrences in Paul's writings, it would not be an exaggeration to say that weakness—not just human but also divine weakness—is a leading theme in his theology. First Corinthians 1:25 is illustrative: "For God's foolishness is wiser than human wisdom, and God's weakness is stronger than human strength."[67] To be weak is not a matter of failing. It is to be shaken at the center of one's being, for the core itself to come apart: "And I came to you in weakness and in fear and in much trembling" (1 Cor 2:3). To be weak is to be in utter perplexity about even what to pray for: "Likewise the Spirit helps us in our weakness; for we do not know how to pray as we ought, but that very Spirit intercedes with sighs too deep for words" (Rom 8:26).

Ancient philosophers well understood weakness and avoided it at all costs.[68] Another name for passion, weakness is a futile desire that does not know what will bring it closure or give it satisfaction.[69] Weakness is thus the opposite of virtue. No friend of weakness, Philo of Alexandria nevertheless takes us straight to the point: "For weakness is brought about by emptiness and strength by fullness."[70] Strength is getting it together, summoning inner resources, and standing firm in the face of difficult circumstances. It is the purposefulness of an unwavering soul. Weakness is spiritual dissipation, the inner person's melting and draining away.[71] Weakness—and in this respect, it resembles hope—is coming unglued with desire for things to be other than they are with no idea how to make them so, a feeling Plutarch disparages as *repentance*:

> So true is it that the purposes of men, unless they acquire firmness
> and strength from reason and philosophy for the activities of life,
> are unsettled and easily carried away by casual praise and blame,

being forced out of their native reckonings. For it would seem that not only our action must be noble and just, but the conviction also from which our action springs must be abiding and unchangeable, in order that we may be satisfied with what we are about to do, and that mere weakness may not make us dejected over actions which have once been accomplished, when the fair vision of the Good fades away.[72]

Plutarch makes it clear that just as a body becomes weak, unable to hold itself up or control its movements or the flow of its fluids, so also the weakened soul flutters when faced with the difficulties of life. The weak soul melts and drains away in desire for something it cannot name.

Thus in his exhortation to bear the weaknesses of others, Paul directs readers away from self-formation, the central enterprise of philosophy in the first century and the reason many readers in the twenty-first century still turn to the Bible. Unlike the author of the Pastoral Epistles, Paul refuses to allow his theory of Scripture to be co-opted by the philosophers, for whom writing was a substitute for the human voice, a useful technology for the preservation of the author's ideas, and a way for teachers to implant strategies of self-improvement in the minds of students. Paul orients writing and reading toward hope in the face of hopelessness. Scripture is there not to help us make something of ourselves or to stabilize communities or to explain how the universe works but to call forth the weak force of hope from us, which is an openness and yes-saying to a future that we cannot imagine.

The Personal Becomes Political: Hospitality

Reading for hope, reading to unleash an unsettling openness to the unknown and unexpected, has political consequences. Hope becomes political when we realize our chance to say yes to unfathomable events rests upon the arrival of strangers and the call to respond to their vulnerabilities, especially their relation to death, with the most gracious hospitality possible. And if the grace is absolute—that is, if the hospitality preserves the visitant in their otherness, their singularity—then that act of hospitality is impossible, but for that reason all the more desirable.[73] Furthermore, if hope dreams the world otherwise, then Paul's reading theory, driven by hope, imagines a paradoxical world where justice reigns, although it is a justice that never allows satisfaction. For this reason, Paul's hope-infused reading theory generates a restlessness about the status quo that refuses to be quieted, refuses to be content with limits on hospitality or what is now called justice. Paul's theory of reading is not really a theory in the normal sense of the word but a plea for readers to suspend the decoding of letters and stop seeking the author's—or, for many readers of the Bible, God's—mind; it propels readers into the public sphere, where suffering never can wait for the reader-centered discovery of meaning. Hope interrupts the task of self-formation. The world's transformation always starts *right now* with the vocalized or silent plea of the excluded other.

Today, *politics* is a dirty word, since it is associated with fearmongering, polarization, manipulation of public opinion, destruction of reputations, and the list goes on. Politics has been narrowed to elections and cynical attempts at governing, always with fundraising and another round of elections in view. What has dropped out of the sphere of the political, for the most part, is the give-and-take of public conversation in a space safe enough for changing minds over matters of common concern. There are, of course, exceptions, but the trend certainly seems to be away from testing ideas and toward apathy, away from positive engagement and toward a resentment paired with acceptance of the way things are. This situation has made the virtue theory of reading Scripture (we read the Bible to form ourselves into better persons) all the more attractive, since many readers of the Bible have come to believe that the only change that they can effect is change within themselves.

So how might we find a path leading from Paul's hoping against hope to political engagement? The first word of Romans 15:1 ("we owe," *opheilomen*) signals that Paul has no interest in beginning this journey with self-formation or virtue. His disinterest, however, should not be confused with apathy about social justice. Instead of virtue, Paul grounds both his theory of reading Scripture and his journey toward political engagement with a conviction that haunts every word in his Letter to the Romans. This letter breathes the conviction that he and his readers are indebted to unnamed and innumerable others. A debt is owed that can only be discharged—and the truth is, it can in principle never be discharged—by fulfilling the infinite call of love in public space, as we read in 13:8–10:

> Owe [*opheilete*] no one anything, except to love one another; for the one who loves another has fulfilled the law. The commandments, "You shall not commit adultery; You shall not murder; You shall not steal; You shall not covet"; and any other commandment, are summed up in this word, "Love your neighbor as yourself." Love does no wrong to a neighbor; therefore, love is the fulfilling of the law.

To think of oneself as always already in debt to unnamed and unknowable others—"neighbors," in the language of the Bible—is a challenging idea for twenty-first-century readers who, when it comes to thinking about social relations, are accustomed to the language of personal virtue or of boundaries and defined duties. Paul has something else up his sleeve. The revolutionary vision Paul places before his readers is a scene of yielding to insatiable love for neighbors.[74]

Paul's idea of a primordial, infinite obligation of each human being to one another (and the other need not be human) is in tune with the Hebrew Bible's emphasis on hospitality to the stranger. Hospitality is a resounding rejection of ancient philosophy's goal of happiness acquired through self-discipline and self-perfection. Paul does not think of ethics as the science of happiness as the Greeks did. Neither does he think as Immanuel Kant does in terms of universal duties applicable in all situations, irrespective of particular circumstances. Instead, he imagines himself already always in debt, always too late on the scene of suffering to take time for the perfection of the self through the discipline of his desires and too devoted to the particularity of the individual standing before him to apply general rules governing the relationship. For that reason, in Romans 1:14, Paul introduces himself to the Roman church and frames the entire letter in a remarkably unphilosophical way. He sidesteps the ancient public leader's customary self-commendation based on moral achievements.[75] Instead, he begins the main argument of his Letter to the Romans by confessing the debt he has to each and every other: "I am a debtor both to Greeks and to barbarians, both to the wise and to the foolish" (1:14). He does not articulate a plan to improve others by teaching them how to control emotions as Clement of Alexandria wishes that he had. Romans gets started with the stunning claim that life itself initiates a debt impossible to repay. Is this a rational way to think about life? Is it even possible to live this way? To whom is the debt owed, and why? I suspect that I ask these questions in order to limit my obligation and preserve my sanity. If I could figure out the *whom* and *how many* questions, I could come up with a payment plan in which my expenditures for others might be calculated. Eventually, I could pay off the debt. So it is important to note Paul's debt is not to God. Neither is it to a single identifiable individual. Nor is it to humanity in general, as if ethical action were a matter of fulfilling abstract duties. It looks like Paul has created an ethical mess. John D. Caputo writes about the deconstruction of ethics that comes about when one begins, as Paul does, with an obligation to every other as totally other:

> You begin to see the effect of the deconstruction of ethics, the double effect of liberating obligation from ethics, or setting it loose from ethics. . . . Obligation becomes a fact (as it were), but a shaky one, with emphasis on the as it were. For I do not know its origin, its whence or its whither. . . . I feel its force but I can prove nothing of its provenance. Obligation is a feeling, the feeling of being bound (*ligare*, *ob-ligare*, *re-ligare*). . . . I cannot get on top of it, scale its heights, catch a glimpse of its rising up. It comes at me, comes over me, overtakes me, seizes hold of me. As soon as I come to be I am already in its grasp.[76]

Similarly, Paul doesn't explain why he is in debt to every person in the world regardless of ethnic origin, or education, or whether they possess virtue. He just is, or in Caputo's words, which would make a great bumper sticker, "Obligation happens."[77] If Paul were able to repay the debt, he would not be Paul.

What I propose is this: We should read all of Romans—all of the New Testament, for that matter—through Paul's phrase "I am a debtor." Reading in this way, we would share in Paul's identity, which, paradoxically, is ever changing (even though he is quite dead), always renewed by the face of the other. As we will see in the next chapter, Paul's identity is stamped by his nonidentity, by his indebtedness rooted in the inexpressible obligation he feels as he faces every singular other. A hopeless impossibility if ever there was one. No wonder reading is for hope! Thank goodness there are writings, sacred and profane, to be read, to be opened, to be played with, with pronouns reassigned and tender examples placed before our eyes of those who have carried in their bodies the coming undone of others.

CHAPTER 4

Faces

THE PASTORAL EPISTLES tire me out. So do Colossians and Ephesians. Reading these letters wearies me of myself, the self my lifelong religious and cultural upbringing tells me I am supposed to be.[1] It is as if they were mirrors held up before my face revealing my deficiencies and condemning me to my own ideal image.[2] Without enthusiasm, I discussed these writings in previous chapters. I had to. Their repressive ideas about self-discipline and household management (*oikonomia*) support a widespread theory about reading Scripture, the belief that when one reads the Bible, one hears the voice of God. But their confusion of text and voice alone does not explain why these letters are so draining.

I think these letters falsely written in Paul's name wear me out because in God's name, they exchange Abraham's and Paul's hoping against hope for the rigor of self-discipline, self-formation, and self-control. I resent their theft of my time (not that it has ever been mine). I do not want to spend what moments remain to me reading exhortations to accomplish what I have not succeeded at so far—making something of myself—all for the sake of obtaining the infinite extension of myself (passing infinite time doing what?) outside of time. So I wonder, Is there a form of living that is a matter neither of spending nor of making? Might I be drawn away from the promised tranquility of soul that perfected selves are said by ancient moral philosophers to enjoy, released from the pseudonymous Paul's promise of eternal salvation, which looks to me, and feels to me, like the curse of everlasting self-preoccupation preceded by a lifetime of self-recrimination?[3]

More wondering. Might it be that another's face has the power to save me from the disciplined self the false Paul wants me to fashion under the guidance of the sacred writings? There are several witnesses to the arresting character of faces: everyday experience, ancient literature, and the Paul of the genuine letters testify that when the eyes of others capture our eyes, an unlooked-for freedom from the idealized self springs up.[4] Love streams from faces.[5] Beauty shines, and so do grace, favor, and charm—all English translations of the untranslatable Greek word *charis*.[6] Faces beam and eyes twinkle, though sometimes they blaze and cast lightning.[7] Either way, faces break the inward gaze of self-examination and crack open time itself, if only for an instant. Perhaps a face can save me from myself.

Here is a literary example of face power. In his fourth-century work *Aethiopica*, the novelist Heliodorus depicts what might be called the infinite deferral of closure, the opposite of what self-discipline aims at in the philosophically minded writing in Colossians, Ephesians, and the Pastoral Epistles. He describes how a face-to-face encounter dislodges the two main characters, Anthia and Habrocomes, from their usual preoccupations. They met, fell in love in a flash, and for "a brief second full of emotion they stood motionless and gazed hard into one another's eyes as if calling to mind a previous acquaintance or meeting." They smile and then blush. Embarrassed, "since passion touched their hearts, their faces blanched. In short, in the space of an instant, an infinity of expression passed across both their faces, as every imaginable alteration in complexion and countenance bore witness to the waves that pounded their souls."[8] If an "infinity of expression" were ever to play out on my face as I gazed on the ever-changing faces of others . . . well, that might be all the rescue from the demand of self-formation I need, although I admit it might also be terrifying.

The thesis (more of a hope, really) of this chapter is that faces, because they promise life (but a life not separated and preserved from death), have the power to change what we look for in Scripture. Faces divert us from the philosophic task of self-formation. They redirect our reading to the terrifying/joyful anticipation of that which, if it happens, will always have been unanticipated. Therefore, since it has not been my intention in this book to update the traditional, phonocentric way of reading the Bible, I now call for a looking up and away from texts and a turning around to face the other, any other, every single other. The apostle Paul reports, with some poetic license, that Moses himself hears this call to move away from writing to gaze at a face. In 2 Corinthians 3, the ancient lawgiver of Paul's imagination does indeed descend Mount Sinai with weighty stone texts, but it is another scene that catches Paul's attention. It is when Moses experiences a face-to-face relation with the divine other: "But when Moses went in before the Lord to speak with him, he took the vail off, until he came out" (Exod 34:34 KJV). Paul wants all his readers to imitate Moses's unveiled gaze:

> Nevertheless when it [or "he"—a reference to Moses] shall turn to the Lord, the vail shall be taken away. Now the Lord is that Spirit: and where the Spirit of the Lord *is*, there *is* liberty. But we all, with open face beholding as in a glass the glory of the Lord, are changed into the same image from glory to glory, *even* as by the Spirit of the Lord. (2 Cor 3:16–18 KJV)

It seems as if Paul imagines his readers not reading books but being transformed into (whose?) image by gazing into each other's faces as if looking into a mirror and seeing . . . what? Their own faces, the faces of others, the Lord's face?

What is required for reading the New Testament in the twenty-first century from Paul's perspective, I think, is to follow Paul's passion—to look at Paul looking at Moses looking at God and to learn from them to look away from texts and to gaze at faces. Then, and only then, ought we to read books. To read the New Testament as the Paul of the genuine Epistles would have us read it—although the apostle himself would not live to see these wildly divergent writings herded together under the title *The New Testament,* and I surmise he would not have thought much of the motley collection—we must begin by not reading it, or any other book, especially the one you have in your hands right now. We must begin with faces.

Warning

Strange as it may sound, in 2 Corinthians 3:6, Paul warns his readers away from reading texts. Texts, he tells them (us), are deadly: "For the letter kills, but the Spirit gives life." In this chapter, I will argue that although the letter/ Spirit distinction—from here on written "letter/spirit" to respect the ancient Greek habit of using letters of uniform height—is the touchstone of biblical hermeneutics, it has attained this status for the wrong reason. What I mean is 2 Corinthians 3:6 does indeed have something very important to say about reading, but it is not what the history of interpretation has claimed—namely, that Christian faith provides exclusive insight into the intention, or the spirit, of the author of creation / the Bible. Christian readers have been told for centuries that to be restored to the life God intended for them, they need to know the creator's thoughts hidden behind the literal sense of the Old Testament. Much of biblical interpretation thinks of itself as giving saving information to readers fallen into sin and ignorance.

I think about 2 Corinthians 3:6 differently: the verse warns readers to stop reading long enough to look at faces and feel the overwhelming urgency to respond to the mystery beyond language harbored in another's gaze. In other words, 3:6 is a plea for readers to suspend book reading and to throw themselves into preserving the otherness of those whose deepest intentions and secrets cannot be known, not even to themselves. The New Testament ought *not* to be read, at least not until a reader becomes familiar with—*shaken by* is more like it—the mysterious, unfulfillable obligation that overwhelms us when another's face has been held in view and holds us in view. With this deep attentiveness to the unknowable other in mind (if this is even possible), we might think of "For the letter kills, but the Spirit gives life" as Paul's version of the Gospel of Mark's "stay awake," a phrase I will explore in the final chapter. So "let the reader understand" (a phrase also discussed in the final chapter; Mark 13:14): stop reading books—yes, you—at least for now. Instead, go read a face and let your face be read. This book, all books sacred and profane, can wait. Waiting is what they do for most of their time on earth anyway. It is, after all, what bookshelves are for.

Before Other Texts: Faces

If you are sounding out the letters making up the words of this sentence that means you have dismissed my interpretation of Paul's warning that the letter kills. Justifiably, I admit, you question my idea that 2 Corinthians 3:6 calls for a moratorium on reading. So in response to your challenge—*Does Paul really privilege faces over texts?*—I answer a faltering yes, aware of how absurd this idea sounds. As I said above, generations of interpreters have understood 3:6 in isolation from Corinthians 3 and have turned the letter/spirit distinction into a motto for Christian hermeneutics.[9] My intention in this chapter is to present a different way of reading 3:6, to think of it as an example of Paul's obsession with faces, an obsession that runs throughout 2 Corinthians 3. Gazing on a face (or not being able to) is obviously a major theme in this portion of the letter, but interpreters have not thought it relevant to the distinction between letter and spirit. I want to change that.

The first step is to think about the face-to-face relation itself. A face seems to give immediate knowledge of the mind behind it, and yet face reading gets complicated with breathtaking speed.[10] Faces give knowledge and at the same time take it away. How does this happen? Imagine a friend seated across from you. Her facial expressions are like word-forming combinations of the alphabet. You see her arched eyebrow, curled lip, darting eyes, and countless other micromovements on the page-like surface of her skin. The language on her face invites you to read her inner self as printed words invite you to know an author's meaning. In other words, her face is a symbol system that communicates her thoughts and feelings. You come to know your friend better by observing the signs written on her face. Theoretically, then, if you were to gaze on her face long enough, you could know her perfectly.[11] *Theoretically*, that is.[12]

Doubtless, there is something lacking in this commonsense account of face reading. I have not yet reckoned with the marvelous mess we get ourselves into when we gaze at a face. Facial expressions are indeed symbolic, and they do invite us to approach the soul of the other. Yet experience also tells us reading faces is not so straightforward. For one thing, as you gaze at your friend, she gazes back, and your face changes in response to what you read on hers. Her arched eyebrow (it leads you to think, *Doesn't she believe me?*) makes your mouth turn down (then she wonders, *Have I saddened him?*). How you appear to her alters what you see as you look at her. A smile crosses your lips (you cannot help it) when you see her take in your sadness, and she responds by lowering her raised eyebrow, and you think, *I've won*, although she knows very well the look of self-satisfaction now coming across your face, that familiar smirk. She frowns, and off you go on another round of tracing each other's thoughts on the other's skin and in their eyes. If there is such a thing as reading faces, it must be far more complex than a subject's observation of an object—unless you insist that she not look back at you or that she keep her expressions frozen, two disastrous ideas for a friendship.

There's more. Face reading gets more complicated the more you think about it, since a face is as much a mirror as it is a book. When your eyes look into your friend's eyes, you see your own reflection in his pupils.[13] You now have two faces to read instead of one, his and yours—or, more accurately, the image of yours *on* his. In addition, since he now sees himself in your pupils, his own gaze confronts him in your gaze. So it goes ad infinitum. And there are even more reasons for perplexity. What if all along he has been mimicking you? What if, just to please you, he shapes his face to be like yours, smiles when you do, and pouts when you do? Or what if he mimics you to mock you? Or what if he turns your naïve confidence in the ability to read the symbols on his face to his advantage precisely to deceive you?[14] These thoughts are tying you in knots. The same vexing thoughts occur to him. Do your suspicions register on your face? Can you keep them from showing? Can he keep his from showing? Your friendship is fraying, or so it seems. Perhaps, though, it is just getting started. Might it be that this confusing, infinite oscillation between knowing and nonknowing, always on the threshold of figuring the other out only to have them withdraw into unknowability, might this deferral of closure be what it is to read another's face? One more question, which might seem out of place

but will soon make sense: Might the open-endedness of reading another's
face be what Paul means by "life" in 2 Corinthians 3:6?

Moving from symbols inscribed on the other's face to the person housed
in the head runs into at least one more wall. What if more than one self is
at home behind the other's face? The usual theory of face reading assumes
that there is a unified subject living within each of us, transparent to itself,
knowing what it wants to do and what it wants to say either in words or by
facial expressions or with pen/keyboard and paper/screen. With a touch
of humor, John D. Caputo explains why this notion of the unitary self has
undergone severe criticism in philosophy, literary criticism, and theology
in the last one hundred years:

> For when we speak of the "I" or "we" or the "self," we are employing
> a certain shorthand that glosses over the complexities, that hastily
> summarizes the current state of an inner anarchic conflict in which
> there are numerous competing forces, constantly shifting, and unsteady
> alliances and unexpected turns yet to be taken. The "I" is like the
> reluctant chairperson of a committee who has been pushed out
> the door to make a progress report and to create the impression of
> consensus, while behind closed doors the committee itself remains
> locked in irreconcilable conflict.[15]

Caputo here sheds light on why gazing at your friend has resulted in more
mystery, not less, and more desire to know her and no satisfaction in what
you have discovered. The more you look, the more uncertain you become
about who you are and who she is, about what she wants from you and
what you must do to respond. You thought you knew her, but you don't
and never will, as long as you pursue the only chance you have of knowing her: gazing face-to-face. She, he, or they—or the multiple selves that
constitute the one her/him/them—are who they are by responding to you,
whom they cannot know any more than you can know yourself (yourselves),
since you also have no single, fixed, or unchanging identity but *live* by

responding to them. Being face-to-face—you are discovering as you prepare to read Scripture as Paul advises by reading faces first—does not promise a path to the full knowledge of the other. Rather, it promises an unending search for the unknowable in which meaning, presence, and immediacy will always be deferred.

Perhaps this deferral is what Paul means by "life." Faces and texts have this in common: to read them, or to *attempt* to read them, is to launch out on a journey, the ending of which, if there will even be an ending, we cannot possibly imagine. The face is a page covered with letters, a surface upon which a symbol system lies, but there is more mystery about faces and texts than a system can contain, since neither a face nor a written page guides us directly to a mind. The other's soul and the author of a text are both hidden from our gaze behind an impenetrable surface. In fact, it is an article of faith that there even *is* a soul behind a face or an author behind a page, although both page and face certainly tempt us to think so and entice us to keep on reading to find out.

What's more, reading a face generates an insatiable desire for knowing the other *and* makes knowledge of the other impossible. Paul, it seems, calls upon readers of books to read in a perpetual quest to know *and* to respond to the text by recognizing it in its longed-for but unreachable otherness, to read with an intense desire to know and continue reading with a confession of the impossibility of ever knowing what a text wants to say to us (as if *it*—ink on paper—could possibly know). When we read, we find ourselves opened, hospitable to the new and the not-yet-even-imagined that arrives in, and in spite of, the symbols we try futilely to master. We expose ourselves to a future that cannot be known, only welcomed or feared—or, better (or, perhaps, worse), welcomed *and* feared. Life, in other words.

The idea I have resisted throughout this book is this: if reasonable and broadly accepted methods for interpreting a text are employed, if we read in light of historical and cultural contexts, and if we search for the intention of the author and what first readers understood the text to mean, there is a good chance we will know what an author meant, and we will be equipped to apply that message to our lives and make something of ourselves and our communities. Now, to be clear, I do not object to method itself. What I object to goes deeper than method to the idea hiding in method—namely, that reading literature ought to be goal oriented, that we read the New Testament to form ourselves as selves or our communities as communities.[16] I see 2 Corinthians 3 pointing us in a different direction, away from satisfaction with a text's determinable meaning and toward the restlessness and insatiability arising from face-to-face relations. Caputo's representation of Derrida's *deconstruction* articulates my hope for what reading the New Testament might become in the twenty-first century:

> There is in Derrida what one might call a certain overreaching, trespassing aspiration, what I have been calling here, all along, a dream, or a desire, a restlessness, a passion for the impossible, a panting for something to come. This passion is not a determinable wish or will for a definable goal or foreseeable objective, however hard any such goal may be to attain. It is not a search for something plannable and foreseeable, the fulfillment of which can be steadily approximated, our progress toward which regularly measured. Over and beyond, beneath and before any such determinate purpose, there is in Derrida, in deconstruction, a longing and sighing, a weeping and praying, a dream and a desire, for something non-determinable, un-foreseeable, beyond the actual and the possible, beyond the horizon of possibility, beyond the scope of what we can sensibly imagine.[17]

Reading any writing, including the New Testament, will be enhanced—in the sense of opening us to the coming of the other—when we tremble before the gap between a text's or a face's promise of delivering an intended meaning and its failure/refusal to do so. I believe, I wonder, I hope (but of course, I do not know) that trembling while facing the other is what Paul means by "life."

Sappho in Saint Paul

In the Christian tradition, the phrase *face-to-face* communicates honesty, immediacy, and straightforward access to the other. Yet for some ancient writers, particularly the poets and novelists who traced the effects of love on those who love, *face-to-face* connoted paradox and indeterminacy. For these writers, the mutual gaze both inflicted and healed (and inflicted again by its healing) a burning desire, always unsatisfied, to know the other. The thesis of this chapter is that 2 Corinthians 3 repeats the *face-to-face* motif that was popular from the seventh century BCE to at least the sixth century CE, and this repetition forms a crucial context for understanding "for the letter kills, but the Spirit gives life."[18]

Sappho helps us see that the many faces appearing to each other in 2 Corinthians 3 communicate something infinitely more *self-shaking* than a subject knowing an object does. She begins her most famous poem by situating a couple face-to-face: "He seems as fortunate as the gods to me, the man who sits opposite [*enantios*] you and listens nearby to your sweet voice and lovely laughter." Then, in a shift in perspective that continues to intrigue scholars, the narrator of the scene herself experiences the lovers' emotions. Her heart trembles. It becomes impossible for her to speak: "My tongue has snapped, at once a subtle fire has stolen beneath my flesh, I see nothing with my eyes, my ears hum, sweat pours from me, a trembling seizes me all over." Here the mutual gaze bestows not knowledge but an experience near to dying.[19]

Three centuries later in the *Argonautica* of Apollonius of Rhodes, the *face-to-face* motif reappears with all the soul-shaking force released in Sappho's poem. The god Eros wounds Medea deep in the heart with a love for the adventurer Jason. Overwhelmed with longing and fear, she is speechless: "She continually cast bright glances straight at [*antia*] Jason, and wise thoughts fluttered from her breast in her distress. She could remember nothing else, for her heart was flooding with sweet pain." The fire of love consumes her, "such was the destructive love that curled beneath her heart and burned in secret. And her tender cheeks turned now pale, now red, in the distraction of her mind."[20] Later in the story, Medea and Jason meet again. Their standing face-to-face leads not to mutual knowledge but to a *lovesick distress* and breathless silence followed by a rush of words like the endless rustling of trees, a powerful metaphor of indeterminacy: "The two stood facing each other [*ephestasan allēloisin*] in speechless silence, like oaks or lofty pines that stand rooted quietly side by side in the mountains when there is no wind, but then, when shaken by a gust of wind, they rustle ceaselessly—thus were these two about to speak a great deal under the force of Love's breezes."[21]

Finally, there is the remarkable sixth-century CE poem of Paulus Silentiarius inspired by Sappho. To my knowledge, no other poem in antiquity so powerfully presents the tension between the desire for knowing the other and the infinite deferral of that knowledge. The poem begins, "I saw the lovers." This is a reminiscence of Sappho, *Fragment* 31. Paulus then goes on to write of "the ungovernable fury of their passion" and of their "yearning, if possible, to plunge into one another's hearts." They try different strategies to cross over to each other, from kissing to the exchange of clothing, the latter an act that might be interpreted as their abandonment of gender markers to achieve the desired communion. Yet nothing satisfies, not even sitting opposite of each other. They cannot quell their shared desire for each to dwell in the other. Their face-to-face relation only increases the desire: "One would more easily pry apart two intertwined stems of a twisted vine that have long merged their tendrils, than those lovers, with their opposed arms [*antiporoisi*] knotting their pliant limbs in a close embrace."[22]

This brief tour of the face-to-face posture in ancient poetry raises intriguing questions. What if there were something of Sappho in Saint Paul? What if the Sapphic spirit of Paulus Silentiarius's insatiable lovers, who never did find closure, filled the apostle's imagination when he wrote about the removal of Moses's veil before the Lord in 3:16 and the people's unveiled faces in 2 Corinthians 3:18? In contrast to the long-held assumption that a face reveals the other's self, might it be the case for Paul, as it was for Heliodorus, that "in the space of an instant, an infinity of expression" passes across faces and defers without end the knowledge of other selves?[23]

Fighting Method with Method

Unlike reading a face, a chapter comes to an end. More of a detour without a destination than a summary of findings, however, this chapter's conclusion is a brief commentary on 2 Corinthians 3. There Paul alludes to Exodus 34:27–35 with all the playfulness of *allude*'s Latin ancestor *ludere* and retells the story of Moses writing a covenant and delivering it to the people of Israel. From the perspective of the ancient Greeks, who interpreted the histories of other peoples in the categories they used to understand their own past, Exodus 34:27–35 was seen as a crucial episode in Israel's *political* history when at Sinai the Jews received their constitution and became a city-state. Second Corinthians 3 retells the story in Exodus 34:27–35 from this political perspective. And as Paul reconfigures Exodus 34:27–35, he opens his readers' imaginations to the church as an assembly of persons held together, living together, by the desire to know and the perpetual deferral of knowing one another.

Why should we pursue a close reading of Paul's reinvention of Exodus 34:27–35? How will it help us think about reading the New Testament in the twenty-first century? As I have already mentioned, 2 Corinthians 3 is the literary home of what Christianity has regarded as one of the two most important formulations of reading theory in the New Testament: "For the letter kills, but the Spirit gives life" (3:6). A famous verse indeed, but as traditionally interpreted, it is toxic to the infinite deferral of knowing that I propose it encourages. Aside from the other classic formulation of reading theory in the New Testament, 2 Timothy 3:16–17, which was discussed in the previous chapter, no passage from the Bible has so effectively assisted phonocentrism's infiltration of Western forms of religion, law, and politics than 2 Corinthians 3:6. So let the reader understand, I am going to put myself in a laughable position. I will venture, without having the time to prove (even if demonstration were my intent), the following thesis: in 2 Corinthians 3:6, Paul intends (my phonocentrism is showing; another cause for laughter!) to challenge phonocentrism, not to promote it as nearly every other commentator on this verse has assumed he is doing.

A chorus of protestors erupts! *How could anyone be so mistaken about Paul? Just read 3:6 and respect what Christian tradition has determined it means.* Here is what the tradition has determined: "Spirit" refers to the author's—*God*'s, for many readers of the Bible—intended meanings contained in written words. Tradition has also determined that "letter" designates the unreliable technology an author has no choice but to use when the living voice is not an option. According to the dominant interpretation of 2 Corinthians 3:6, then, writing "kills" in the sense that it does not provide certainty about the author's intention. The spirit as voice "gives life" in the sense of informing readers of the author's mind.[24]

I am proposing a very different interpretation of 2 Corinthians 3:6. The letter kills, yes, but not by obscuring an author's (or God's) meaning. Rather, the letter kills by bringing closure to the deferral of knowledge that face-to-face relations generate. And for its part, the spirit gives life not by imparting knowledge of salvation but by fostering face-to-face relations and opening readers (of faces or of texts) to unknowable others. Stated in another way, 2 Corinthians 3:6 is not about hermeneutics as traditionally defined—that is, the science of determining an author's meaning.[25] Rather, it is about radical politics, people living with one another in the stubborn restlessness of interpreting that which presents itself as clear and in no need of interpretation. The politics of 2 Corinthians 3 (the churchly minded might rename politics *ecclesiology*) is a social dis-ease of hoping against hope for a peace that passes beyond understanding's grasp. "For the letter kills, but the Spirit gives life" is more of a political or ethical slogan than a hermeneutical one, although its importance for how we think about texts, all texts and not just the Bible, cannot be emphasized enough.

In what follows, I want to ask what it means that 3:6 is only a small piece of 2 Corinthians 3, the literary site where Paul reinvents Exodus 34:27–35. By the standard of the last 150 years, mine is a very conventional approach. I want to understand 3:6 with the help of the first principle of the historical-critical method—namely, that a text's meaning depends on its context. But in another sense, this commentary will be unusual, since it opens itself to as many contexts as these pages have room for and I have the knowledge to speak about. To get started, here is one context, a translation of the Septuagint's translation of Exodus 34:27–35. I have italicized words and phrases that made their way as allusions or quotations into 2 Corinthians 3:

> And the Lord said to Moyses: *Write* for yourself these words. For on the basis of these words I have made a *covenant* [*diathēkēn*] with you and Israel. And Moyses was there *before the Lord* for forty days and forty nights. He did not eat bread and he did not drink water. *And he wrote these words on the tablets of the covenant* [*tōn plakōn tōn tēs diathēkēs*], the Ten Words. And as Moyses was descending from the mountain, the two *tablets* [*plakes*] were also in Moyses' hands. Now as he was descending from the mountain, Moyses did not know that *the appearance of the skin of his face was charged with glory while he was speaking to him* [*dedoxastai hē opsis tou chrōmatos tou prosōpou autou en tō lalein auton autō*]. And Aaron and all the elders of Israel saw Moyses, and *the appearance of the skin of his face was charged with glory* [*ēn dedoxasmenē hē opsis tou chōmatos tou prosōpou autou*], and they were afraid to come near him. And Moyses called them, and all the rulers of the congregation *turned* [*epestraphēsan*] to him, and Moyses spoke to them. And after these things all the sons of Israel drew near to him, and he commanded them all the things that the Lord said to him on the mountain, Sina. And when he stopped speaking to them, *he placed a covering over his face* [*epi to prosōpon autou kalymma*]. *But whenever Moyses would enter in before the Lord to speak with him, he would remove the covering* [*hēnika de an eiseporeueto Mōysēs enanti kyriou lalein autō, periēreito to kalymma*] until coming out. And when he came out, he would tell all the sons of Israel what the Lord commanded him. And the sons of Israel saw *the face* [*to prosōpon*] *of Moyses that it was charged with glory* [*dedoxastai*], and *Moyses put a covering over his face* [*periethēken Mōysēs kalymma epi to prosōpon heautou*] until he went in to converse with him.[26]

Exodus 34:27–35 and 2 Corinthians 3 are only two contexts for the interpretation of 2 Corinthians 3:6. Paul's relationship with the Corinthian church is another, and I will point out the emotions, events, expectations, and actions of key players that moved Paul to write 2 Corinthians. Other contexts come into play too. As I mentioned above, a comparison with ancient political writings suggests the Corinthians might have regarded Moses as the lawgiver (*nomothetēs*) of the Jews and the covenant of Sinai as their constitution (*politeia*). Significantly, ancient political theory borrowed philosophy's notion of writing as recorded voice and voice as the reflection of the lawgiver's (or God's) intention to order individual and communal life by putting an end to confusion and deferral. Philosophy also provided political thinkers with the definition of leadership: real leaders use frank speech (*parrēsia*; see 3:12). And philosophy (along with medicine) gives us a framework for understanding Paul's statement about spirit (*pneuma*) in 3:6, a key term in the ancient physiology of perception. Finally, of course, ancient literature (poetry and novels) will come into play as they already have in the case of the face-to-face motif discussed above. Again, my method is this: to interpret 2 Corinthians 3:6 in as many contexts as I am able to.

Endless Conclusion:
A Brief Commentary on 2 Corinthians 3

2 CORINTHIANS 3:1

Do we begin again to commend ourselves? Or do we need, as some do, letters of recommendation [*systatikōn epistolōn*] to you or from you?[27]

Paul takes a jab at his opponents in Corinth. They are the "some" who rely on letters of recommendation, the traditional means in antiquity for travelers to acquire legitimacy and financial support in new surroundings.[28] The fact that the opponents rely on such letters is Paul's chief objection to their manner of leadership. They show no interest in face-to-face relations with the Corinthians, since they substitute writing—in this case, letters of recommendation—for the open-ended relations Paul links to the spirit in 3:6. Here is the first hint of what Paul might mean by "for the letter kills."

But what do letters of recommendation have to do with covenants, the type of writing at issue in 2 Corinthians 3? Why does Paul start a discourse about Moses and the covenant with what seems to be an unrelated discussion of letters? Possibly, he starts with epistles because from the perspective of the ancient theory of reading, letters and covenants are closely related. In fact, they are structurally the same; that is, both covenants and epistles are composed of alphabetic letters (*grammata*) thought to communicate the author's intention. They employ the same information technology, writing, to bring closure to the confusing and distressing affairs of human life. The first-century BCE historian Diodorus Siculus acknowledges the shared characteristics of epistles and covenants when he reports how Charondas, an ancient lawgiver like Moses, set reading and writing above every other kind of learning. He explains, "For it is by means of them [reading and writing] that most of the affairs of life and such as are most useful are concluded [*epiteleisthai*; note the *tel* root that signifies *end* and hints at death], like votes, letters, covenants, laws, and all other things which make the greatest contribution to orderly life."[29] Writing brings closure and establishes order. Diodorus continues,

> For it is by such knowledge [reading and writing] alone that the dead are carried in the memory of the living and that men widely separated in space hold converse through written communication with those who are at the furthest distance from them, as if they were at their side and in the case of covenants in time of war between states or kings the firmest guarantee that such agreements will abide is provided by the unmistakable character of writing. Indeed, speaking generally, it is writing alone which preserves the cleverest sayings of men of wisdom and the oracles of the gods, as well as philosophy and all knowledge, and is constantly handing them down to succeeding generations for the ages to come. Consequently, while it is true that nature is the cause of life, the cause of the good life is the education which is based upon reading and writing.[30]

For Diodorus, epistles and covenants make life possible by preserving and communicating knowledge. Both bring an end to ignorance, confusion, and uncertainty by revealing the writer's intention. In Diodorus's view, a life worthy of the name *life* is the result of reading and writing. Second Corinthians 3:6, however, claims the opposite: writing, the kind of writing found in letters and covenants, brings death. And yet Paul's argument is more complicated than this simple opposition. As we will see next, there is another kind of writing in Paul's imagination, one that brings life without bringing closure, although Diodorus would not have recognized it as writing, nor would he have agreed such writing brought life.

2 CORINTHIANS 3:2 (A)

You yourselves are our letter [*hē epistolē*] . . .

Here Paul introduces a metaphorical writing that does not kill. Exodus 34:27–35 does not speak of it, but Paul finds it there anyway. (See comments on 2 Cor 3:16 below.) Philosophers occasionally employed writing as a metaphor but with quite a different aim than the use by poets, novelists, and Paul.[31] Consider the famous Cynic philosopher Diogenes of Sinope and his refusal to write a letter of recommendation for a certain Menodorus:

> The Megarian youths appealed to me to introduce Menodorus the philosopher to you, a very ridiculous introduction, for you will know that he is a man from his portraits, and from his life and words whether he is also a philosopher. For, in my opinion, the sage provides his own introduction.[32]

Paul rejects the metaphor of writing used in self-legitimation (3:5), but like a lover who longs for an absent beloved, whose world *is* the beloved, Paul names the Corinthians themselves, written on his heart, as the only recommendation he needs.

2 CORINTHIANS 3:2 (B)

. . . written in our hearts [eggegrammenē en tais kardiais hēmōn] . . .

As we have seen, Paul refuses to use conventional letters of recommendation
and a normal, written covenant to mediate his relationship to the Corinthian
community. Instead, the spirit's writing on his heart creates their bond.
Writing on the heart was a well-known erotic motif in Greek literature.[33]
An expert on love in Achilles Tatius's novel *Leucippe and Clitophon* reports
that writing on the heart feeds lovesickness, a disorder of insatiable desire:

> The pleasure which comes from vision enters by the eyes and
> makes its home in the breast; bearing with it ever the image of the
> beloved, it impresses it upon the mirror of the soul and leaves there
> its image [*anaplattei tēn morphēn*]; the emanation given off by beauty
> travels by invisible rays to the lovesick heart and imprints [*enaposphra-
> gizei*] upon it its photograph.[34]

Plutarch relies on the fact that *graphein* meant not only "to write" but also
"to paint" and even "to burn":

> Someone has said that the images entertained by the poetic imagina-
> tion, because they impose themselves so vividly, are dreams of those
> wide awake; but this is much truer of the images entertained by the
> imagination of lovers who speak to the beloved and embrace him or
> chide him as though he were present. For our sight seems to paint its
> other pictures on wet plaster: they fade away quickly and slip from
> mind; the images of the beloved, however, burned [*graphomenai*] into
> the mind by sight as if using encaustic technique, leave behind in the
> memory shapes that move and live and speak and remain forever
> and ever.[35]

This popular motif of lovers' interior writing suggests that in 2 Corinthians 3, the "new covenant" is the face-to-face relation that inscribes the

other on the heart. Unlike the writing of epistles and covenants, writing on the heart finalizes nothing and does not put longing to rest. Rather, it turns the heart over to an infinite desire to know the other. This desire is what I am suggesting Paul means by "life" in 3:6.

2 CORINTHIANS 3:2-3

. . . known and read by all people, manifesting [*phaneroumenoi*] that you are a letter of the anointed one [*christou*] served [*diakonētheisa*] by us . . .[36]

Paul's openness to "all people" is a matter of face-to-face relations. His readability contrasts with the veiled face of Moses in 3:13–14. Moreover, Paul manifests not only himself but also the Corinthians. Everywhere he goes, he frankly confesses both his attachment to them and the deep emotional distress he suffered after sending them the "letter of tears" (2:3–4). The community's face-to-face relation with Paul is "a letter of Christ" and the only legitimacy he claims. The opponents, on the other hand, rely on letters of recommendation—dead documents.

On his journey through Asia Minor and Macedonia to meet Titus, Paul reports he spoke frankly about his love for the Corinthian community and his regret for having sent the letter of tears. A confession like this, however, would have made him appear slave-like to his opponents. Since courage to speak one's mind was the basic requirement of leadership, if the opponents' charge of flattery went unanswered, Paul was in danger of losing the Corinthians' confidence. Yet in defiance of his opponents' charge, Paul doubles down and embraces the designation *slave*. He portrays himself as a slave (*diakonos*) of Christ's letter of recommendation—that is, the *diakonos* of the Corinthians themselves written on his heart. This is not the first time in 2 Corinthians that Paul presents himself as a slave, nor is it the last.

A striking example of the slavery motif occurs in 2:14: "To God be thanks, who always leads us in a triumphal procession [*thriambeuonti*] in the anointed one" (my translation). As a passage from Ovid illustrates, ancient poets transformed the triumphal procession into a scene of wounded lovers accepting the servitude imposed on them by Eros, the god of love:

> Look, I confess! I am new prey of thine, O Cupid; I stretch forth my hands to be bound, submissive to thy laws. . . . In thy train shall be captive youths and captive maids; such a pomp will be for thee a stately triumph. Myself, a recent spoil, shall be there with wound all freshly dealt, and bear my new bonds with unresisting heart. Conscience shall be led along, with hands tied fast behind her back, and Modesty, and all who are foes to the camp of Love. Before thee all shall tremble; the crowd, stretching forth their hands to thee, shall chant with loud voice: "Ho Triumph!" Caresses shall be at thy side, and Error, and Madness—a rout that ever follows in thy train. With soldiers like these dost thou vanquish men and gods; strip from thee aids like these, thou wilt be weaponless.[37]

Paul is the Corinthians' slave (see 4:5), a status that seems to contradict his claim to possess frank speech (*parrēsia*; see 3:12) and freedom (*eleutheria*; see 3:17). It was a cliché in ancient literature that the slave and the free person differ precisely in this: slaves have no free speech.[38] Free speech, however, was understood in at least three ways: (1) in the Greek political assembly as a citizen's right to speak every thought; (2) as biting moral criticism, and this was the understanding of the opponents and some in the Corinthian church (see 2 Cor 11:20; 13:2–3);[39] and (3) as speaking openly about one's own emotions.[40] Paul asserts he does use frank speech but not the reviling kind employed by his critics (see 2 Cor 11:19–20). His frank speech reveals his regret and self-recrimination over sending the letter of tears.[41]

2 CORINTHIANS 3:3 (A)

. . . written [*eggegrammenē*] not with ink but with the spirit of the living God . . .

Ink and spirit (*pneuma*) are materials that make the two kinds of writing possible. Their materiality implies that "spirit" does not refer to the intention of the author / God as the Christian tradition teaches. Rather, ancient physiology defined spirit (*pneuma*) as a combination of fire and air penetrating all matter. Spirit in this sense made seeing, hearing, tasting, touching, and smelling possible by writing external entities on the heart, which, according to some medical thinkers and philosophers, was the seat of perception rather than the brain.[42] Thus spirit writing is more direct than writing with ink, since the latter requires mental transformations of alphabetic letters that encode the author's voice; readers must process phonetic letters by pronouncing them to reactivate the author's voice, itself only a reflection of the intended meaning.[43] Note that 2 Corinthians 2:14 claims that knowledge of God comes not by reading texts, or even by listening to the apostle speak, but by smelling him, an odd thought for modern readers. Paul's odor signals the crucial role perception plays in 2 Corinthians 3.[44] Second Corinthians 2:14–15 claims the opponents have faulty perceptions (see 4:3–5): for them, Paul smells of death. Those who are being saved, however, perceive that Paul smells of life.[45] This is an additional interpretive clue to "the spirit makes life" in 3:6 (my translation).

2 CORINTHIANS 3:3 (B)

... not on stone tablets but on hearts of flesh tablets [*plaxin kardiais sarkinais*].

Paul turns from the materials of writing (spirit and ink) to writing surfaces. "Stone tablets" resist textual alteration. "Hearts of flesh," however, are open to infinite emendation because they are soft. That is, texts inscribed on stone remain unaffected when they are read. A fleshy heart, in contrast, receives continual textual revision as one reads ever-changing sentences written on the other's face, which, like a mirror, reflects the other's heart, or so it was said.[46]

2 CORINTHIANS 3:4–5

We have such confidence through Christ toward God. Not that we are
competent from ourselves to be accounted anything from ourselves,
but our competency is from God who made us competent to be slaves
[*diakonous*] of a new covenant [*kainēs diathēkēs*].

Why is Paul so interested in confidence and competence? Assume for a
moment that instruments of finality like letters, covenants, and laws make
the good life possible, and assume leaders are responsible for securing the
good life for others. Then Paul's talk of the spirit's writing of the Corinthians
on his heart appears to be sentimentality masking his incompetence. That
is the conclusion his opponents drew.

How does Paul respond to this charge? When the mission and methods
of ancient philosophers were criticized, they pointed to their self-mastery
(see 2 Cor 4:5 and 1 Tim 3:1–7). Furthermore, they claimed to have received
a divine call.[47] Paul shuns self-mastery (3:5), however, and describes the
post to which he was called by placing the word "new" (*kainos*) in front
of "covenant" (*diathēkē*). The new covenant, which he serves as a slave,
is neither an improvement of the old covenant nor its replacement but a
political/familial arrangement (which is the literal meaning of *diathēkēs*) of
persons in the face-to-face relation.[48] It is new because it refuses closure and
lives from the *kai* (and) of *kainos* (new).[49] Thus Paul legitimates his frank
speaking without the help of philosophy. He presents himself as a slave of
the constantly changing and always new arrangement/covenant (*diathēkē*)
of face-to-face relations.[50]

These relations might be joyful, but it is important to note that earlier, Paul
writes frankly of his self-condemnation, depression, and thoughts of suicide:

We want you to know, brothers and sisters, of our affliction that happened in Asia: we were so weighed down, beyond measure, beyond
power, that we were in great doubt even about living. But we ourselves
in ourselves had the sentence of death in order that we might not base
our confidence in ourselves but in the God who raises the dead, who

out of such a death rescued us, and will rescue, in whom we have hoped that he will yet rescue even as you also work together for us with a plea that the favor [*charisma*] coming to us from many faces might be received with thanksgiving for us through many.[51] (2 Cor 1:8–11; my translation)

What gave rise to Paul's emotions in his passage? Second Corinthians 2:3–4 and 7:7–8 refer to a letter (some scholars call it *the letter of tears*) in which Paul portrays himself weeping over the church's inaction against an individual who had injured him. Ancient handbooks on letter writing tell us that grieving self-presentation communicated strong rebuke.[52] Paul's tearful rebuke was effective, perhaps *too* effective. First, Titus reports that although the Corinthians shun the offender, the letter of tears causes them grief. Second, Paul thinks the church has gone too far in its discipline and fears the offender will commit suicide.[53] Thus rather than a motto for biblical hermeneutics, the phrase "the letter kills" corresponds to a specific situation of grief and the possibility of suicide in Corinth.

2 CORINTHIANS 3:7 (A)

If the service [*diakonia*] of death inscribed in letters [*grammasin*] on stone tablets happened in *doxa* . . .

I have left the term *doxa* untranslated. "Glory," which has a visual connotation, is the usual translation, but *doxa* also has a temporal connotation as reflected in the translation "expectation."[54] *Doxa* as "expectation" suggests an openness to the future, and this is reflected in another possible translation, "hope." Like "hope," *doxa* is a yes-saying to that which is always yet to come. This explains how Paul moves without explanation from *doxa* in 3:11 to "hope" in 3:12. My point is this: the challenge of translating *doxa* into English calls attention to the tension between the *doxa* that defers knowledge and the *doxa* that puts an end to the quest for knowing the other. On one hand, the letter as the textual technology that brings closure kills; likewise, visual *doxa* overwhelms the viewer. On the other hand, the spirit, which was thought to make perception possible, gives life—life as perpetual deferral of an end—just as *doxa* gives hope.

How does *doxa*/glory put an end to *doxa*/expectation? The following passage from Chariton's first-century CE novel *Callirhoe* describes the effects of Callirhoe's radiant face on the people of Miletus. Her shining beauty might remind readers of the effect of Moses's glorious face on the people of Israel in 2 Corinthians 3:7–11. Callirhoe enters Miletus, crowded with expectant onlookers, but her splendor is too much for them. Her beauty crushes their expectation:

> Her great fame [*kleos mega*] had spread all over Asia, and already the name of Callirhoe had come to the attention of the Great King as one excelling even Ariadne and Leda. On this occasion, however, she surpassed all expectation [*tēs doxēs*]. She appeared dressed in black, her hair loose and her face radiant [*astraptousa de tō prosōpō*]; with her bare arms and feet she seemed more beautiful than the Homeric goddesses "of the white arms" and "of the fair ankles." In fact not a single one there could withstand her dazzling beauty. Some turned their heads away as though the sun's rays shone into their eyes, and others actually knelt in homage; even children were affected. Mithridates, the governor of Caria, fell speechless to the ground like a man unexpectedly [*aprosdokētou*] struck by a missile. . . . She alone held every eye in thrall.[55]

Callirhoe's divine beauty destroys the hope harbored in the anticipation of her appearance. Her *doxa* (as beauty) surpasses the *doxa* (as expectation) of her eager onlookers and overpowers them. Her magnificence enslaves their eyes. Like the face of Moses, Callirhoe's shining face becomes a deadly weapon, a missile that strikes Mithridates dumb and puts him on his last legs.[56] Like Moses, Callirhoe, equal to the form of a goddess, unintentionally carries out a ministry of death. *Doxa* as glory kills *doxa* as expectation. That, I believe, is what Paul is getting at in 2 Corinthians 3:7–11.

2 CORINTHIANS 3:7 (B)

... so that the people of Israel could not gaze [*atenisai*] at Moses' face [*to prosōpon Mōyseōs*] because of his face's *doxa* [*tēn doxan tou prosōpou autou*] that was being made of no effect [*katargoumenēn*] ...

When reading this verse in light of Exodus 34:27–35, it is clear that Paul invents expectant onlookers. The people of Israel try to stare (*atenizein*) at Moses's face; Chariton too has the crowd stare in expectation at another one of Callirhoe's public appearances:

> At that moment everyone strained [*exeteinan*] not only their eyes but their very souls, and nearly fell over each other in their eagerness to be first to see and get as near as possible. Callirhoe's face shone with a radiance which dazzled the eyes of all, just as when on a dark night a blinding flash is seen. Struck with amazement, the Persians knelt in homage.[57]

Normally, eyes wide open in a stare would allow an image to enter and be inscribed on the viewer's soul, but neither Callirhoe's nor Moses's radiant face permits such interior writing. The way Paul tells it, the people of Israel are unable to stare at Moses, since *doxa* beams from his face. Little do they know, however, the *doxa* on Moses's face is itself being made of no effect (*katargoumenēn*).

2 CORINTHIANS 3:8

... how much more will the service [*diakonia*] of the spirit be in *doxa*?

Note the shift in tense between verses 7 and 8. In 3:7, the service of death "happened," and *doxa* as splendor overwhelmed expectation, but in 3:8, the service of the spirit "will be" in temporal *doxa*. That is, the spirit will keep anticipation alive. Thus Paul doubles elements of Exodus 34:27–35 that were originally univocal. Second Corinthians 3 has two kinds of *doxa*, two kinds of covenants, two kinds of writing. And this doubling takes us back to 2 Corinthians 3:6, where Paul asserts there are two kinds of language. One, a language of breath or spirit (*pneuma*) spoken when persons face each other and perpetuate each other's desire and unknowing; the other, a language that writes things down, captures meaning, pins it to the ground, and kills it.

2 CORINTHIANS 3:9

For if the service of condemnation [*diakonia tēs katakriseōs*] is *doxa*, much more does the service of justice [*diakonia tēs dikaiosynēs*] abound in *doxa*.

Readers expect "in" rather than "is." "Is" suggests the rather odd meaning that the service of condemnation is itself *doxa*. What is going on here? One explanation is that *doxa* in its visual sense carried a further connotation: "the opinion that others have of one"—that is, "repute."[58] If this is the case here, then the negation of *doxa* (as "reputation") is equivalent to "condemnation" and reminds readers of 1:8–9, where Paul narrates his self-condemnation for having caused grief to the Corinthians. "Condemnation" also points to the church's decision to shun the individual who had injured Paul (see 2:5–11).

2 CORINTHIANS 3:10

Indeed, that which has been *dox-ed* [*to dedoxasmenon*] has not been *dox-ed* [*ou dedoxastai*] in this respect: on account of the surpassing/deferring/postponing [*hyperballousēs*] *doxa*.

Paul continues to move back and forth between the visual and the temporal denotations of *doxa*. Moses's face both is and is not charged with *doxa*. Yes, his face certainly beams with divine splendor, but that form of *doxa* prevents a face-to-face relation with the people of Israel and inhibits the *doxa* as expectation/hope. Thus Moses's shining face is made of no effect in this sense: its overwhelming splendor ruins the possibility of a mutual gaze with the people of Israel. While glory kills the face-to-face relation as

we saw in Callirhoe's case, Paul implies expectation and hope would have
fueled the relationship of Moses and the people.

2 CORINTHIANS 3:11–12

For if what was being made of no effect [*to katargoumenon*] happened
through *doxa*, much more does that which abides happen in *doxa*.
Therefore, because we have such hope [*elpida*] we use much frank
speech [*pollē parrēsia chrōmetha*].[59]

Recall that Paul's opponents accused him of not speaking his mind. Here
he refutes the accusation, although his brand of frank speaking is not the
biting and shaming speech the superapostles and even some of the Corinthians (see 13:2–3) expected to hear from a leader. His frank speech refuses
to hide emotions. What gives him the confidence for self-disclosure? The
open-endedness of the face-to-face relation, hope.

2 CORINTHIANS 3:13

And [we are] not like Moses, who placed a veil [*kalymma*] on his face
[*prosōpon*] to keep the people of Israel from gazing [*atenisai*] at the end
[*telos*] of that which was being made of no effect [*tou katargoumenou*].

So far, I have pointed out how Paul retells Exodus 34:27–35 by doubling the
following elements of the story: writing, covenant, and *doxa*. In this verse,
Paul doubles Moses also. He first makes of Moses what ancient rhetorical
theory called a negative example. Unlike Paul, Moses hides his emotions
from the sight of those whom he leads. In 3:16, however, when the veil is
removed and he turns to face the Lord, Moses becomes a positive example
for Paul and for all the readers of the letter (see the "we all" in 3:18 [my
translation]).[60]

Exodus 34:33 itself does not explain why Moses veiled his face. The
Septuagint's silence on this point provides an opening for Paul to supply a
motive: Moses veils himself to prevent the people of Israel from staring at
his face. Unlike many ancient and modern interpreters, however, I do not

think Paul wants his readers to conclude Moses hides his face for a sinister reason—for example, to keep the people from noticing that his glory is fading. The motif of covering one's head in Greek literature suggests another reason: Moses veils his face not to deceive but to hide strong emotion. The most famous example of this motif is the Homeric portrayal of Odysseus as he falls apart longing for home:

> Odysseus grasped his great purple cloak with his stout hands, and drew it down over his head, and hid his handsome face [*kalypse de kala prosōpa*]; for he felt shame before the Phaeacians as he let fall tears from beneath his eyebrows. Indeed, as often as the divine minstrel ceased his singing, Odysseus would wipe away his tears and draw the cloak from off his head, and taking the two-handled cup would pour libations to the gods. But as often as he began again, and the Phaeacian nobles urged him to sing, because they took pleasure in his song, Odysseus would again cover his head and groan. Now from all the rest he concealed the tears that he shed, but Alcinous alone was aware of him and noticed, for he sat by him, and heard him groaning heavily.[61]

Covering the head kept pain (grief, shame, regret, etc.) secret. Paul's Moses does not want to be seen suffering. Contrast this with Paul, who quite openly confesses his regret (1:8–9).

2 CORINTHIANS 3:14 (A)

But their minds [*ta noēmata*] were hardened [*epōrōthē*].

Often, commentators have remarked that "their minds were hardened" is Paul's accusation that the people of Israel resist the allegorical reading of Scripture; in other words, that they reject interpretations built on privileged Christian insights into God's intention hidden behind the so-called dead and deadly letter. Interpreting Scripture, however, is not at issue in this verse. The relation between leader and people is. What I think Paul is driving at is how a written text—any text, including his own writings—functions like a veil obstructing the face-to-face relation. On the people's side, their hardened surfaces make the inscription of Moses himself on their hearts impossible. Thus writing (the nonmetaphorical kind) prevents a face-to-face relation between Moses and the people of Israel, an idea that Paul develops in the next two verses. But before moving on, I want to be clear: I am *not* making the traditional, phonocentric point that Paul believes the Christian law of love has superseded the old testament and the people of Israel are allegedly unable to grasp the divine mind whose intent is love. What I think Paul is getting at is more complicated and profound. He contests his contemporaries' (whether they are Jews or Greeks) view of writing that says a text discloses the author's intention, brings certainty, and protects life from that which cannot be contained in and by language.

2 CORINTHIANS 3:14 (B)

For to this very day, the same veil remains at the reading [*anagnōsei*] of the old covenant [*palaias diathēkēs*] since it is not being unveiled [*mē anakalyptomenon*], because it [the veil] is being made of no effect in the anointed one [*en Christou katargeitai*].

The idea of repetition infuses this verse and the next: "this very day," "the same veil," "reading" (*anagnorisis*; literally, "a knowing again"), "old" (*palaios*; related to *palin*, "again"). Writing establishes social relations mediated by repetition. Expectation of the anointed one, who is always yet to come, however, interrupts writing/repetition by unveiling the veil, or as Paul puts it, by making the veil of no effect.

2 CORINTHIANS 3:15

But until today, whenever Moses is read a veil [*kalymma*] lies on their hearts [*kardian*].

We are now closing in on an interpretation of "the letter kills." In this verse, consider the violence hidden within the phrase "Moses is read." Even though it was a common practice in the first century, as it is now, to use an author's name to refer to their literary corpus (e.g., *Have you read Dickens lately?*), this practice eradicates the person behind the book. In other words, when we call a book by the name of the author, we unintentionally kill the author. We are complicit in a murderous repetition of alphabetic letters that refer to the author by taking the author's place.[62] That is, by calling the book *Moses*, we transfigure the human Moses (as if *human Moses* were any less lethal to Moses) into the written word *Moses*. Moses becomes *Moses*, the ink dried into scratches on papyrus or paper—quotable, repeatable, and detached from the flesh-and-blood Moses. His death by writing, his condemnation to limitless repetition of the letters that compose his name, does indeed make him available to readers, but only as a book, only as his literary *corpus*. Thus the book steals his name for its title, and this means that Moses is read but never reads back. Readers—Jews, Christians, Muslims, any and all readers—stare at alphabetic letters that preserve the sounds (adjusted for having been removed from the Hebrew tongue) that once joyfully announced love. One might delight in imagining Pharaoh's daughter caressing Moses's face and speaking the words "Moses, my son." But now when *Moses* is pronounced, Moses no longer gazes back as he once might have at Pharaoh's daughter, any more than this ink or these pixels shaped into *M-o-s-e-s* gaze at you. According to *P-a-u-l*, who for nearly two thousand years has been a string of letters pointing to a once-beating-heart-tablet made of flesh, the same veil that obscured Moses's emotions lies over the people's hearts. This means that any person reading the old covenant, then or now, like anyone reading any writing not written on hearts—including, I will say it again, the writings collected under the title *The New Testament*—will repeat the endlessly repeatable letters in order to say the same words. Finally, we have arrived. This is how the *letter kills*. By repetition of the same. By boredom. By closure. By the being of the signifier purchased by the blood of the signified. By commentaries like the one now in your hands.

2 CORINTHIANS 3:16–17

When he turned [*epistrepsē*] to the Lord, the veil is taken away.[63]
The Lord is the Spirit and where the Spirit of the Lord is—freedom
[*eleutheria*].

At this point, Paul's story of Moses takes an unexpected turn. Moses no
longer writes the Lord's commands. No longer does he repeat divine words
to the people of Israel or find his name repeated as the people of Israel or
the people of Corinth read the word *Moses* or the book called *Moses*, both
word and book presenting an unalterable, preprogrammed Moses that
depends on the once living Moses's nonpresence. In the midst of all these
deadly letters that Christians call Holy Scripture, Moses miraculously turns,
and his veil is removed, and he finds himself face-to-face with the Lord,
who is none other than the spirit, which is the materiality of the face-to-
face relation. Then, with no books in sight, there is no end to reading but
a ceaseless face reading, a life.[64]

2 CORINTHIANS 3:18

I began this chapter with a complaint that self-formation in the Pastoral
Epistles and hierarchical order in Colossians and Ephesians are wearisome,
tedious, and oppressive. I have taken advantage of every context I could
discover (scriptural, historical, philosophical, rhetorical, cultural, political,
and literary) to make *Paul*—who for me is a name standing for what I think
all the alphabetic letters of 2 Corinthians 3 strung together in words and
sentences hint about life—share my exhaustion. The Paul of my imagination is equally desperate for a way of existing that escapes order and finality. With these contexts in mind, and with others that operate in me with
little or no awareness on my part, I have stolen Paul's famous line "For the
letter kills, but the spirit gives life" from the traditional theory of reading,
which privileges coming to know an author's intentions over any other
impact reading might have. I have twisted Paul's words to see if they could
support a perennially suppressed impact of reading, the infinite deferral of
knowing the other. I have come to think of this deferral as life itself. I took

a detour through the common (yet extraordinary!) experience of face reading and briefly traced the history of the *face-to-face* motif in ancient erotic
literature. And here in 2 Corinthians 3:18, Paul (unquestionably the *Paul*
of my imagination, but only of my imagination?) writes what I have come
to think I think about living in a community of insatiable face readers.
Moses's freedom in the face-to-face relation with the Lord ("with unveiled
faces") is Paul's freedom, and it belongs to all ("And all of us"). The politics
of this community (will it ever exist?), the politics of the new covenant, is
perpetually open ended in the stunning change ("are being transformed")
into the same image, an image that no one has ever seen, since it is the face
of the Christ, the anointed one, the one who is always yet to come.

CHAPTER 5

The One and Many Ends

> But when you see the desolating sacrilege set up where it ought not
> to be (let the reader understand), then those in Judea must flee to the
> mountains. (Mark 13:14)

A STRANGE THING happens when reading this verse. An illusion
vanishes and a future opens. What illusion? That readers are *there* observing what Jesus, the crowds, and the disciples did and said. Dispelled is the
perception of the Gospel of Mark as a video-audio recorder defying time,
playing back events, and making Jesus present to the reader. What future
opens as the illusion closes? That I cannot say, since it is not for me to know
my future, and I would be a fool to speak about the world's coming days.
In any case, this final chapter faces up to an instant, the time it takes for us
to pronounce "let the reader understand," when we are robbed of a world
an inscribed surface seduces us to create. We are left with our lives and the
text we hold in our hands. And a ghostly remainder: a plea ringing in our
ears for understanding.

Do not get me wrong. I am all for the illusions of literature, the mind-transporting effects of ink on paper or electrons inside a screen. To read
is to release oneself into a world created by scratch marks on a surface or
pulsations in a gas. I have read the Gospel of Mark hundreds of times, and
each time, I suspend the judgment of my eyes, since they, in a conspiracy
with one part of my brain, insist I am merely viewing inky squiggles grouped
together to form words and words grouped together to form sentences and

so on. When I read intently, I, or another part of my brain that also claims to be *me*, lose track that I am a reader and that I am using a technology called *writing*. As I buy into the text's narration of events and the characters' words, I experience a story unfolding as if I were in the story or the story in me, and I do not notice the confusion of location. Without the illusion of presence created by written words, we would never want to pick up a book; with the illusion in place, a story's characters hold interest for us and we care about what happens to them, although the illusion lives only as long as the reader does what readers must do: forget what writing most assuredly is. Ink on paper.

The strange thing about Mark 13:14 is this: it calls attention to itself as a text—a material thing in the world you can spill coffee on or have censors rip from library shelves. And the verse confronts us with the undeniable fact that we are readers: "But when you see the desolating sacrilege set up where it ought not to be (let the reader understand), then those in Judea must flee to the mountains." The NRSV, however, lessens the illusion-dissolving effect of "let the reader understand" by cordoning the phrase off with parentheses. There was no such punctuation in ancient Greek texts; capital letters ran together without word breaks, commas, semicolons, and parenthetical signs. Ancient eyes saw letters strung together without SPACINGBETWEENWORDS and without punctuation, as in the case of THETEXTYOUAREREADINGRIGHTNOW, and there were no periods. Thus the urging of the reader to "understand" emerges without warning from the preceding letters, and once it proclaims itself, the plea recedes into the following letters. To what effect? Since we readers take the letters to be visual cues stimulating our breath, teeth, and tongue to reproduce the sound of a written Jesus speaking about the end, they prompt us to play a trick on ourselves.[1] We say "let the reader understand," creating ourselves as the very readers addressed by Jesus and urged by him to understand. What I am getting at is this: a textual Jesus interrupts the story, and before we know what we are doing, we help him do it. We enable Jesus to speak directly to us ghostly creatures.

Yes, we readers of the Gospel of Mark are ghosts. From Jesus's perspective, we are nothing but fictional characters who are not really walking around Galilee accompanying him to Jerusalem or listening to him predict the destruction of the temple or the destruction of the cosmos or the destruction of his body. We are holding open a book (or looking at a screen), perhaps clumsily drinking coffee and just about to yell at the dog for barking at the mail carrier like the mutt does every morning around ten thirty. The textual Jesus needs us who *now* are (though each of us has a someday when the *now* passes away and we become even more ghostlike) flesh-and-blood readers to let him make his plea for us to "understand."

Imagine the effect Mark 13:14 might have had on readers of the first century. Whether they read Mark aloud or silently, Jesus's voice—the voice that sounds out in their mouths or minds as they read the words, the voice from the past that had predicted the world's disastrous future—this voice suddenly speaks directly to them from them and to us from us, and for a brief moment across time, we are all confronted with the indisputable fact that we are *readers*. Not viewers. Not listeners. Someone calls us readers, whether the invisible narrator or the letters *J-e-s-u-s*, and we confirm the address, since we do in fact read the very words that beg/command (which is it?) us to recognize that we are readers. And when we wake up to the fact that we are readers, the illusory world of reading is spoiled. We are no longer silent characters sitting close enough to Jesus at the Mount of Olives, across from the temple, to hear him speak about the end of the world; we do not witness his arrest; and we do not see him abandoned, even though good story, well told as the Gospel of Mark certainly is, tries mightily to get us to think that we are right in the middle of things, these things like ghosts that do and do not exist.

So what if we were to defy the NRSV and remove the parentheses from Mark 13:14? When the parentheses go away, the phrase "let the reader understand" sneaks up on our reading-induced illusion of presence. The surprise happens something like this: Imagine you are attending a theatrical performance.[2] The play is nearly over, and you have been drawn deeply into it—so much so that you push the cares of everyday life to the back of your mind. You lose track of time—that is, the events of the play have masked the consciousness of *your* time. What you see and hear on the stage has moved you, and you feel part of the drama's time and strain forward to find out what will happen next. Without warning, the actors freeze and the main character looks out at the audience and says, "You do know that this is a play, don't you? I implore you, please, please understand." And then, as quickly as the play was suspended, it begins again as if the plea for understanding (understanding what?—that this is a play and not real life?) had never been spoken. Yet *you* have been changed. Yes, you will probably watch the rest of the play. Maybe your emotions will pick you up where they left you off and involve you once again in the characters' lives, but you will always wonder what it was exactly you were supposed to understand or what your life would now be like if that actor had not decided to speak to you. And most of all, you will be haunted by the anxious thought that you might again without warning, in the midst of your usual entertainments, be implored to understand (understand what?).

Here is my point: Readers of the New Testament in the twenty-first century must make a decision. Either we respond to the voice addressing us from the stage and say *Yes, we know it's a play, but yes, keep on playing* or we leave the theatre in a huff, so angry at an actor's impromptu address ruining our fantasies that we never again venture beyond the safety of our imagined facts and simulated certainties. My fear is that we will run from literature, run from poetry, run from theatres—any place that we are vulnerable to surprise—and run into churches to listen to an authoritative voice that for repressive political purposes feeds and organizes our anger at voices that interrupt our reading-induced reverie. This choice, I believe, is what John D. Caputo is getting at in his proposal for *radical hermeneutics*, in which

> the sacred texts are treated, not as the Divine Revelation that defini-
> tively props up the authority of some confessional faith or ecclesiastical
> office, nor as the record of some extraordinary empirical event from

long ago that tells us *wie es eigentlich gewesen ist* [how it really happened], as if human history was literally launched approximately six thousand years ago by two painfully naked and parentless people who made the big mistake of being drawn into a conversation with a sneaky snake. Historical-critical studies (not to mention science and common sense) should have long ago doused the fires of fundamentalism and inerrantism, but that does not settle the question of the appeal or the claim that issues from such texts. *For these texts are solicitations that call for a response, appeals coming from I know not where about a way to be, a style of existence, about a poetic possibility that we are invited to transform into existential actuality.*[3]

Back to Mark 13:14. I think I have made the case that "let the reader understand" has the potential of ruining, at least for a moment, the illusion of presence that literature creates in us as we allow ourselves to sink into the time and space of the story. Good readers sink like rocks. Inspired by good literature, they forget they are reading. I have seen these readers and envied them as they stare at a page, transfixed on what the page opens them to. Drawn into a world that exists only in their heads, they overcook the chicken, they neglect fastening their seat belts in turbulence, and they let that other world—the one often called *real*—go by as if it were not there, all because of a textual surface that contains something that does not exist in time and space, a story. Now, what intrigues me is that the Gospel of Mark, which is so good at capturing our attention, also jolts us out of our reverie by addressing us as readers. "Let the reader understand" does not let us remain the eavesdroppers whom our own acts of good reading turn us into. Here is what I have wanted to say in this book (and why I am pleased to have had Jesus or the narrator of Mark say it for me): readers of the New Testament in the twenty-first century (of any century) have to come to terms with the fact that *we are readers* and that we live here and now. Astonishing: to have the main character of a fictional otherworld turn to you, the reader, and say "Wake up! You are reading! Understand!"

I take responsibility for those exclamation points. I sense desperation in Jesus's imperative for readers to understand. The word "let" signals a plea more urgent than a simple request or even a command. Yes, of course, Mark 13:14 *could* be read as an authoritative command coming from on high, as in the famous "Let there be light" of Genesis 1:3, though even this archaic imperative too might harbor a plea or a wish that is powerless to bring itself about.[4] In any case, I cannot stop wondering whether Mark 13:14 is Jesus's (or someone's—it does not matter) desperate and insistent prayer to us readers, a solicitation of our hearts and minds to respond to some dire state of affairs. What affairs? What future is opening before us?

There might be a simple reason to think Jesus's plea to readers is impassioned: he had no one else to turn to. His disciples understand nothing in Mark's Gospel, and he could no longer endure being misunderstood. At every turn in the narrative up to chapter 8, the disciples fail to recognize Jesus for what he is, the Messiah. Mark 8:14–21 summarizes their ignorance in the first half of the Gospel. Then Peter makes a breakthrough and figures Jesus out, or so it seems in 8:29: "He [Jesus] asked them, 'But who do you say that I am?' Peter answered him, 'You are the Messiah.'" In this moment, Peter was about to discover that Jesus's identity is a moving target even in the moment of the Messiah's dying words. After making the technically correct confession, Peter still does not understand (8:33). He cannot incorporate suffering and death into his hope for the Messiah. And who in their right mind blames him?[5]

The disciples' failure to understand Jesus has received considerable scholarly attention, and rightly so. Given the disciples' mindlessness in Mark's Gospel, it is not unreasonable for Jesus to have grown desperate as he seeks someone to understand him, anyone, even those who did not exist yet and might never come into existence—in other words, to imagine that Jesus is desperate for us readers to understand. It is as if Jesus (or was it the author, the one in charge of writing?) ran out of possibilities of being understood by anyone living in the textual world he inhabits, and he must turn to no-ones, the nonexistent, impossible beings like us. Jesus—that is, the textual Jesus of the Gospel of Mark—cries out for understanding from anyone who stumbles across the words "let the reader understand." Right now, that is you and me.

Here is an illuminating contrast. The disciples in the Gospel of Matthew are not the dunderheads they are in the Gospel of Mark.[6] In fact, Matthew portrays the disciples as avid and perceptive students. Matthew's disciples *get* Jesus: he is the Teacher, and they know themselves as his *students*, which is how *mathētai* (usually translated as "disciples") might also be translated. There is a great deal at stake in these students' comprehension of their teacher's words, nothing less than the church itself, since in the Gospel of Matthew, the church is built upon the teacher-student relationship of Jesus and the disciples. Unlike the Gospel of Mark, which closes with (and one can't even imagine what Christianity would have become if it had listened to) the stunned silence of Mary Magdalene, Mary the mother of James, and Salome (Mark 16:8), Matthew ends the story by emphasizing the disciples' task of repeating Jesus's teachings:

> Then the eleven disciples went to Galilee, to the mountain where Jesus had told them to go. When they saw him, they worshiped him; but some doubted. Then Jesus came to them and said, "All authority in heaven and on earth has been given to me. Therefore go and make disciples [*mathēteusate*; literally, 'teach'] of all nations, baptizing them in the name of the Father and of the Son and of the Holy Spirit, and teaching [*didaskontas*] them to obey everything I have commanded you. And surely I am with you always, to the very end of the age." (Matt 28:16–20 NIV)

Matthew's Jesus does a quick bit of biblical teaching in 24:15–16. I do not sense desperation in his words: "So when you see the desolating sacrilege standing in the holy place, [and at this point, Matthew adds the next eight words—ten in Greek] as was spoken of by the prophet Daniel (let the reader understand), then those in Judea must flee to the mountains." Matthew's Jesus has suppressed the desperation of Mark's Jesus, and instead of the latter's open-ended plea for understanding (to anyone reading, living or not yet living), Matthew supplies the reader with an example of biblical prophecy *fulfilled*. In other words, that which Mark leaves unexplained Matthew pins down. Matthew does not allow the question *understand what?* to arise in the reader's mind. Mark certainly does.

Understand What?

Back to Mark's Jesus. What exactly is the reader (i.e., the reader who refuses to fill in Mark's gaps with Matthew's explanatory addition "as was spoken of by the prophet Daniel") supposed to understand in 13:14? If we do not consult Matthew—and to preserve the integrity of Mark's narrative, I believe we should not—what exactly is Jesus asking readers to understand? To get at this question, I look to two unnamed women who enter the story in Mark 12:41–44 and 14:3–9. What makes them special? Jesus implies that *they* understand, even as the disciples are mired in misunderstanding. If we come to know what they know, and in the way that they know it, we might be able to respond to the imperative to understand in Mark 13:14. We might become readers who understand.

First, the poor widow:

> He [Jesus] sat down opposite the treasury, and watched the crowd putting money into the treasury. Many rich people put in large sums. A poor [*ptōchē*] widow came and put in two small copper coins, which are worth a penny. Then he called his disciples and said to them, "Truly I tell you, this poor widow has put in more than all those who are contributing to the treasury. For all of them have contributed out of their abundance; but she out of her poverty has put in everything she had, all she had to live on." (Mark 12:41–44)

Next, a woman who breaks a jar of perfume and anoints Jesus:

> While he was at Bethany in the house of Simon the leper, as he sat at the table, a woman came with an alabaster jar of very costly ointment

of nard, and she broke open the jar and poured the ointment on his head. But some were there who said to one another in anger, "Why was the ointment wasted in this way? For this ointment could have been sold for more than three hundred denarii, and the money given to the poor." And they scolded her. But Jesus said, "Let her alone; why do you trouble her? She has performed a good service for me. For you always have the poor with you, and you can show kindness to them whenever you wish; but you will not always have me. She has done what she could; she has anointed my body beforehand for its burial. Truly I tell you, wherever the good news is proclaimed in the whole world, what she has done will be told in remembrance of her." (Mark 14:3–9)

How are the women alike? Each understands how to give without knowing she understands anything about giving. To put it another way, we read about their actions rather than their intentions or motives. Each gives a gift, and in their giving, both women contravene the way gifts were, and still are, given. Their giving just happens. As far as readers know, they give without seeking a return and without intending to create a sense of obligation. Such divergence from the give-and-take of normal giving is what makes these two women exemplary.

Social historians of both Greece and Rome stress the importance of gift giving for the stability of ancient society. While it must be admitted that the ancient system of benefaction (or patronage, as it is sometimes called) did feed (some) people and public buildings were indeed built, these benefits nevertheless came at a cost to the poor in terms of dignity. Here is how patronage worked. A wealthy person gave gifts of all kinds (loans, food, buildings and other types of infrastructure, letters of recommendation, and so forth) to cities, clubs, and persons of a lower social and economic status relative to the giver. The recipient was expected to pay back the gift not in kind but by gratitude and by honoring the benefactor. Thus there was a circle of gift giving, an economy of giving and getting back.[7] Yet this economy did not extend to all. Recipients had to possess some social standing to make their gratitude valuable to benefactors. Therefore, these two women do something quite out of the ordinary, perhaps even revolutionary: they deform the circularity of gift giving. In other words, they break the habit in which one gives in order to get. Each gives but not in such a way as to get back. In this way, against all expectation, without the intention to do so, and unlike the disciples, they *get* Jesus. Therefore, if we want to understand Jesus's imperative in Mark 13:14 for readers to understand, we should pay careful attention to their gifts.[8]

The first woman is a poor widow (12:42–43). The word "poor," however, does not do justice to the extremity of her living conditions. "Beggarly" is a better translation because of the revulsion she provoked and the contempt onlookers of her poverty might have held her in.[9] Perhaps, with desperation matching the plea "let the reader understand," she might have begged others for the two coins she throws into the treasury.[10] We do not know, and it is not possible to know, because she is a fiction who has no other existence than the one springing up in our heads as this text is read and as her story insists on coming into existence in the gifts we are inspired to give.[11] Nevertheless, even though her back history is not available, we do get to wonder about her action in print. What does it mean that, in spite of her circumstances—or, more likely, because of them—she *acts* as if she understands what it means to give a gift?

A brief detour through 2 Corinthians 8 helps explain why Christianity—any religion, in fact—has so much at stake in the paradox that true gifts can only be given by beggars, the point I think Mark's Jesus makes when he calls attention to the widow.[12] The word "gift" or "grace" (*charis*) is paired with "beggarly" (*ptōchos*; 8:2, 9–10) in 2 Corinthians 8 (8:1, 4, 6–7, 9, 19). While Paul appears to be preoccupied with the details of a fundraising campaign in 2 Corinthians 8 and 9, something else is going on. In these verses, the pure gift meets the real world, and Paul feels responsible to both. These verses plead with the church in Corinth to make good on its earlier commitment of a donation to relieve the difficulties experienced by the church in Jerusalem. In other words, Paul asks for a gift on behalf of others. These verses are interesting for what Paul struggles mightily *not* to say as he asks for money. Here is the problem he faced: if it was the dream of an absolute or pure gift that drove Paul's theology, and I think it was, then any Corinthian contribution to the church in Jerusalem would run the risk of being perceived by both the givers and the recipients as an act of benefaction. A gift like that would accentuate the difference in social power between the two communities. The contribution would obligate the recipients to give back in some way, by their gratitude if nothing else. And then Paul's theology of grace would be compromised.

Paul faced a challenge: to encourage the giving of a gift *and* to defend the gift against the social convention that demanded a gift must always be repaid, ingratitude being the worst sin imaginable. Defense of the absolute gift is at the heart of 8:9, where Paul says something very strange and quite unexpected for his first-century readers but resonates with Mark's beggarly widow: "For you know the generous act [*charin*] of our Lord Jesus Christ, that though he was rich, yet for your sakes he became poor [*eptōcheusen*], so that by his poverty [*ptōcheia*] you might become rich."

On first reading, there is nothing odd about this verse, and the translation "generous act" has a noble ring to it. Yet nobility is the reason this translation needs to be called into question. Persons in the position to be generous perform acts of generosity. They give out of their abundance (that is noble), they give from what they have (even nobler), or they give until it hurts (the noblest). The Greek word *charis* named gift giving in all three situations, so the translation is not incorrect, but "generous" locks us into thinking that Paul is satisfied with benefaction, a system in which patrons, men (almost always) of substance, from their superior position of having substance gave to those lacking substance. Yet in this passage, it is not by his generosity but by his insubstantial, beggarly life (*ptōcheia*) that Jesus Christ enriches others.[13]

Second Corinthians 8:9 points to the same paradoxical giving out of nothingness that we see in the beggarly widow of Mark 12. If "she" is the true benefactor, then the word "true" starts to deconstruct the concept of benefactor. Such deconstruction is the force of Jesus's speech about her (see 12:43–44). Her style of gift giving undermines the logic of benefaction among the rich who give out of their abundance. If we take a measurement (but doing so violates the spirit of pure giving), she gives far more than patrons do, even though she gives far less. What Mark 13:14 pleads with us to understand is that true gift giving, genuine grace, longs to escape the economic logic of giving-in-order-to-get-a-return.[14]

Some philosophers and theologians have taken absolute gift giving quite seriously lately.[15] They begin with the paradox of the gift and try hard *not* to resolve it but to let the *aporia* it contains drive them to new thoughts and new acts of giving. Caputo explains Jacques Derrida's position on the gift, which Derrida himself states succinctly in the last sentence of the following quotation:

> The conditions that make the gift possible simultaneously make it impossible. For in the act A gives B to C, C comes to be indebted to A, if only by gratitude, which means that C has not been given something but has been put in debt. A, on the other hand, has not given anything anyway, but has been taking under the guise of giving, having acquired credit, whether material or symbolic, even if only silently in A's own mind, just in case A chose to remain an anonymous donor. "For there to be a gift, there must be no reciprocity, return, exchange, countergift, or debt."[16]

The moment you decide to give a gift, you have spoiled it. Why? Because along with your intention to give, you also have thoughts about putting the gift into an economy of exchange. Those thoughts are often unconscious. Even though you think you do not expect a return on the gift, get honest. You do. If you donate anonymously to your favorite charity, for example, you derive satisfaction even though no one else aside from the Internal Revenue Service knows that you donated. Or think about the gift from the perspective of a recipient. How do *you* feel when you are taken out for dinner, or have a car door opened for you, or an unexpected check comes in the mail from a relative? Grateful, maybe. But obligated, certainly, and perhaps a little suspicious. Gifts create debts. The debt often can be discharged with a simple *thank-you*, but if the gift is big, you worry the *thank-you* will not be big enough. Gifts go bad so quickly that they seem not to have a chance.

Yet we still dream of gifts.[17] We cannot let go of the possibility of an impossibility, of our giving pure gifts and of receiving them. Would it not be marvelous, miraculous even, to give a perfect gift, one that creates no obligation to you in the recipient's mind and no expectation of return in yours? Would it not also be marvelous to receive a gift, not knowing who gave it or why, just that it is there for the sheer joy of it, no strings attached? But this is impossible. For this pure dream gift to happen, the giver would have to be unaware that she was giving it; otherwise, the gift creates an asymmetrical relationship between giver and recipient, and both know it. The gift, once it has been given, begins a relation of domination and control, however well intentioned the original impulse to give. Similarly, for a dream gift to happen, recipients must be in the dark. They must never know they are getting a gift lest the gratitude lowers their eyes in the presence of the giver. For the true gift, there must be nonknowing all the way around. You would not know if you gave it or from whom you got it. Like the Messiah's problem with appearing, if a gift shows up with a name attached, it is not a gift.[18]

The widow nudges the patronage system toward something new by giving out of her nothingness.[19] She obligates no one (two coins—a debt?) and puts herself at risk of death. Her understanding of the gift is not lost on Jesus. He contrasts her gift with those of big donors who give out of their excess and generate a class of persons: recipients-grateful-to-donors. She gets Jesus, perhaps not consciously, and Jesus gets her (12:44). Without access to her mind, he interprets her *action*. The widow gets what the obtuse disciple in 13:1 ("Look, Teacher, what large stones and what large buildings!") fails to grasp and what the reader is begged to understand in 13:14, that the *logical* part of theo*logical* is not the logic of a transaction. A new logic thinks *God* without thinking *purpose* or *payback*, if that is possible.

A comparison with Matthew 23:37–39 is instructive. In order to place grace/gift into an economy of giving and receiving, the author erases the widow from the story. As a result, Matthew avoids Mark's Mini-Apocalypse, although he repeats nearly all the words in Mark 13. Matthew leaves out the widow's apocalyptic (revelatory) way of giving out of her emptiness. And as odd as it sounds, he replaces her with a bird:

> Jerusalem, Jerusalem, the city that kills the prophets and stones those who are sent to it! How often have I desired to gather your children together as a hen [*ornis*; better, "bird"] gathers her brood under her wings, and you were not willing! See, your house is left to you, desolate. For I tell you, you will not see me again until you say, "Blessed is the one who comes in the name of the Lord." (Matt 23:37–39)

Matthew's Jesus speaks as if he were God threatening Jerusalem (which stood for Jews and, perhaps in this context, the Pharisees; see 23:29) with destruction for rejecting his gift of protection from the Roman army. Note the logic of retribution. God is a benefactor wishing to give protection, and the Jews, pictured by the author of Matthew as ingrates, refuse to acknowledge the gift. I cannot emphasize enough the difference between Mark and Matthew on this point. Mark's Jesus wants the reader to think about the signs of the world's end in terms of the widow's impossible gift, but in Matthew, the end is a time of revenge, repayment for rejection of God's gift. Unlike readers of Matthew, who must carefully calculate their actions and know their intentions lest they find themselves one day walking off with the goats rather than the sheep (Matt 25:31–46), the readers of Mark are asked to put aside the logic of retribution and embrace the beggarly widow's grace. Matthew's calculating Jesus, who speaks for Matthew's calculating God, ruins the grace within the gift.[20]

Another Benefactor

Back to Mark. We were exploring how the widow's gift clarifies the plea for understanding in 13:14. Without saying a word, she teaches that to understand is to seek to give a gift. Another benefactor appears in Mark 14:3–9 and teaches the same lesson. Like the poor widow, this unnamed woman loosens the strict, economic logic of patronage. She works her new logic in the presence of Jesus's dining associates and angers them as she counters the logic of benefaction. They think she is wasteful: "But some were there who said to one another in anger, 'Why was the ointment wasted in this way? For this ointment could have been sold for more than three hundred denarii, and the money given to the poor.' And they scolded her" (14:4–5). Jesus retorts that she has done "a good work [*kalon ergon*]" (14:6 KJV) and indicates that he has a contrary opinion of her.

He thinks she is very good at giving a gift, but the quality of her giving rests in her *not* knowing that she is giving. No one knows her motives; the omniscient narrator of the Gospel of Mark does not fill us in. The text does not have a portal to her intentions. For all we know, she has selfish motives, or maybe she does not know why she interrupted the dinner. Perhaps she got the address of the dinner party she intended to crash wrong. In any case, our not-knowing and her no-knowing are essential for the deconstruction of the ancient system of gift giving. If she knew why she was giving, then she would have already understood her gift as a means to an end, like the alms that feed the poor (which *do* feed the poor, though seldom enough, and must not be dispensed with in the name of the pure gift). Her gift is safe. The text tells us nothing about her motives or her intentions. Jesus views her *action* as the preeminent example of giving, indeed so outstanding that the gospel will not have been preached at any time or anywhere in the world if what she did—that is, what she gave and how she gave it—will not also have been spoken of (14:9). A sobering thought for Christian preachers who have not heeded Jesus's requirement that proclaiming the gospel will always speak of her. Of what she *did*.

What She Did

Remember, we are trying to understand what Jesus pleads with readers to understand in Mark 13:14. The plea itself is undefined but framed by two women who give gifts. The beggarly woman's gift is her minuscule donation to the treasury given out of desperate and despised poverty, a gift that originates from outside the circle of economic exchange, but she does not disdain the circle. What is the perfume-bearing woman's gift? How does she give it? And how does her gift escape the logic of benefaction in which the giver gives in order to get a return and the recipient feels obligated to give back? How, in other words, does she free the grace of giving from the law of giving?

She touches Jesus.[21]

And not just metaphorically. True, Jesus defends her with a sweeping pronouncement: "What she has done will be told in remembrance of her" (14:9). He is moved by her action. She touches him in that sense. Yet the text does not spiritualize her touch. Her touch is material, one body mourning another body, her flesh and blood reaching out to his isolation and contacting his flesh and blood. The Greek word *katacheō*, translated here as "poured on," also points to the shedding of tears, particularly at funerals. Jesus makes this association with funerary ritual explicit in verse 8: "She has done what she could; she has anointed my body beforehand for its burial." Note that it is Jesus who interprets her action in this way. What *she* thinks she is doing, if she thinks anything, we do not know. Yet her lack of self-awareness does not detract from her understanding of how to give. If anything, it makes it possible. Grace happens. It happens, we pray, whether we plan for it or not. Jesus proclaims the event of her grace. He says he is the first in a long line of proclaimers who will preach what she did "in memory of her" (14:9 NIV).

Her gift, the pressure of her perfume-laden hands on his head, neck, and shoulders, releases, if only for a moment, the pain of isolation arising from his arrest, trial, and ultimately, crucifixion, when he suffers isolation beyond anyone's kind touch.[22] The disciples, on the other hand, do not understand. Three of them will sleep through another crisis of abandonment when Jesus prays three times to the One who ignores him, the One who is perhaps not even there to hear his pleas, the One whom Jesus thinks can do all things, even grasp the cup, take it away, and give him more time (14:32–42). Instead of giving Jesus more time, the woman's saving touch transforms a moment of the time Jesus has left. The awkward instant when an uninvited woman touches a doomed man in a gathering of men who care more about the glory of almsgiving than about a God-forsaken man, a desolating sacrilege—this is not ordinary time. Not for Jesus, anyway. Perhaps Simon the leper—repulsive, whom no one touches—understands what she is doing. What she gives to Jesus is not the measurable time he will soon be asking God for at Gethsemane, one moment expiring before the next, before the next, before the next, each *now* consumed with the pain of abandonment. Her gift is not more of that time. Her gracious touch dissolves measurement, interrupts repetition, but only for an unrepeatable moment.

In her touch, the economic time of sacrifice, repayment, reward, and punishment is opened to something incalculable. Her touch shocks us and returns us to this life, this body, this now, when opportunities to give as she gives present themselves, if only we have eyes to see. What Mark 13:14 pleads with us readers to understand is the gift of touch, of a gracious movement toward Jesus in the isolation of his abandonment. *Readers*, if ever such beings hear the address that calls them into existence, will understand not with the head but with the heart and give as she gave as they wake from reading to see and touch isolated ones, whose numbers are legion. A moment of release and freedom spring from the touch of a dinner-crashing woman who anoints a man headed for execution. If such a term might be allowed, she *myrrhifies* the body that Jesus is becoming. Her touch and the beggarly woman's gift of near nothingness, these stories of gift giving give us a chance to become readers in the Markan sense, ones who get lost in written narratives, losing track of our own time and place as good readers always do yet keeping alive the hope that in our time and in our place, in our bodies, the only time and place that we have, we will hear a voice emerging from what we read without warning and without reason pleading with us to understand. To understand what the two women *did*. Pleading with us to stay awake to their style of giving, their brand of grace, their blind movement toward another's abandonment and pain.[23]

Signs of the Ends

Mark 13 is about signs of the end, but there is ambiguity (to put it mildly) about which end or whose end these signs point to. This chapter in Mark, often called the Mini-Apocalypse supposedly because its sole purpose is to reveal (*apokalyptein*) the secret of the world's end, has a reputation for frightening readers.[24] I want to read the end signs of Mark 13 differently. Unlike the Gospel of Matthew and the interpreters who have followed its lead, I do not limit what the signs point to. That is, might a sign point to the end of the world *and* to the death of Jesus *and* to the isolation of anyone excluded because they are different and resist assimilation? Were the signs of the world's demise in Mark 13 also signs of Jesus's end in chapters 14–15? And was the death of Jesus a sign that points beyond itself to everyone in the course of history who has been violently disposed of as Jesus was? Does every unjust and violent death signify the End? These questions are unsettling, since of these deaths, there has been no end, and I fear there will be none.

Our reading of Mark 13 acknowledges the widow's gift (12:41–44). Unknowingly, she contested benefactors' top-down gift giving that had funded the construction of the temple and provoked the pie-eyed admiration of one of Jesus's disciples. Such admiration was the effect the erection of impressive structures was calculated to have on Jews and Gentiles alike. In 13:1, we read, "As he came out of the Temple, one of his disciples said to him, 'Look, Teacher, what large stones and what large buildings!'"[25] Jesus's ambiguous reply to this inane observation—it was directed to a man about to be crucified and not on an architectural tour of the wonderful buildings benefactors had once given to the nation—has been obscured by the NRSV, which reads, "Then Jesus asked him, 'Do you see these great buildings? Not one stone will be left here upon another; all will be thrown down [*katalythē*]'" (13:2).[26] "Thrown down" suggests a brief point in time, perhaps the days it takes an army to raze a large building. That is indeed what happened when the Romans overran Jerusalem and destroyed the temple in 70 CE. Mark 13 anticipates this catastrophe as a sign of the end of history, but *katalythē* also points in another direction, to Jesus's body, since the Greek word meant not "throw down" but "dissolve," "break apart," and "become undone" as a rope unravels. *Katalyō* signified a process spread out over time and that, if it is a person who suffers such dissolution and not a stone, seems never to end, unless someone steps in to touch the dying flesh. Jesus refers to the stones, certainly, but there is also a hint it is more than the temple that will come undone. Here is what I am getting at: when Jesus speaks of the impending destruction of the temple, readers (especially re-readers of the Gospel of Mark) might think he is also talking about the destruction of his own body. Jesus's use of *katalyō* does not of course rule out the destruction of the temple; according to first-century Jewish apocalyptic thought, the house of God in rubble would indeed be a sign of the end of history, and there is no question that Mark 13 dedicates itself to giving signs for just such an end. But Mark 13 is more complicated than that.

Mark 13 is Jesus's ambiguous response to the disciples' question about the timing of the one grand end of history: "When he was sitting on the Mount of Olives opposite the temple, Peter, James, John, and Andrew asked him privately, 'Tell us, when will this be, and what will be the sign that all these things are about to be accomplished?'" (13:3–4). A philosophic presupposition about history shines through the word "accomplished." The author puts into these disciples' mouths a deterministic concept of history. According to the chief proponents of such a view, the Stoics, time is like a rope or cable coming uncoiled.[27] A character in one of Cicero's dialogues explains:

> Moreover, since, as will be shown elsewhere, all things happen by Fate, if there were a man whose soul could discern the links that join each cause with every other cause, then surely he would never be mistaken in any prediction he might make. For he who knows the causes of future events necessarily knows what every future event will be. But since such knowledge is possible only to a god, it is left to man to presage the future by means of certain signs which indicate what will

follow them. Things which are to be do not suddenly spring into existence, but the evolution of time is like the unwinding of a cable: it creates nothing new and only unfolds each event in its order. This connexion between cause and effect is obvious to two classes of diviners: those who are endowed with natural divination and those who know the course of events by the observation of signs. They may not discern the causes themselves, yet they do discern the signs and tokens of those causes. The careful study and recollection of those signs, aided by the records of former times, has evolved that sort of divination, known as artificial, which is divination by means of entrails, lightning's, portents, and celestial phenomena.[28]

The sequence of events for all of time has already been set. Each moment constructs the conditions of possibility for the next, and no event not pre-programmed could ever take place. Of course, this understanding of time is ruinous for the *always yet to come* time of the Messiah, to say nothing of ruining hope, faith, justice, and the gift. The neatly coiled rope at the beginning of time contains within itself all the moments of time. There can be no surprises.[29]

With something like this time ticking in their heads, Peter, James, John, and Andrew ask Jesus for a sign when the rope will completely uncoil. And the disciples are not the only ones with a deterministic understanding of history. Jesus, too, speaks as if the secret of time's ending lay hidden in the mind of God before the beginning of time: "But about that day or hour no one knows, neither the angels in heaven, nor the Son, but only the Father" (13:32).[30] As Revelation illustrates, apocalyptic literature delights in disclosing the contents of God's mind in horrifying detail, as if its author had ascended into heaven and inspected the rope wound up in God's head. Yet here is the problem with reading Mark 13 as a condensed version of Revelation—that is, as if it intended to pass on information about the timing of the end. *Nowhere in this chapter or in the Gospel of Mark does the Father tell the secret of time.* Nowhere do the signifiers of the end, which the disciples are so eager to discover and for which they are so capable of staying awake (unlike their failed vigil for Jesus at Gethsemane), guide us safely to the signified end. In fact, the one whom Jesus calls Father does not speak in the last part of the Gospel, aside from 14:27, a verse that provides no assurance. The Father's silence might come as a surprise to first-time readers of Mark, since approving pronouncements from heaven in Mark 1:11 and 9:7 carry Jesus and the reader safely through the story from one crisis to the next. At the end of the Gospel, however, no one hears God speak.[31] Perhaps the point of the Father's silence in Mark 13–16 is this: the *I*, the *ego* of God, has no information for us about the timing of the end of time.

The Gospel of Mark thus places readers between two orders of endings. Of the one kind, the big one, we cannot be certain when it is coming, even if we are convinced by scientists who predict a run for the solar system in billions of years. Only the Father knows, and according to Mark 13:32, he is not talking: "But about that day or hour no one knows, neither the angels in heaven, nor the Son, but only the Father."[32] But endings of the other order repeat themselves with appalling regularity in the mockery and exclusion of any human, in any moment of desolation, in any moment when the words "My God, My God, why have you forsaken me?" are spoken aloud or silently.[33] Then the many microapocalypses take place, whenever there is a crying out for the gift of touch.

The Gospel of Mark challenges us: under the circumstance of discovering (perhaps to our dismay) that we are the readers begged by a literary figure named Jesus to understand, will we stay awake for the many ends? Will we take Mark's Jesus at his word when he says that signs will take place in his generation, as we generate his speech, when we read the letters that cue our teeth, tongue, lips, and breath to pronounce "Truly I tell you, this generation will certainly not pass away until all these things have happened" (Mark 13:30 NIV)? If this verse refers only to the single, cataclysmic end, then the textual Jesus is mistaken about the timing of the end. But if the verse refers to other ends, the microapocalypses happening in Jesus's own lifetime (which would not be much longer), then his words ring true with a truth not limited to what actually happened. The Gospel of Mark pleads with its readers to understand that before the unknowable, cataclysmic end rings down the curtain of history, there are knowable ends of time, but only if we, unlike the disciples, stay awake for them.

One of these innumerable apocalypses is Jesus's end:

Then the soldiers led him into the courtyard of the palace (that is, the governor's headquarters); and they called together the whole cohort. And they clothed him in a purple cloak; and after twisting some thorns into a crown, they put it on him. And they began saluting him, "Hail, King of the Jews!" They struck his head with a reed, spat upon him, and knelt down in homage to him. After mocking him, they stripped him of the purple cloak and put his own clothes on him. Then they led him out to crucify him. . . . It was nine o'clock in the morning when they crucified him. The inscription of the charge against him read, "The King of the Jews." And with him they crucified two bandits, one on his right and one on his left. Those who passed by derided him, shaking their heads and saying, "Aha! You who would destroy the temple and build it in three days, save yourself, and come down from the cross!" In the same way the chief priests, along with the scribes, were also mocking him among themselves and saying, "He saved others; he cannot save himself. Let the Messiah, the King of Israel, come down from the cross now, so that we may see and believe." Those who were crucified with him also taunted him. When it was noon, darkness came over the whole land until three in the afternoon. At three o'clock Jesus cried out with a loud voice, "Eloi, Eloi, lema sabachthani?" which means, "My God, my God, why have you for-saken me?" When some of the bystanders heard it, they said, "Listen, he is calling for Elijah." And someone ran, filled a sponge with sour wine, put it on a stick, and gave it to him to drink, saying, "Wait, let us see whether Elijah will come to take him down." Then Jesus gave a loud cry and breathed his last. And the curtain of the temple was torn in two, from top to bottom. Now when the centurion, who stood facing him, saw that in this way he breathed his last, he said, "Truly this man was God's Son!" (Mark 15:16–20, 25–39)

Now think again of Mark 13:14: "But when you see the desolating sacrilege set up where it ought not to be (let the reader understand), then those in Judea must flee to the mountains." Notice three themes drawn together: (1) desolation (*erēmōsis*), (2) revulsion (a better translation of *bdelygma* than "sacrilege"), and (3) flight from the object of disgust. Mark 13:14 predicts the destruction of the temple. I do not deny that. And yet since the Greek word for "reading" is literally "knowing again" (*anaginōskō*), the plea addresses not only first-time readers but re-readers too.[34] The latter group will have already witnessed Jesus's desolation, his accusation against God, and the disciples' flight. Re-readers will have noticed that the darkening of the sun predicted in 13:24 takes place in 15:33. The readers addressed by the Gospel, because they are good readers and get lost in what they are *knowing again*—such is the power possessed by ink on a page to create illusions—will have already witnessed Jesus's mocked and deserted body, repulsive in the torture of crucifixion.[35] They will have witnessed his isolation. Yet unmoved to reach through the page to his flesh, hasty readers anxious for the end of the story will have already turned the page on him.[36] What I think Mark 13:14 asks us to stop and wonder at is this: the crucified Jesus himself is the/a desolating sacrilege. The crucified one is the/an end and a sign of the ends of all who are mocked, isolated, and dying from grief.[37] Let the reader understand that.

A comparison of Mark 13:14 with Matthew 24:15–16 is instructive. Matthew allows "desolating sacrilege" to refer to just one thing: the coming profanation of the temple in Jerusalem so monstrous that it will drive God out and signal the end of time. In Daniel 9, the angel Gabriel gives a time line that resembles the coiled rope of the Stoics. The time line is Matthew's key to the reinterpretation of Mark 13:14:

So consider the word and understand the vision: "Seventy weeks are decreed for your people and your holy city: to finish the transgression, to put an end to sin, and to atone for iniquity, to bring in everlasting righteousness, to seal both vision and prophet, and to anoint a most holy place. Know therefore and understand: from the time that the word went out to restore and rebuild Jerusalem until the time of an anointed prince, there shall be seven weeks; and for sixty-two weeks it shall be built again with streets and moat, but in a troubled time. After the sixty-two weeks, an anointed one shall be cut off and shall have nothing, and the troops of the prince who is to come shall destroy the city and the sanctuary. Its end shall come with a flood, and to the end there shall be war. Desolations are decreed. He shall make a strong covenant with many for one week, and for half of the week he shall make sacrifice and offering cease; and in their place shall be an abomination that desolates, until the decreed end is poured out upon the desolator." (Dan 9:23–27)

What is so striking about Gabriel's speech is the Stoic-like concept of history it presupposes: events in history occur by necessity. Gabriel and Matthew add an agent to determinism, the biblical God, who measures time by enforcing an economy and carefully calculating repayment as summarized in this famous saying: "All who take the sword will perish by the sword" (Matt 26:52). Divine retribution is the force that moves one moment of time to the next. Discernable to the eye of belief, the plan requires God to repay sinners for the evil they have done, and each moment has to take place in just the way it does in order to set up the conditions for the next moment. The process of one moment making inevitable the next goes on forever (but only ten thousand years in orthodox Stoics doctrine), but the One who initiated this passing of time, a passing that resembles the crashing down of dominoes, knows that there is a final event, retribution handed out to the one who desolates. I have been using the word *economic* for this kind of time, since punishment in the end cancels out the evil that has been done. When the evil is infinite, as it seems to be in Matthew 24:15–16, then the punishment must be eternal.

By directing the reader to the book of Daniel, Matthew makes sure there is no mystery about what the reader must understand. For Matthew, history makes sense as the ticking of a clock makes sense. The temple will be profaned. Abomination will force God out. God will repay evil. History will end. According to Matthew, that and only that is what we need to bring to bear on *desolating sacrilege* for its proper interpretation. The Scriptures—in this case, the book of Daniel—say what must happen and in what way it must happen.

What I Say to You I Say to All

Mark has no time for Daniel and inevitable events. Let the reader understand, time has been, is, and will be coming to an end all around us, over and over again. An apocalypse takes place in front of Peter, James, and John, and they sleep through it, even though Jesus has begged them, repeatedly, to stay awake for it (14:32–42). These friends of Jesus may keep watch with him, so intimate are they that he invites them to eat his body and drink his blood (14:17–21). But they sleep:

> They went to a place called Gethsemane; and he said to his disciples, "Sit here while I pray." He took with him Peter and James and John, and began to be distressed [*ekthambeisthai*][38] and agitated [*adēmonein*]. And he said to them, "I am deeply grieved, even to death; remain here, and keep awake [*grēgoreite*]." And going a little farther, he threw himself on the ground and prayed that, if it were possible, the hour might pass from him. He said, "Abba, Father, for you all things are possible; remove this cup from me; yet, not what I want, but what you want." He came and found them sleeping [*katheudontas*]; and he said to Peter, "Simon, are you asleep [*katheudeis*]? Could you not keep awake one hour [*grēgorēsai*]? Keep awake [*grēgoreite*] and pray that you may not come into the time of trial; the spirit indeed is willing, but the flesh is weak." And again he went away and prayed, saying

the same words. And once more he came and found them sleeping [*katheudontas*], for their eyes were very heavy; and they did not know what to say to him. He came a third time and said to them, "Are you still sleeping [*katheudete*] and taking your rest? Enough! The hour has come; the Son of Man is betrayed into the hands of sinners. Get up, let us be going. See, my betrayer is at hand." (Mark 14:32–42)

They may play the part of the gracious, perfume-bearing woman who touches Jesus's body and suspends his pain, winning an unsought fame that Christianity's own drowsiness has obscured. They may. Yet they sleep, even though Jesus has pleaded with them to keep awake for the end time, his end time, the end of anyone's time:

But about that day or hour no one knows, neither the angels in heaven, nor the Son, but only the Father. Beware, keep alert [*agrypneite*]; for you do not know when the time will come. It is like a man going on a journey, when he leaves home and puts his slaves in charge, each with his work, and commands the doorkeeper to be on the watch [*grēgorē*]. Therefore, keep awake [*grēgoreite*]—for you do not know when the master of the house will come, in the evening, or at midnight, or at cockcrow, or at dawn, or else he may find you asleep [*katheudontas*] when he comes suddenly. And what I say to you I say to all: Keep awake [*grēgoreite*]. (Mark 13:32–37)

Again, Mark 13:37 says, "And what I say to you I say to all: Keep awake." A strange thing happens every time we read these words, whether aloud in a public gathering or when a reader (like you, right now) silently scans the letters. An illusion is destroyed. What illusion? That readers are *there* observing what Jesus does and says and what the disciples, the crowds, and Jesus's opponents do and say. In other words, the illusion that gets disillusioned is our thinking of the Gospel of Mark as a technological device like a video-audio recorder defying time in its ability to replay events and to re-present Jesus to the reader. In a moment, in the time it takes for us to say "And what I say to you I say to all: Keep awake," we readers have robbed ourselves of the imaginary world the inscribed surface helps us create, and all we are left with is our lives and the text we hold in our hands. And one other thing. We are left with the pleas of ones soon to be executed ringing in our ears: "Keep awake."

Notes

Introduction

1 The writings of John D. Caputo have helped me understand many things and will be a constant companion in this book; they have especially helped explain why I have become increasingly reticent to use the word *God*. To understand my hesitation, substitute *it* for *the event* in the following quotation from Caputo's *The Insistence of God: A Theology of Perhaps* (Bloomington: Indiana University Press, 2013), 10:

> Once I say I know the name of the event, once I can say, this is God, the event is God, then the event ceases to be an event and becomes something that I have added to my repertoire, brought within the horizon of my experience, knowledge, belief, identification, and expectation, whereas the event is precisely what always and already, structurally, exceeds my horizons. What I mean by the event is the surprise, what literally over-takes me, shattering my horizon of expectation. God is *a* name for the event, but the very idea of an event prevents us from saying the event *is* God, because the very idea of the event is that I cannot see it coming. For the event, names are always lacking, even the name of God.

Maria Lichtman has confirmed for me that the mystery *it* opens me to is deeply embedded in the history of Christian theology, though habitually overlooked. See her "Negative Theology in Marguerite Porete and Jacques Derrida," *Christianity and Literature* 47, no. 2 (1998): 213–27.

2 For a critique of this way of conceiving time (Edmund Husserl's), see John D. Caputo, *Radical Hermeneutics: Repetition, Deconstruction, and the Hermeneutic Project* (Bloomington: Indiana University Press, 1987), 133–47; and John D. Caputo, *The Prayers and Tears of Jacques Derrida: Religion without Religion* (Bloomington: Indiana University Press, 1997), 77–87. See also Andrea Hurst, *Derrida Vis-à-Vis Lacan: Interweaving Deconstruction and Psychoanalysis* (New York: Fordham University Press, 2008), 24–27.

3 For Jacques Derrida's appreciation of the apophatic quandary (i.e., how to speak of the One that cannot be spoken of), see Caputo, *Prayers and Tears*, 41–57.

4 The concept of a supreme being itself has a history, but judging by the following passage (*On the Cosmos* 397b9–26, falsely attributed to Aristotle), it is remarkable how little the concept of God has changed since the opening centuries of the Common Era:

> It now remains to speak in summary fashion about the cause holding the universe together, as has also been done about the rest; for it would be wrong when speaking about the cosmos—even if not in detail, then at least for a knowledge in outline—to pass over that which is most important in the cosmos. There is indeed an ancient account, native to all people, that all things have come into existence from god and because of god, and that no thing by itself is self-sufficient, if deprived of the preservation deriving from him. Therefore some of the ancients were also led to say that all these things that appear to us through the eyes and hearing and every sensation are full of gods, presenting an idea appropriate to the divine power, not however to the divine essence. For god is really the preserver of all things and the begetter of everything however it is brought about in this cosmos, without indeed enduring the hardship of a creature hard at work for itself, but by making use of an untiring power, by means of which he prevails even over things that seem to be far away. He has been allotted the highest and first place, and is therefore called supreme.

Translation is Johan C. Thom, *Cosmic Order and Divine Power: Pseudo-Aristotle, "On the Cosmos"* (Tübingen, Germany: Mohr Siebeck, 2014), 43.

5 Symeon the New Theologian, *Hymns* 22.53–56. Translation is Daniel K. Griggs, *Divine Eros: Hymns of St. Symeon the New Theologian* (Crestwood, NY: St. Vladimir's Seminary Press, 2010), 159.

6 My flirtation here with apophatic theology is only that, a flirtation. In the mystical theologian's confidence that the God beyond being is even more transcendent than the supreme being, I hear the melody of kataphatic theology, only at a higher pitch. On this point, see Caputo, *Prayers and Tears*, 1–19. A less technical treatment of this issue can be found in John D. Caputo, *Hoping against Hope: (Confessions of a Postmodern Pilgrim)* (Minneapolis: Fortress, 2015), 23–39.

7 Caputo, *Hoping against Hope*, 1–22.

8 John D. Caputo, *The Weakness of God: A Theology of the Event* (Bloomington: Indiana University Press, 2006), 91. Just as Caputo's objections to kataphatic theology should not be interpreted as atheism pure and simple, so also his qualified appreciation of apophatic theology should not be mistaken as a covert defense of the Christian metaphysical God. See John D. Caputo, "Unprotected Religion: Radical Theology, Radical Atheism, and the Return of Anti-religion," in *The*

Trace of God: Derrida and Religion, ed. Edward Baring and Peter E. Gordon (New York: Fordham University Press, 2015), 151–77.

9 For a reflection on the Holocaust and the question of God that avoids taking advantage of the former as I have done, see Richard Kearney, *Anatheism: Returning to God after God* (New York: Columbia University Press, 2010), 57–82.

10 See Caputo, *Prayers and Tears*, 15–17. For the association of *is* with God, which is the problem of putting God into the box of metaphysics, see Caputo, *Hoping against Hope*, 114–22. For a fuller treatment, see Caputo, *Insistence of God*, 24–38.

11 Safe, that is, if we would all pledge to honor and protect the singularity of every individual's unique opening onto their world. See Michael Naas, *The End of the World and Other Teachable Moments: Jacques Derrida's Final Seminar* (New York: Fordham University Press, 2015), 46–61.

12 For an example of the philosophic predecessor to the Christian doctrine of God's self-sufficiency, see Epictetus, *Discourses* 3.13.4–7:

> Why, if being alone is enough to make one forlorn, you will have to say that even Zeus himself is forlorn at the World-Conflagration, and bewails himself: "Wretched me! I have neither Hera, nor Athena, nor Apollo, nor, in a word, brother, or son, or grandson, or kinsman." There are even those who say that this is what he does when left alone at the World-Conflagration; for they cannot conceive of the mode of life of one who is all alone, starting as they do from a natural principle, namely, the facts of natural community of interest among men, and mutual affection, and joy in intercourse. But one ought none the less to prepare oneself for this also, that is, to be able to be self-sufficient, to be able to commune with oneself; even as Zeus communes with himself, and is at peace with himself, and contemplates the character of his governance, and occupies himself with ideas appropriate to himself, so ought we also to be able to converse with ourselves, not to be in need of others, not to be at a loss for some way to spend our time.

Translation is W. A. Oldfather, *Epictetus. Discourses, Books 3–4. Fragments. The Encheiridion*, Loeb Classical Library 218 (Cambridge, MA: Harvard University Press, 1928), 89–91.

13 David Wood, "Things at the Edge of the World," in *Phenomenologies of the Stranger: Between Hostility and Hospitality*, ed. Richard Kearney and Kascha Semonovitch (New York: Fordham University Press, 2011), 68.

14 For encouraging reflections on how to live with a tradition by contesting it, see Michael Naas, *Taking on the Tradition: Jacques Derrida and the Legacies of Deconstruction* (Palo Alto, CA: Stanford University Press, 2003), xvii–xviii.

15 Eusebius, *The Proof of the Gospel* 1.1. Translation is W. J. Ferrar, *The Proof of the Gospel: Eusebius* (Eugene, OR: Wipf & Stock, 2001), 3–4. Where did Eusebius get these ideas? Hebrews is one of his sources, but Stephen's recapitulation of Israel's history in Acts 7 is another. Notice how the author of Acts puts into Stephen's mouth an ethnic slur and an accusation of murdering the Messiah:

> You stiff-necked people, uncircumcised in heart and ears, you are forever opposing the Holy Spirit, just as your ancestors used to do. Which of the prophets did your ancestors not persecute? They killed those who foretold the coming of the Righteous One, and now you have become his betrayers and murderers. You are the ones that received the law as ordained by angels, and yet you have not kept it. (Acts 7:51–53)

16 Eusebius, *Proof of the Gospel* 1.5. Translation is Ferrar, *Proof of the Gospel*, 25 (my emphasis).

17 Anthony Grafton and Megan Williams, *Christianity and the Transformation of the Book: Origen, Eusebius and the Library of Caesarea* (Cambridge, MA: Belknap, 2006), 137.

18 For the false and insidious distinction between Judaism as a religion of law and Christianity as a religion of love, see Caputo, *Prayers and Tears*, 234–43. See also Merriam Leonard, "Derrida between 'Greek' and 'Jew,'" in *Derrida and Antiquity*, ed. Miriam Leonard (Oxford: Oxford University Press, 2010), 135–58.

19 For the paradox of getting started by means of the impossible, a major theme in Caputo's writings, see his *Prayers and Tears*, 51–66, 306–11; "Temporal Transcendence: The Very Idea of *à venir* in Derrida," in *Transcendence and Beyond: A Postmodern Inquiry*, ed. John D. Caputo and Michael J. Scanlon (Bloomington: Indiana University Press, 2007), 190–91; and "The Experience of God and the Axiology of the Impossible," in *The Experience of God: A Postmodern Response*, ed. Kevin Hart and Barbara Eileen Wall (New York: Fordham University Press, 2005), 21–22.

20 See Caputo, *Radical Hermeneutics*, 11–35.

21 Ancient novels can help us out here. They associate the new with paradox, surprise, the marvelous, and the sublime. See Stefan Tilg, *Chariton of Aphrodisias and the Invention of the Greek Love Novel* (Oxford: Oxford University Press, 2010), 172–97.

22 Another example of language's playfulness is the word *palaios* (old). The Greek for *again* is *palin*, suggesting that every time first-century readers took "old" from the page into their minds, they might for an instant have thought they were bringing in "again." The point is this: in the Greek language, repetition is built into the word *old* as well as into the concept of the old.

23 Augustine, *Sermons* 187.3. Translation is Thomas Comerford Lawler, *St. Augustine: Sermons for Christmas and Epiphany* (Westminster, MD: Newman Press, 1952), 87.

24 For a witty discussion of the issue, see Theodoret of Cyrus, *Eranistes*. I wonder how Christianity might have turned out differently if something like Caputo's understanding of *flesh* had informed the doctrine of the incarnation? See his reflections on *flesh* in "Hospitality and the Trouble with God," in Kearney and Semonovitch, *Phenomenologies of the Stranger*, 94–97. Caputo's ideas about *flesh* have antecedents. See, for example, John of Ford, *Sermons* 83.2:

> So, from the very moment that "the Word was made flesh," the Lord Jesus bore his cross, truly from then on "a man of sorrows, acquainted with grief." In fact, we hold that the evangelist intended to reveal this by saying that "the Word was made flesh," *the word "flesh" standing deliberately for his capacity to suffer and feel compassion.* If you think of it, what in all creation is weaker than human flesh, or more tender. Weakness implies suffering and tenderness implies compassion, the two factors from which, as from two bars of wood, the cross of Christ was fashioned.

Translation is Wendy Mary Beckett, *John of Ford: Sermons on the Final Verses of the Song of Songs* (Kalamazoo, MI: Cistercian, 1984), 6:2–3 (my emphasis).

25 For "become" (*ginomai*) marking events of stunning metamorphosis, see Richard Buxton, *Forms of Astonishment: Greek Myths of Metamorphosis* (Oxford: Oxford University Press, 2009), 23, 38, 111, 122, 131, 166–77.

26 Augustine, *Sermons* 187.3–4. Translation is Lawler, *St. Augustine*, 87–88.

27 For a more sympathetic account of Augustine's theory of language than I give here, see Philip Burton, *Language in the Confessions of Augustine* (Oxford: Oxford University Press, 2007), 88–108. Contrast Augustine's theory of language with that of Gregory of Nyssa (*Homilies on the Song of Songs* 3.87), which is friendlier to the arguments in this book.

28 Adam Kamesar, "The *Logos Endiathetos* and the *Logos Prophorikos* in Allegorical Interpretation: Philo and the D-Scholia to the Iliad," *Greek, Roman, and Byzantine Studies* 44, no. 2 (2004): 163.

29 For a concise statement of this ancient linguistic theory, a theory that is still very much in force in contemporary understandings of the relation between mind and language, see Philo, *The Worse Attacks the Better* 39–40. For a thorough examination of the ancient sources, see Jaap Mansfeld, "'Illuminating What Is Thought': A Middle Platonist *Placitum* on 'Voice' in Context," *Mnemosyne* 58, no. 3 (2005): 358–407. See also Casper C. de Jonge, *Between Grammar and Rhetoric: Dionysius of Halicarnassus on Language, Linguistics and Literature* (Leiden: Brill, 2008), 53–59.

30 See Caputo, *Weakness of God*, 175:

> An event (*événement*) is a certain "happening" that is "linked" but not bound causally to antecedent and consequence, not bound by efficient causality to the past or by teleological causality to the future, but is taken for itself, in its own singularity. The event has a certain free-floatingness, an innocence and gift likeness; it is a happening over which we have no mastery, in which things happen to us, overtake and overcome us.

As Caputo often reminds readers, to define *event* is to risk self-contradiction because of an event's resistance to assimilation into any preexisting system—in this case, the system of language that supplies the tools of definition (in other words, words). Geoffrey Bennington also notes (and thoroughly appreciates the irony) of the event's resistance to definition in the definition of the event he offers; see his *Not Half No End: Militantly Melancholic Essays in Memory of Jacques Derrida* (Edinburgh: Edinburgh University Press, 2010), 40–44.

31 See John D. Caputo, *More Radical Hermeneutics: On Not Knowing Who We Are* (Bloomington: Indiana University Press, 2000), 41–59. Caputo's admiration for Gadamer but preference for Derrida is similar to my approval of the historical-critical method matched by a desire to move beyond it for the sake of radical hospitality:

> The difference between Gadamer and Derrida, in my view, is that deconstruction in virtue of its more radical anti-essentialism, provides for a more radical conception of friendship and hospitality, of putting oneself at risk, and if hermeneutics means putting one's own meanings at risk, as Gadamer has beautifully written, then deconstruction also effects a more radical hermeneutics. (58)

32 Quoted from Caputo, *Prayers and Tears*, 16–17.

33 Caputo, 17.

34 See Paola Ceccarelli, *Ancient Greek Letter Writing: A Cultural History (600 BC–150 BC)* (Oxford: Oxford University Press, 2013), 359. See also Antiphanes, *Fragments* 196.17–21, on which see Yopie Prins, "Sappho's Afterlife in Translation," in *Re-reading Sappho: Reception and Transmission*, ed. Ellen Greene (Berkeley: University of California Press, 1996), 46–48.

35 See Ceccarelli, *Ancient Greek Letter Writing*, 65–67, 188–99, 258–64. Plato, however, accused writing of weakening the power of memory. See Plato, *Phaedrus* 275A.

36 Quoted by Ps.-Plutarch, *The Education of Children* 14C. Translation is Frank Cole Babbitt, *Plutarch. Moralia*, vol. 1, *The Education of Children. How the Young Man*

Should Study Poetry. On Listening to Lectures. How to Tell a Flatterer from a Friend. How a Man May Become Aware of His Progress in Virtue, Loeb Classical Library 197 (Cambridge, MA: Harvard University Press, 1927), 69.

37 *The Greek Anthology* 9.401. Translation is W. R. Paton, *The Greek Anthology*, vol. 3, *Book 9: The Declamatory Epigrams*, Loeb Classical Library 84 (Cambridge, MA: Harvard University Press, 1917), 223. In Aeschylus's play *Prometheus Bound*, Prometheus boasts of his several gifts to miserable humanity, one of which was writing: "I also invented for them the art of number, supreme among all techniques, and that of combining letters into written words, the tool that enables all things to be remembered and is mother of the Muses" (459–61). Translation is Alan H. Sommerstein, *Aeschylus. Persians. Seven against Thebes. Suppliants. Prometheus Bound*, Loeb Classical Library 145 (Cambridge, MA: Harvard University Press, 2009), 493.

38 For Derrida's notion of *force*, which I am alluding to here, see Sarah Wood, *Derrida's "Writing and Difference"* (London: Continuum, 2009), 27–46.

39 For a discussion of what Maurice Blanchot called the relation of dissymmetry, see Caputo, *Prayers and Tears*, 84–85; at greater length, see Kevin Hart, *The Dark Gaze: Maurice Blanchot and the Sacred* (Chicago: University of Chicago Press, 2004), 191–222.

40 For an explanation of Derrida's famous line *there is nothing outside the text*, see Bennington, *Not Half No End*, 86–99.

41 See Caputo, *Hoping against Hope*, 63–72.

Chapter 1

1 See John D. Caputo, *Hermeneutics: Facts and Interpretation in the Age of Information* (London: Pelican Books, 2018), 307–10.

2 See Caputo, *Weakness of God*, 56–65.

3 See, for example, Caputo, *Radical Hermeneutics*, 146–47. For an explanation of how Derrida radicalized hermeneutics (though Caputo reports Derrida himself had little use for the word *hermeneutics* because of its association with presence, meaning, and stability), see Caputo, *Hermeneutics*, 117–41.

4 Plato, *Republic* 450E–451A. See also Chrysippus, *Fragmenta logica et physica* 44.3–4.

5 For the first person in the work's preface establishing the historiographer's expertise, see Georgina Longley, "'I, Polybius': Self-Conscious Didacticism?," in *The Author's Voice in Classical and Late Antiquity*, ed. Anna Marmodoro and Jonathan Hill (Oxford: Oxford University Press, 2013), 176–77. Luke 1:1–4 is an example of what Ps.-Demetrius (*On Style* 19) called *historical period*, a compositional style in which the ending of the phrase is safe and secure.

Note the snug fit between the preface's style and its stated intention; both are about safety.

6 See *LSJ* 1739.

7 See Origen, *Homilies on Luke* 1.6.

8 These pressures can be detected in Acts 9:2; 19:9, 23; 22:4; 24:14, 22.

9 Epictetus, *Discourses* 3.16.7–11. Translation is Oldfather, *Epictetus. Discourses, Books 3–4*, 107.

10 This verse is a brilliant piece of writing but a little bizarre, since in an English translation, we encounter a Greek text reporting Jesus's translation into Hebrew of a line from a tragedy originally written in Greek. When, we are left wondering, did the risen Jesus find time to read and translate Euripides into Hebrew?

11 See also Luke 1:22. For the dream/vision report, see John Hanson, "*Dreams* and *Visions* in the Graeco-Roman World and Early Christianity," in *Aufstieg und Niedergang der römischen Welt 2.23.2*, ed. Hildegard Temporini and Wolfgang Haase (Berlin: de Gruyter, 1972), 1395–427. One might compare the double dream in the Peter and Cornelius episode of Acts 10:1–33 with Apuleius, *Metamorphoses* 11. For gods communicating their plans through dreams and visions, see Mary Beard, "Cicero's 'Response of the Haruspices' and the Voice of the Gods," *Journal of Roman Studies* 102 (2012): 20–39; see further William V. Harris, *Dreams and Experience in Classical Antiquity* (Cambridge, MA: Harvard University Press, 2009), 123–202; and Jan N. Bremmer, *Greek Religion and Culture, the Bible and the Ancient Near East* (Leiden: Brill, 2008), 215–34.

12 The saying seems to have circulated independently of the play like Clint Eastwood's "Go ahead, make my day" has taken on a life of its own apart from the 1983 movie *Sudden Impact*.

13 Julian, *Orations* 8.246B. Translation is Wilmer C. Wright, *Julian. Orations 6–8. Letters to Themistius, to the Senate and People of Athens, to a Priest. The Caesars. Misopogon*, Loeb Classical Library 29 (Cambridge, MA: Harvard University Press, 1913), 181.

14 For personal harm resulting from resistance to the divine will, see Brad Inwood, *Reading Seneca: Stoic Philosophy at Rome* (Oxford: Clarendon, 2005), 157–59.

15 See Daniel S. Richter, *Cosmopolis: Imagining Community in Late Classical Athens and the Early Roman Empire* (Oxford: Oxford University Press, 2011), 7–8.

16 The ancient preface clarified the author's role as teacher and warranted the work's information. See Jason König, "Conventions of Prefatory Self-Presentation in Galen's *On the Order of My Own Books*," in *Galen and the World of Knowledge*, ed. Christopher Gill, Tim Whitmarsh, and John Wilkins (Cambridge: Cambridge University Press, 2009), 45–47. For an approach to the preface of Luke similar to my own, see Rick Strelan, "A Note on *Asphaleia* (Luke 1.4)," *Journal for the Study of the New Testament* 30 (2007): 170.

17 Note Paul's references to catechesis in Gal 6:6.

18 Dionysius looks down his nose at previous attempts at writing Roman history. The author of Luke–Acts does the same, obliquely criticizing the Gospel of Mark for lacking an overarching, explanatory structure.

19 For other occurrences of the list, see Acts 1:1; 10:36–42; 18:24–25; 28:31.

20 Luke–Acts leads the reader to certainty in the light of divine providence. Caputo shows the underside of certainty in *Hoping against Hope*, where he criticizes Western culture's obsession with the *why* question, which he calls "means-and-ends thinking." He believes the unrelieved quest for explanation, for getting answers, is one of the main contributors to human misery:

> For me religion means living in constant exposure to the unconditional, open to something excessive, exceptional, unforeseeable, unprogrammable, something slightly mad relative to the rationality of means-and-ends thinking. To lack the religion of which I speak is to allow the series of conditions to surround and submerge us. We would see no farther than our noses, have only a nose for a good investment, for making a profit, so that our lives would be consumed by consuming, swallowed up by winning, where everything has a price. (Caputo, 37)

Caputo affirms what he calls the *nihilism of grace*, which bears a striking resemblance to Martin Luther's *justification by grace through faith*. See Caputo, 30.

21 See Abraham J. Malherbe, "'Not in a Corner': Early Christian Apologetic in Acts 26:26," in *Light from the Gentiles: Hellenistic Philosophy and Early Christianity*, ed. Carl Holladay et al. (Leiden: Brill, 2013), 1:209–27. See also R. Walzer, *Galen on Jews and Christians* (Oxford: Oxford University Press, 1949), 42–56; and Robert Wilken, *The Christians as the Romans Saw Them*, 2nd ed. (New Haven, CT: Yale University Press, 2003), 68–93.

22 For the influence of Stoic thought on Luke–Acts and other ancient histories, see John T. Squires, *The Plan of God in Luke–Acts* (Cambridge: Cambridge University Press, 1993), 37–77.

23 See Jonas Grethlein, *Experience and Teleology in Ancient Historiography: "Futures Past" from Herodotus to Augustine* (Cambridge: Cambridge University Press, 2013), 224.

24 See Nicolas Wiater, "Writing Roman History—Shaping Greek Identity: The Ideology of Historiography in Dionysius of Halicarnassus," in *The Struggle for Identity: Greeks and Their Past in the First Century BCE*, ed. Thomas A. Schmitz and Nicolas Wiater (Stuttgart, Germany: Franz Steiner, 2011), 61–64.

25 Origen worried some readers might think Luke 1:1 is a criticism of the Gospel of Mark. See Origen, *Homilies on Luke* 1.1: "The words 'have tried' imply an accusation against those who rushed into writing gospels without the grace of the Holy Spirit. Matthew, Mark, John, and Luke did not 'try' to write: they wrote their Gospels when they were filled with the Holy Spirit." Translation is Joseph T. Lienhard, *Origen: Homilies on Luke: Fragments on Luke* (Washington, DC: Catholic University of America Press, 1996), 5.

26 Dionysius of Halicarnassus, *Roman Antiquities* 1.5.2–4. Translation is Earnest Cary, *Dionysius of Halicarnassus. Roman Antiquities*, vol. 1, *Books 1–2*, Loeb Classical Library 319 (Cambridge, MA: Harvard University Press, 1937), 17–19. Today's readers might object to Dionysius's arrogance, but his haughty attitude masks a more serious issue. There is something deeply wrong when historians, even the humble ones, weave disasters and suffering into a narrative that comes to a grand and glorious end. This applies to theologians as well. For this critique, see Caputo, *Weakness of God*, 253–57; and Caputo, "Hearing the Voices of the Dead: Wyschogrod, Megill, and the Heterological Historian," in *Saintly Influence: Edith Wyschogrod and the Possibilities of Philosophy of Religion*, ed. Eric Boynton and Martin Kavka (New York: Fordham University Press, 2009), 161–74.

27 If the prefaces of Dionysius and the author of Luke–Acts seem heavy handed, it should be noted that these authors were by no means unique in their desire to control how their texts would be understood by readers. See Helen Morales, *Vision and Narrative in Achilles Tatius' Leucippe and Clitophon* (Cambridge: Cambridge University Press, 2004), 77.

28 In the modern period, of course, the word *divine* often drops out. Yet although some contemporary theorists wish to break away from theology's stranglehold on hermeneutics, programming still finds a way into their conceptions of interpretation. See Caputo, *Hermeneutics*, 145–70.

29 For Hermes as leader or guide, see Artemidorus, *Oneirocritica* 4.72. See also Athanassios Vergados, *The Homeric Hymn to Hermes: Introduction, Text and Commentary* (Berlin: de Gruyter, 2013), 221–23. Note that Gabriel in Luke 1:19–20 also resembles Hermes.

30 See Maurizio Bettini, *The Ears of Hermes: Communication, Images, and Identity in the Classical World*, trans. William Michael Short (Columbus: Ohio State University Press, 2011), 131–68; and Vergados, *Homeric Hymn to Hermes*, 234, 529. Another word for interpretation is exegesis (related to *hēgoumenos* in v. 12). In theological seminaries, exegesis is another name for the interpretation of biblical texts. Like Hermes, who conveyed messages from immortals to mortals, students of the Bible are trained to lead meaning out of biblical texts—that is, to bring clarity to nonexegetes concerning the authors' (or God's) intended meanings. Aspiring

Christian exegetes, who learn to interpret in order to preach, might be alarmed to discover they stand in a long tradition that includes ancient Greek interpreters of oracles. See Robert Parker, *On Greek Religion* (Ithaca, NY: Cornell University Press, 2011), 40–45.

31 For the tradition of Hermes's clever theft of Apollo's cows, see Vergados, *Homeric Hymn to Hermes*, 283–97.

32 For this characterization of Hermes, see Cornutus, *On Greek Theology* 16.

33 For "way" (*hodos*) as a philosophic term designating a series of choices making up the life of virtue, see Anton Cornelis van Geytenbeek, *Musonius Rufus and Greek Diatribe* (Assen, Netherlands: Van Gorcum, 1962), 23. See also 2 Tim 4:7.

34 For the early history of this idea, see Katharina Volk, "Letters in the Sky: Reading the Signs in Aratus' *Phaenomena*," *American Journal of Philology* 133 (2012): 209–40.

35 See Joshua W. Jipp, "Paul's Areopagus Speech of Acts 17:16–34 as Both Critique and Propaganda," *Journal of Biblical Literature* 131, no. 3 (2012): 567–88. The irony is that by the first century, many intellectuals were functioning monotheists; see Michael Frede, "The Case for Pagan Monotheism," in *One God: Pagan Monotheism in the Roman Empire*, ed. Stephen Mitchell and Peter Van Nuffelen (Cambridge: Cambridge University Press, 2010), 53–81.

36 Scholars have recognized that the theological ideas of the Paul of Luke–Acts are at odds with the undisputed Pauline Epistles. See Philipp Vielhauer, "On the 'Paulinism' of Acts," in *Studies in Luke–Acts*, ed. Leander E. Keck and J. Louis Martyn (London: SPCK, 1968), 33–50. The conception of God in Acts 17 has been heavily influenced by Stoicism (more on this below), whereas the Paul of the undisputed letters fights to save the name of God from the Stoic concepts elite males in the first century counted on to preserve their privileged status in the churches. For a nuanced account of Stoic influence on the Areopagus speech, see David L. Balch, "The Areopagus Speech: An Appeal to the Stoic Historian Posidonius against Later Stoics and Epicureans," in *Greeks, Romans, and Christians: Essays in Honor of Abraham J. Malherbe*, ed. David L. Balch, Everett Ferguson, and Wayne A. Meeks (Minneapolis: Fortress, 1990), 52–79.

37 *LSJ* 400.

38 See *antiballō* in Luke 24:17.

39 Suetonius, *Greek Terms of Abuse* 6; Hesychius, *Lexicon* S 1468.

40 For ancient attitudes toward curiosity, see Alexander Kirichenko, "Satire, Propaganda, and the Pleasure of Reading: Apuleius' Stories of Curiosity in Context," *Harvard Studies in Classical Philology* 104 (2008): 340–45.

41 For Roman distrust of religious movements arising in Egypt and migrating to Rome, see the classic study of Arthur Darby Nock, *Conversion: The Old and the New*

in Religion from Alexander the Great to Augustine of Hippo (Oxford: Oxford University Press, 1933), 71–76.

42 For ancient prejudice against novelty, see Jipp, "Paul's Areopagus Speech," 574–75.

43 See Richard Hunter and Donald Russell, eds., *Plutarch: How to Study Poetry ("De audiendis poetis")* (Cambridge: Cambridge University Press, 2011), 147, 195.

44 See Dale B. Martin, *Inventing Superstition: From the Hippocratics to the Christians* (Cambridge, MA: Harvard University Press, 2004), 5–9.

45 For the religious dimension of Stoic thought, see Keimpe Algra, "Stoic Philosophical Theology and Graeco-Roman Religion," in *God and Cosmos in Stoicism*, ed. Ricardo Salles (Oxford: Oxford University Press, 2009), 224–52.

46 For a detailed account of the Stoic doctrines in these verses, see Balch, "Areopagus Speech," 52–79.

47 See Abraham J. Malherbe, "Pseudo-Heraclitus, Epistle 4: The Divinization of the Wise Man," in Holladay et al., *Light from the Gentiles*, 2:606–19.

48 Several study Bibles correctly direct readers of v. 28 to Aratus of Soli (early third century BCE). The Stoic philosopher Epictetus would have applauded the line "For we too are his offspring." See Epictetus, *Discourses* 1.3.

49 Jesus too was said to have been beside himself (Mark 3:21). For the connection of *ekstasis* to madness in ancient medical writings, see below, note 53. For trembling, silence, and madness, see Posidonius, *Fragmenta* 436. In a statement that has long puzzled scholars, in 2 Cor 5:13, Paul points both to his madness and to being in a right mind. Generally, ancient doctors and philosophers regarded the two states to be mutually exclusive. See Galen, *De propriorum animi cuiuslibet affectuum dignotione et curatione* 5.22.1–5.23.3; Plutarch, *Sayings of Kings and Commanders* 188A; Plutarch, *Table-Talk* 693A–B; and Plutarch, *Whether an Old Man Should Engage in Public Affairs* 791C.

50 For hermeneutics as the ordering of *the things* into a coherent explanation, see Diogenes Laertius, *Lives of Eminent Philosophers* 9.13; and Diogenes Laertius, *Lives of Eminent Philosophers* 10.2. The term *diermēneuō* (and cognates) often refers to the philosophic, phonocentric understanding of interpretation; see Philo, *That the Worse Is Wont to Attack the Better* 127; Philo, *On the Contemplative Life* 28; Philo, *Life of Moses* 2.129; and Philo, *The Migration of Abraham* 79–81.

51 For example, note the Stoic terminology in Acts 2:23: "this man, handed over to you according to the definite plan [*tē hōrismenē boulē*] and foreknowledge [*prognōsei*] of God." For a brief introduction to the Stoic doctrine of providence, see Epictetus, *Discourses* 1.6.

52 For the twofold sense of *eulogein*, see Philo, *The Migration of Abraham* 71–74. See also Arius Didymus, *Liber de philosophorum sectis* 64.2.20–21.

53 See Ps.-Galen, *Introductio seu medicus* 14.740.12–14.

54 See Galen, *De melancholia* 6.9.94–111. See also Peter Toohey, "Some Ancient Histories of Literary Melancholia," *Illinois Classical Studies* 15, no. 1 (1990): 143–47.

55 For a discussion of Rufus's dates, see Vivian Nutton, "Rufus of Ephesus in the Medical Context of His Time," in *On Melancholy: Rufus of Ephesus*, ed. Peter E. Pormann (Tübingen, Germany: Mohr Siebeck, 2008), 140–41.

56 Translation is Peter E. Pormann, "Appendix 2: Isḥāq ibn ʿImrān on 'Scholarly Melancholy,'" in Pormann, *On Melancholy*, 291.

57 Peter Toohey, "Rufus of Ephesus and the Tradition of the Melancholy Thinker," in Pormann, *On Melancholy*, 222–25.

58 Translation is Pormann, "Appendix 2," 293. For the scholar's love of *paideia* as the cause of insanity, see Chiara Thumiger, "Aretaeus's 'Stomachic' Patients: Comic Features in a Medical Discussion?," *Illinois Classical Studies* 43, no. 2 (2018): 482.

59 See Galen, *De melancholia* 6.9.56–64. See also Toohey, "Some Ancient Histories," 146–47.

60 Simon Swain, "Social Stress and Political Pressure: *On Melancholy* in Context," in Pormann, *On Melancholy*, 135. Even a Roman emperor felt the sting of the "imputation . . . of being somewhat slow and dull of apprehension." For these revealing comments, see Marcus Aurelius, *Meditations* 5.5. Translation is C. R. Haines, *Marcus Aurelius*, Loeb Classical Library 58 (Cambridge, MA: Harvard University Press, 1916), 103.

61 The fourth-century BCE physician Diocles of Carystus located the cause of *mania* in the *zesis* of blood around the heart; see Anonymi Medici, *De morbis acutis et chroniis* 18.1.5–8. For the connection of anger and *zesis*, see Peter N. Singer, "Galen and the Philosophers: Philosophical Engagement, Shadowy Contemporaries, Aristotelian Transformations," in "Philosophical Themes in Galen," ed. Peter Adamson, Rotraud Hansberger, and James Wilberding, supplement, *Bulletin of the Institute of Classical Studies*, no. 114 (2014): 28. For *pneuma* (breath or spirit) as the medium of madness rather than blood, see Peter E. Pormann, "Commentary," in Pormann, *On Melancholy*, 108–9. For an example of boiling spirit in nonmedical writers, see A. M. G. McLeod, "Physiology and Medicine in a Greek Novel: Achilles Tatius' Leucippe and Clitophon," *Journal of Hellenic Studies* 89 (1969): 97–105.

62 See Luke 1:3. It should be noted that Philo of Alexandria conceived of hermeneutics exactly in this way, as a "more accurate" explanation of facts, where "accurate" means contextualizing historical occurrences within the order of divine providence. See Philo, *De vita contemplativa* 31–32, 75–76; and Philo, *Who Is the Heir of Divine Things?* 63.

63 The second-century CE physician Aretaeus of Cappadocia places *aporia* second after *loathing* in a list of melancholy-like mental disorders; see Thumiger, "Aretaeus's 'Stomachic' Patients," 480–81.

64 George Kazantzidis, "Haunted Minds, Haunted Places: Topographies of Insanity in Greek and Roman Paradoxography," in *Landscapes of Dread in Classical Antiquity: Negative Emotion in Natural and Constructed Spaces*, ed. Debbie Felton (New York: Routledge, 2018), 228–29.

65 For fear (*phobos*) as a symptom of madness, see Galen, *De locis affectis libri vi* 8.192.7. Staring at the ground is another symptom of madness; see Toohey, "Rufus of Ephesus," 232–33.

66 See Plutarch, *Table-Talk* 623C; see *lērēsis* as "delirium" in Diogenes Laertius, *Lives of Eminent Philosophers* 7.118. See also Philip J. van der Eijk and Peter E. Pormann, "Appendix 1: Greek Text, and Arabic and English Translations of Galen's *On the Affected Parts* iii. 9–10," in Pormann, *On Melancholy*, 267–68.

67 For madness (*ekstasis*) as an incapacity to believe the marvelous and a fluttering of the soul, see Philo, *Who Is the Heir of Divine Things?* 251.

68 The Stoic wise man marvels at nothing; see Diogenes Laertius, *Lives of Eminent Philosophers* 7.123. For the connection of astonishment to dread, see Kazantzidis, "Haunted Minds, Haunted Places," 229–31.

69 For the beginning of the end of dialogue in early Christianity, see Simon Goldhill, "Why Don't Christians Do Dialogue?," in *The End of Dialogue in Antiquity*, ed. Simon Goldhill (Cambridge: Cambridge University Press, 2008), 1–11.

70 See Katarzyna Jazdzewska, "From *Dialogos* to Dialogue: The Use of the Term from Plato to the Second Century CE," *Greek, Roman, and Byzantine Studies* 54, no. 1 (2014): 17–36.

71 See Andrew Ford, "The Beginnings of Dialogue: Socratic Discourses and Fourth-Century Prose," in Goldhill, *End of Dialogue*, 36.

72 See Phrynichus, *Eclogae* 188; and Suda, *Lexicon* E 2817. For playing ball as a metaphor for dialogue, see Artemidorus, *Oneirocritica* 4.69.

73 The motif was not limited to Peripatetics, however; see Timothy M. O'Sullivan, *Walking in Roman Culture* (Cambridge: Cambridge University Press, 2011), 91–96, 110–15.

74 See Acts 16:14; 17:3. On this point, see Cătălin Enache, "Character, Voice and the Limits of Dietetics in Hippocrates' De victu I 36," *Wiener Studien* 129 (2016): 76–83.

75 See Galen, *Quod animi mores corporis temperamenta sequantur* 4.788.11–789.3; Plutarch, *Whether Land or Sea Animals Are Cleverer* 963E–F; and Ps.-Hippocrates, *Epistles* 12.13–14.

76 See Galen, *De locis affectis libri vi* 8.342.1–10; and Philo, *On Sobriety* 6. For the centrality of dread in ancient understandings of insanity, see note 64 above.

77 See Ps.-Aristotle, *Physiogomics* 812a2–4; and Dio Chrysostom, *Orations* 16.1–3.

78 See Galen, *De locis affectis libri vi* 8.190.10–191.3; and Plutarch, *That Epicurus Actually Makes a Pleasant Life Impossible* 1093A; 1104E. See also Eijk and Pormann, "Appendix 1," 283.

79 See Epictetus, *Enchiridion* 33.16.

80 See Galen, *In Hippocratis prorrheticum i commentaria iii* 16.612.10–613.11.

81 See Toohey, "Some Ancient Histories," 154.

82 See Plutarch, *On Tranquility of Mind* 473E–474B. Some things never change; for the misrepresentation of Jacques Derrida and Heraclitus as mere instigators of sullenness, see Erin O'Connell, "Derrida and Presocratic Philosophy," in Leonard, *Derrida and Antiquity*, 81–100.

83 For the gloominess of Heraclitus, see Diogenes Laertius, *Lives of Eminent Philosophers* 6; Heraclitus, *Epistles* 5.3; Lucian, *Philosophies for Sale* 14; and Hippolytus, *Refutation of All Heresies* 1.4.1. For Empedocles, see Diogenes Laertius, *Lives of Eminent Philosophers* 8.73; Lucian, *Dialogues of the Dead* 6.4; and Lucian, *The Runaways* 2. For Xenocrates, see Plutarch, *Caius Marius* 2.3; and Xenocrates, *Fragments* 2. For Diogenes of Sinope, see Lucian, *Philosophies for Sale* 7. For Chrysippus, see Lucian, *Philosophies for Sale* 20. For the gloominess of philosophers in general, see Lucian, *The Dead Come to Life* 12, 14, 37.

84 See Hippocrates, *De morbis i–iii* 1.30.5–8; Ps.-Galen, *Definitiones medicae* 19.416:7–8; Menander, *Aspis* 305–9; Philo, *On the Cherubim* 69; Philo, *Who Is the Heir of Divine Things?* 249–50; and Eijk and Pormann, "Appendix 1," 268–69.

85 For the element of ridicule in the phrase, see Peter N. Singer, "The Mockery of Madness: Laughter at and with Insanity in Attic Tragedy and Old Comedy," *Illinois Classical Studies* 43, no. 2 (2018): 300, 316. See also Aesop, *Fables* 128, on which see William A. Ross, "'Ὦ ἀνόητοι καὶ βραδεῖς τῇ καρδίᾳ': Luke, Aesop, and Reading Scripture," *Novum Testamentum* 58, no. 4 (2016): 369–79. For other examples, see Philo, *On Dreams* 2.181; Plutarch, *Sayings of Spartans* 224E–F; and Plutarch, *On the Fortune or the Virtue of Alexander* 329E.

86 See Philo, *De cherubim* 116; and Musonius Rufus, *Discourses* 20.33–36.

87 For the impairment of perception in the state of madness, see Galen, *De locis affectis libri vi* 8.200.13–15. For slow perception in Hippocratic medicine, see Enache, "Character, Voice," 77–83.

88 For the association of internal overheating with mental disease, see Hippocrates, *De morbis i–iii* 1.30.1–13.

89 For rage, see Singer, "Galen and the Philosophers," 28. For erotic desire, see Sappho, *Fragments* 48; Aristophanes, *Lysistrata* 9; and *The Greek Anthology* 12.83, 130.

90 See Pormann, "Commentary," 105–8; and Toohey, "Rufus of Ephesus," 224–25.

91 See Toohey, "Some Ancient Histories," 152–55.

92 See Zeno, *Fragments* 206: "Pathos esti ptoia psychēs." For similar formulations, see Chrysippus, *Fragmenta moralia* 378.5, 663.3–5; Ps.-Hippocrates, *Epistles* 12.18; Timaeus, *Fragments* 222.13–20; and Erotianus, *Vocum Hippocraticarum collectio* 107.3–4. For further discussion, see David E. Fredrickson, "Hellenistic Philosophy and Literature," in *The Oxford Handbook of New Testament, Gender, and Sexuality*, ed. Benjamin Dunning (Oxford: Oxford University Press, 2019), 249–50.

93 See Ps.-Galen, *Introductio seu medicus* 14.740.16–18; and Plutarch, *Whether Land or Sea Animals Are Cleverer* 963E–F. See further Kazantzidis, "Haunted Minds, Haunted Places," 16; and Chiara Thumiger, "Mental Insanity in the Hippocratic Texts: A Pragmatic Perspective," *Mnemosyne* 68, no. 2 (2015): 218–20.

94 For the spirit going up from the body to the soul, causing madness, see Plutarch, *The Dialogue on Love* 758D–E; Galen, *De melancholia* 6.9.73–75; and Eijk and Pormann, "Appendix 1," 269, 281.

Chapter 2

1 Elizabeth A. Castelli, *Imitating Paul: A Discourse of Power* (Louisville, KY: Westminster John Knox, 1991), 17.

2 For the growing appreciation of the importance of emotions in biblical interpretation, see F. Scott Spencer, "Getting a Feel for the 'Mixed' and 'Vexed' Study of Emotions in Biblical Literature," in *Mixed Feelings and Vexed Passions: Exploring Emotions in Biblical Literature*, ed. F. Scott Spencer (Atlanta: Society of Biblical Literature, 2017), 1–41. Focusing on emotions in the Pauline writings is not the only way to extricate Paul from his reputation as a world-denying, body-hating autocrat. Ward Blanton's *A Materialism for the Masses: Saint Paul and the Philosophy of the Undying Life* (New York: Columbia University Press, 2014) seeks to push past Friedrich Nietzsche's flawed but influential characterization of Paul's theology.

3 It is important to distinguish between nostalgia and longing. Nostalgia is a desire to return to a familiar past. In theory, this desire could be satisfied. But longing in Paul's letters opens itself to the impossibility of attaining rest like the infinite restlessness expressed in the subtly self-contesting words of Maya Angelou: "I long, as does every human being, to be at home wherever I find myself." For an illuminating discussion of this line, see Naas, *Jacques Derrida's Final Seminar*, 83–87. Derrida's preference for melancholy over so-called successful mourning corresponds to ancient poetry's and Paul's affirmation of longing. For mourning's resistance to closure in Derrida's thought, see Bennington, *Not Half No End*, 38–40.

4 See John Lee White, *The Form and Function of the Body of the Greek Letter: A Study of the Letter-Body in the Non-literary Papyri and in Paul the Apostle* (Missoula, MT: Society of Biblical Literature, 1972), 49.

5 See Ruth Padel, *In and Out of the Mind: Greek Images of the Tragic Self* (Princeton, NJ: Princeton University Press, 1992), 12–48.

6 See Clayton Zimmerman, *The Pastoral Narcissus: A Study of the First Idyll of Theocritus* (Lanham, MD: Rowman & Littlefield, 1994), 41–70.

7 Homer, *Odyssey* 19.203–9. Translation is A. T. Murray, *Homer. Odyssey*, vol. 2, *Books 13–24*, revised by George E. Dimock, Loeb Classical Library 105 (Cambridge, MA: Harvard University Press, 1919), 249.

8 See *The Greek Anthology* 5.279, 281, 288, 290, 303; 12.22, 49, 81, 83, 99. For fire, melting, and emptying as erotic tropes, see David E. Fredrickson, *Eros and the Christ: Longing and Envy in Paul's Christology* (Minneapolis: Fortress, 2013), 45–65.

9 See A. A. Long, *From Epicurus to Epictetus: Studies in Hellenistic and Roman Philosophy* (Oxford: Oxford University Press, 2006), 377–94; and Margaret Graver, *Stoicism and Emotion* (Chicago: University of Chicago Press, 2007), 61–108.

10 See Epictetus, *Discourses* 1.1.

11 See John M. Rist, "The Stoic Concept of Detachment," in *The Stoics*, ed. John M. Rist (Berkeley: University of California Press, 1978), 259–72.

12 Epictetus addresses the topic of dealing with another's grief in *Discourses* 3.4, whose heading summarizes what he would likely have said to a mourner: "That we ought not to yearn for the things which are not under our control."

13 The NIV, RSV, and KJV do not have "me," but they do have "his."

14 Caputo, *Hoping against Hope*, 106.

15 For the philosophers' dim view of shared suffering, see David E. Fredrickson, "Paul, Hardships, and Suffering," in *Paul in the Greco-Roman World: A Handbook, Volumes 1 and 2*, ed. Paul Sampley, 2nd ed. (New York: T&T Clark, 2016), 2:172–97.

16 This is also the case in Phil 1:7, which could be translated as either "I have you in my heart" or "You have me in your heart." Perhaps the two translations taken together reveal the intimacy Paul wished for with the church at Philippi.

17 For the motif of *consolatio amoris*, see Richard Hunter, *Theocritus and the Archeology of Greek Poetry* (Cambridge: Cambridge University Press, 1996), 220–42; and Alison Sharrock, *Seduction and Repetition in Ovid's "Ars Amatoria II"* (Oxford: Clarendon, 1994), 53–61.

18 For this ambiguity expressed with other words, see Theocritus, *Idylls* 11.80–81; and Euripides, *Hippolytus* 348. The *consolatio amoris* motif is closely associated with an adjective Sappho invented to describe the ambivalence of love: bittersweet (*glukupikros*). See Fredrickson, *Eros and the Christ*, 39–42.

19 Joan Booth, "All in the Mind: Sickness in Catullus 76," in *The Passions in Roman Thought and Literature*, ed. Susanna Morton Braund and Christopher Gill (Cambridge: Cambridge University Press, 1997), 150–68.

20 Gilbert of Hoyland, *Sermons on the Song of Songs* 19. Translation is Lawrence C. Braceland, *Gilbert of Hoyland: Sermons on the Song of Songs* (Kalamazoo, MI: Cistercian, 1979), 2:239.

21 *Tapeinophrosynē* in Phil 2:3 does not mean "humility." Since *tapeinos* means "low" and the root *phrosynē* points to perception, "sadness" or "depressed state of mind" are better translations. For the sense of degradation attached to the slavery of love, see R. O. A. M. Lyne, "*Servitium Amoris*," *Classical Quarterly* 29, no. 1 (1979): 117–30. For philosophers on the topic of the lover's depressed spirit, see Ps.-Aristotle, *Physiognomics* 808a7–12. See further David Sedly, "Chrysippus on Psychophysical Causality," in *Passions and Perceptions: Studies in Hellenistic Philosophy of Mind*, ed. Jacques Brunschwig and Martha Nussbaum (Cambridge: Cambridge University Press, 1993), 329. For lovesickness as depressed spirit, see Plutarch, *The Dialogue on Love* 753B; and *The Greek Anthology* 12.101, 158. The best study on this topic is Peter Toohey, *Melancholy, Love, and Time: Boundaries of the Self in Ancient Literature* (Ann Arbor: University of Michigan Press, 2004), see especially 72–79. For the inevitability of mourning at the origin of friendship, see Robert D. Stolorow, "Friendship, Fidelity, and Finitude: Reflections on Jacques Derrida's *The Work of Mourning*," *Comparative and Continental Philosophy* 2 (2010): 143–46.

22 See Regina Höschele, "Meleager and Heliodora: A Love Story in Bits and Pieces?," in *Plotting with Eros: Essays on the Poetics of Love and the Erotics of Reading*, ed. Ingela Nilsson (Copenhagen: Museum Tusculanum, 2009), 121–27.

23 See Amanda Wilcox, *The Gift of Correspondence in Classical Rome: Friendship in Cicero's "Ad Familiares" and Seneca's "Moral Epistles"* (Madison: University of Wisconsin Press, 2012), 64–72, 132–42; and Stanley K. Stowers, *Letter Writing in Greco-Roman Antiquity* (Philadelphia: Westminster Press, 1986), 68–69.

24 Thousands of actual letters from antiquity have survived, and thousands more if those of the first millennium CE are counted, as indeed they should, since the theory of letter writing during this period did not change substantially. That is why the standard works on letter writing range over several centuries. See Klaus Thraede, *Grundzüge griechisch-römisher Brieftopik* (Munich: C. H. Beck, 1970); and Heikki Koskenniemi, *Studien zur Idee und Phraseologie des griechischen Briefes bis 400 n. Chr.* (Helsinki, Finland: Finnish Academy, 1956). Even letters from the tenth century shed light on first-century practices; see Gustav H. Karlsson, *Idéologie et cérémonial dans l'épistolographie byzantine: Textes du Xe siècle analysés et commentés* (Uppsala: Almqvist & Wiksell, 1959). One reason for the epistolary tradition's stability was the generations of students of rhetoric learning from handbooks to write letters of recommendation, condolence, blame, grief, thanks, apology, and many more types. See Abraham J. Malherbe, *Ancient Epistolary Theorists* (Atlanta: Scholars Press, 1988), 1–11.

25 See Ceccarelli, *Ancient Greek Letter Writing*, 3, 9, 81–85, 257–58; and Wilcox, *Gift of Correspondence*, 89–90. Ancient epistolary theorists thought that one particular type, the *friendly letter*, was the source of the other letter types. Accordingly, theorists based claims about the defining characteristics of letters on the friendly letter. See Koskenniemi, *Studien zur Idee*, 34–47.

26 Synesius, *Epistles* 138. Translation is Augustine FitzGerald, *The Letters of Synesius of Cyrene* (London: Oxford University Press, 1926), 231–32. See also Synesius, *Epistles* 26–27, 31, 49, 60, 68, 80, 94, 96, 127, 132, 145, 148, 150, 152. Many of the 166 letters of Procopius of Gaza (ca. 465–ca. 528) also testify to the endurance of this theme.

27 Synesius, *Epistles* 123. Translation is FitzGerald, *Letters of Synesius*, 213–14.

28 What I am calling *the double effect* was identified by ancient rhetoricians by other names. See Ruth Webb, "Imagination and the Arousal of the Emotions in Greco-Roman Rhetoric," in Braund and Gill, *Roman Thought and Literature*, 117.

29 See Malherbe, *Ancient Epistolary Theorists*, 58–61.

30 Seneca, *Epistles* 40.1. Translation is Richard M. Gummere, *Seneca. Epistles*, vol. 1, *Epistles 1–65*, Loeb Classical Library 75 (Cambridge, MA: Harvard University Press, 1917), 263–65. For further analysis, see Mathilde Cambron-Goulet, "Orality in Philosophical Letters," in *Between Orality and Literacy: Communication and Adaptation in Antiquity: Orality and Literacy in the Ancient World*, ed. Ruth Scodel (Leiden: Brill, 2014), 10:151–56.

31 See Julian, *Epistles* 77.

32 Pliny, *Epistles* 6.7. Translation is P. G. Walsh, *Pliny the Younger: Complete Letters* (Oxford: Oxford University Press, 2006), 137–38. See Julian, *Epistles* 12. See also Anna De Pretis, "'Insincerity,' 'Facts,' and 'Epistolarity': Approaches to Pliny's *Epistles* to Calpurnia," *Arethusa* 36, no. 2 (2003): 27–46.

33 For various artifacts accentuating absence by giving the illusion of presence, see Maurizio Bettini, *The Portrait of the Lover*, trans. Laura Gibbs (Berkeley: University of California Press, 1999), 7–17.

34 Pliny, *Epistles* 6.7. Translation is Walsh, *Pliny the Younger*, 137–38.

35 Augustine, *Epistles* 27. Translation is Sister Wilfrid Parsons, *Saint Augustine: Letters* (Washington, DC: Catholic University of America Press, 1951), 88. Here Augustine is more love poet than theologian as he confesses that presence and absence cannot be disentangled. This is surprising, however, if we recall his sermon on John 1:14 (see the introduction). There he was committed to the hierarchical

organization of binaries and steered clear of the plain sense of the verse, which does indeed confuse the finite and the infinite, a distinction closely related to absence and presence. "And the Word became flesh" is not, however, the focus of what follows. Rather, we will explore the phrase "he emptied himself" in Phil 2:7 CSB.

36 For criticism of the traditional interpretation, see Sheila Briggs, "Can an Enslaved God Liberate? Hermeneutical Reflections on 2 Philippians 2:6–11," *Semeia* 47 (1989): 137–53.

37 For the effect of "form of God" on first-century readers, see Buxton, *Forms of Astonishment*, 182.

38 See Gianpiero Rosati, "'Latrator Anubis': Alien Divinities in Augustan Rome, and How to Tame Monsters through Aetiology," in *Paradox and the Marvelous in Augustan Literature and Culture*, ed. Philip Hardie (Oxford: Oxford University Press, 2009), 273.

39 A related motif was beauty as a weapon. See Karlheinz Kost, *Musaios, Hero und Leander: Einleitung, Text, Übersetzung und Kommentar* (Bonn, Germany: Bouvier, 1971), 283.

40 For fuller treatments than I am able to offer here, see Kathryn J. Gutzwiller, *Poetic Garlands: Hellenistic Epigrams in Context* (Berkeley: University of California Press, 1998), 136–37; and Fredrickson, *Eros and the Christ*, 85–104. For female divinities abducting young men, see Giuliana Lanata, "Sappho's Amatory Language," trans. William Robins, in *Reading Sappho: Contemporary Approaches*, ed. Ellen Greene (Berkeley: University of California Press, 1996), 193. For gods transforming themselves in order to abduct humans, see Buxton, *Forms of Astonishment*, 158–64. Imperial Rome advertised its absolute power through monumental art depicting scenes of erotic abduction; see Katherine A. Shaner, "Seeing Rape and Robbery: ἁρπαγμαός and the Philippians Christ Hymn (Phil. 2:5–11)," *Biblical Interpretation* 25 (2017): 342–63.

41 Emily Vermeule, *Aspects of Death in Early Greek Art and Poetry* (Berkeley: University of California Press, 1979), 163–64.

42 See Katia Margariti, "Lament and Death Instead of Marriage: The Iconography of Deceased Maidens on Attic Grave Reliefs of the Classical Period," *Hesperia* 87, no. 1 (2018): 91–176; and Buxton, *Forms of Astonishment*, 126–34, 148. As liminal experiences, marriage and death implied each other; see Artemidorus, *Oneirocritica* 2.49: "For both marriage and death are considered 'ends' [*telē*] for men and are indicated by each other." Translation is Daniel E. Harris-McCoy, *Artemidorus' "Oneirocritica": Text, Translation, and Commentary* (Oxford: Oxford University Press, 2012), 235. See further Artemidorus, *Oneirocritica* 2.65.

43 See Shaner, "Seeing Rape and Robbery," 342–63.

44 Caputo's allusions to kenotic theory for the most part do not support the interpretation of Phil 2:7 I am advancing here. Rather, they reflect his interest in apophatic theology, wherein God empties Godself of the attributes that according to kataphatic theology constitute God's divinity. See Caputo, *Prayers and Tears*, 37–45. In his discussion of dying in the writings of Maurice Blanchot, however, Caputo comes very close to what I elsewhere have argued (Fredrickson, *Eros and the Christ*, 57–83) is the erotic sense of *kenosis* in ancient poetry and in Phil 2:7:

> By "dying" Blanchot appears to be drifting in the direction of Levinas, of what Levinas means by substitution, being-for-the-other, transcendence as the absolute passivity of being-already-delivered over to the other before any conscious act or choice. In Blanchot, dying does not mean getting sick or growing old, which are visible events in ordinary time, but a kind of ontological erosion of the self, a hollowing out of self-ishness, I-hood, which begins to take on the look of Levinasian substitution, of turning the self inside out—not my death but the death of the other—of a deep responsiveness before all responsible action to the approach, to the step of the other at my door. (Caputo, *Prayers and Tears*, 82)

For erotic understandings of the crucified Christ in medieval Christianity that bear some similarity to what Caputo describes here, see Mary Frances Wack, *Lovesickness in the Middle Ages: The "Viaticum" and Its Commentaries* (Philadelphia: University of Pennsylvania Press, 1990), 24–27. For the ancient erotic sense of *draining*, see Gutzwiller, *Poetic Garlands*, 131–32.

45 See Martin Luther, *Lectures on Galatians*, ed. Jaroslav Pelikan and Walter A. Hansen, trans. Jaroslav Pelikan, vol. 26 of *Luther's Works* (Saint Louis, MO: Concordia, 1963), 288; and Martin Luther, "The Freedom of a Christian," in *Luther's Works*, ed. and rev. Harold J. Grimm, trans. W. A Lambert (Philadelphia: Muhlenberg Press, 1957), 31:366.

46 Guerric of Igny, *Sermon* 29.1. Translation is the Monks at Saint Bernard Abbey, *Guerric of Igny: Liturgical Sermons* (Spencer, MA: Cistercian, 1971), 2:55–56.

47 See Fredrickson, *Eros and the Christ*, 65–78. And yet it must be observed that the aggressors in ancient poetry often portrayed themselves as victims or slaves and their victims as masters and aggressors. For this sort of manipulation, see Sharon L. James, "Her Turn to Cry: The Politics of Weeping in Roman Love Elegy," *Transactions of the American Philological Association* 133, no. 1 (2003): 99–122.

48 For the philosophers' disdain of the slave of love, see Epictetus, *Discourses* 4.1.15–23.

49 See Owen Hodkinson, "'Novels in the Greek Letter': Inversions of the Written-Oral Hierarchy in the Briefroman 'Themistocles,'" in *Seeing Tongues, Hearing Scripts: Orality and Representation in the Ancient Novel*, ed. Victoria Rimell

(Groningen, Netherlands: Barkhuis, 2007), 257–78. Paul alludes to the epistolary cliché *absent in body but present in spirit* in Phil 2:12 but in a way that emphasizes his absence only at the moment the letter is read.

50 God—in need of nothing, according to the philosophers—is the supreme example of fullness. Therefore, males who are mature or perfect (*anēr teleios*) are full (see Col 4:12) like God is full. On the other hand, gourmands, the sexually insatiate, and women empty themselves and are therefore perpetually in need. Furthermore, to be empty is to be in pain; see Jacques Jouanna, *Hippocrates*, trans. Malcom B. DeBevoise (Baltimore: Johns Hopkins University Press, 1999), 335–38.

51 "Head" (*kephalē*) in Colossians and Ephesians is best explained in terms of the close but complex relationship between ancient philosophy, literature, and medicine, on which see Christopher Gill, *Naturalistic Psychology in Galen and Stoicism* (Oxford: Oxford University Press, 2010), 23–43. Medicine was not just for doctors. For the mutual influence of medical concepts and literary criticism, see Jacqueline Michelle Arthur-Montagne, "Symptoms of the Sublime: Longinus and the Hippocratic Method of Criticism," *Greek, Roman, and Byzantine Studies* 57, no. 2 (2017): 325–55.

52 For a few examples of the philosophic theme of self-control in the New Testament, see 1 Cor 7:37; Jas 3:2; Heb 2:10; 5:9, 14; 6:1; 7:28.

53 The KJV translates accurately: "unto a perfect man."

54 See Galen, *The Diagnosis and Cure of the Soul's Passions* 5.34, 55. For the *anēr teleios*, see James Hankinson, "Actions and Passions: Affection, Emotion, and Moral Self-Management in Galen's Philosophical Psychology," in Brunschwig and Nussbaum, *Passions and Perceptions*, 198–204.

55 See Arius Didymus, *Liber de philosophorum sectis* 78.1.7–9; Philo, *On the Special Laws* 4.140; Dio Chrysostom, *Orations* 8.16; and Galen, *The Diagnosis and Cure of the Soul's Passions* 5.14.9–10. In the ancient philosophic construction of gender, the opposite of the perfect male was the fluttering female, who, like a child, lacked the power of self-control. See Eph 4:14; and Plato, *Republic* 439D.

56 Plutarch, *How a Man May Become Aware of His Progress in Virtue* 84D–E (my emphasis). Translation is Babbitt, *Plutarch. Moralia*, 1:449.

57 Diane Enns, *Love in the Dark: Philosophy by Another Name* (New York: Columbia University Press, 2016), 14. Enns does not distinguish between Paul and the pseudonymous Paul of Colossians and Ephesians, but this does not diminish her insight about the latter's view of marriage. Her remarks could be directed against Plutarch as well; see Plutarch, *Advice to Bride and Groom* 142E.

58 See Plutarch, *Advice to Bride and Groom* 140A.

59 Caputo, *Prayers and Tears*, 78.

Chapter 3

1 Around the time of the Pastoral Epistles, Plutarch also emphasized the same connection between reading and self-formation. See Hunter and Russell, *Plutarch*, 170–83, 191–95, 200–209; and Richard Hunter, *Critical Moments in Classical Literature: Studies in the Ancient View of Literature and Its Uses* (Cambridge: Cambridge University Press, 2009), 169–201. For Seneca on reading and self-improvement, see Christopher Star, *The Empire of the Self: Self-Command and Political Speech in Seneca and Petronius* (Baltimore: Johns Hopkins University Press, 2012), 173–83.

2 I have left *sophisai* untranslated for the moment, not because the NRSV's "instruct" is incorrect (it is not), but because it does not allow English readers to recognize the theme of self-discipline in the word *sōphrosynē* and its cognates. See 1 Tim 2:9, 15; 3:2; 2 Tim 1:7; Titus 1:8; 2:2, 4, 5, 6, 12. Other philosophic terms in 1 Tim pertaining to self-discipline are "reproof," "training," "righteousness," and "correction." For the last term, see Irene Peirano, *The Rhetoric of the Roman Fake: Latin Pseudepigrapha in Context* (Cambridge: Cambridge University Press, 2012), 39.

3 For the formation of the self in ancient Greece, see Michel Foucault, *The History of Sexuality*, vol. 2, *The Use of Pleasure*, trans. Robert Hurley (New York: Pantheon, 1985), 63–77. For the motif of self-control in Paul's writings, see Stanley K. Stowers, "Paul and Self-Mastery," in Sampley, *Paul in the Greco-Roman World*, 2:270.

4 The author of the Pastoral Epistles and Epictetus both refer to this disaster as "shipwreck." See 1 Tim 1:18–20; and Epictetus, *Discourses* 2.16.20.

5 See 1 Tim 1:2; 2 Tim 1:2; Titus 1:4. As a Lutheran eighth grader, I had to memorize this verse in preparation for the rite of confirmation. Now I know why. Second Tim 3:16 guarantees the truth of the entire Bible. Of course, if anyone were to ask what guarantees the guarantee—that is, what bestows on this single verse such mystical power that it not only preserves the Bible from critical thought but also places itself beyond doubt—questioners are likely to encounter stern looks. Yet it is neither fair nor logical to cite Second Tim 3:16 to prove the truth of Second Tim 3:16. If the questioner persists, the knowledgeable defender of Lutheran orthodoxy has recourse to obscure terms built on the word *self* (*autos*), like *autalētheia* (self-established truth) and *autopistos* (credible in itself), that discourage interrogation, put questioners in their place, and exemplify the main features of phonocentrism: "When we have once learned that the Scriptures are divine and contain the Word of God, we no longer believe the Scriptures on account of the Church, but on account of themselves; because, viz., they are the voice of God, which is *autalētheia*, and hence, *autopistos*, which we know must be believed on its own account and immediately." Heinrich Schmid, *The Doctrinal Theology of*

the Evangelical Lutheran Church, trans. Charles A. Hay and Henry E. Jacobs, 3rd ed., rev. (Minneapolis: Augsburg, 1899), 40. In short, the Bible is true because it is the reduction of God's word (i.e., the divine voice) to writing. To read Scripture is to reanimate God's voice. Since voice is the reflection of the mind, the divine intention in every word of Scripture is absolutely clear. Nevertheless, the eighth grader in me still says, "Yeah, right."

6 For the acceptance of fakes in antiquity, see Peirano, *Roman Fake*, 53, 66–67; and A. D. Morrison, "Authorship and Authority in Greek Fictional Letters," in Marmodoro and Hill, *Author's Voice*, 287–312. Pseudonymous letters were attempts to control the interpretations of a tradition's doctrines and practices. See Benjamin Fiore, *The Function of Personal Example in the Socratic and Pastoral Epistles* (Rome: Biblical Institute Press, 1986), 102–63.

7 First Tim 3:14 refers to hope but only as an epistolary cliché. "I hope to come to you soon" was a polite way of saying, "Don't count on me coming; regard this letter as a substitute for my arrival."

8 Interpreters sometimes claim the Pastoral Epistles were adaptations of Paul's thought for a new generation. This is too charitable an assessment in light of the vicious pronouncements in the Pastoral Epistles on women in general and men who did not conform to ancient philosophic ideals of masculinity, the latter theme powerfully exposed by Manuel Villalobos Mendoza, *When Men Were Not Men: Masculinity and Otherness in the Pastoral Epistles* (Sheffield: Phoenix Press, 2014). The letters' repressive ideology might be ignored, so defenders argue, as antiquated attitudes of fearful believers in the hostile context of the Roman Empire. For an eye-opening account of the reception history of the Pastoral Epistles, see Jay Twomey, *The Pastoral Epistles through the Centuries* (Chichester, UK: Wiley-Blackwell, 2009).

9 Note how Caputo weaves *the logic of impossibility* through the final pages of his *Hoping against Hope*, 185–200. See also his *Insistence of God*, 3–23.

10 For hope as yearning, see Douglas Cairns, "Metaphors for Hope in Archaic and Classical Greek Poetry," in *Hope, Joy, and Affection in the Classical World*, ed. Ruth R. Caston and Robert A. Kaster (Oxford: Oxford University Press, 2016), 17–21.

11 Caputo, *Hoping against Hope*, 198. For other treatments of hope in Caputo's writings, see Caputo, "Experience of God," 20–41; and Caputo, "Postmodern Hope," in *Postmodern Apologetics? Arguments for God in Contemporary Philosophy*, ed. Christina M. Gschwandtner (New York: Fordham University Press, 2013), 242–64.

12 Some writers of erotic poetry also embraced the paradox. See, for example, Ovid, *Heroides* 20.16.

13 Yet what exactly is *salvation* in the Pastoral Epistles? It is not only a future reward but also self-mastery in the here and now that gains the ultimate reward. For salvation as a turning away from ignorance to knowledge and virtue in order to obtain everlasting life, see Titus 2:11–14; 2 Pet 1:3–11.

14 Similarly, readers of 1 Thess 5:8 committed to philosophical ways of thinking would have scoffed at Paul's substitution of hope for reason in his playful reworking of the *armor of the sage* motif. See Abraham J. Malherbe, *The Letters to the Thessalonians: A New Translation with Introduction and Commentary* (New York: Doubleday, 2000), 297–98. For rationality as a defense against the onslaughts of misfortune, see Miriam Griffin, "The Younger Pliny's Debt to Moral Philosophy," *Harvard Studies in Classical Philology* 103 (2007): 451–81; and Star, *Empire of the Self*, 25–41.

15 Ps.-Seneca, *De Spe* 1–5. Translation is Michael S. Armstrong, *"Hope the Deceiver": Pseudo-Seneca "De Spe" (Anth. Lat. 415 Riese)* (Hildesheim, Germany: Georg Olms, 1998), 49–51. For hope as the "common deceiver of all mankind," see Laurel Fulkerson, "'Torn between Hope and Despair': Narrative Foreshadowing and Suspense in the Greek Novel," in Caston and Kaster, *Hope, Joy, and Affection*, 82.

16 See Cairns, "Metaphors for Hope," 13–44. For hope in the ancient novels, see Fulkerson, "'Hope and Despair,'" 75–91.

17 For cognates of the verb *tassō* (order), see 1 Tim 1:1; 2:11; 3:4; Titus 1:3, 5; 2:5, 9, 15; 3:1.

18 For connections between the ancient Greek household and political theory, see Grant A. Nelsestuen, "*Oikonomia* as a Theory of Empire in the Political Thought of Xenophon and Aristotle," *Greek, Roman, and Byzantine Studies* 57, no. 1 (2017): 74–104; Richter, *Cosmopolis*, 3–18; and Carlo Natali, "*Oikonomia* in Hellenistic Political Thought," in *Justice and Generosity: Studies in Hellenistic Social and Political Philosophy*, ed. Andre Laks and Malcolm Schofield (Cambridge: Cambridge University Press, 2009), 100–109, 117–18. For the analogy of emperor and head of household, see Teresa R. Ramsby and Beth Severy, "Gender, Sex, and the Domestication of the Empire in Art of the Augustan Age," *Arethusa* 40, no. 1 (2007): 43–71; and Kristina Milnor, *Gender, Domesticity, and the Age of Augustus: Inventing Private Life* (Oxford: Oxford University Press, 2005), 11–31.

19 For the analogy between imperial power and individual self-control, see Star, *Empire of the Self*, 25–52.

20 See Aristotle, *On Interpretation* 16a5–7: "Words spoken are symbols or signs of affections or impressions of the soul; written words are the signs of words spoken." Translation is H. P. Cooke and Hugh Tredennick, *Aristotle. Categories. On Interpretation. Prior Analytics*, Loeb Classical Library 325 (Cambridge, MA: Harvard University Press, 1938), 115.

21 For a helpful collection of philosophic texts illustrating the ideology of household management, see David L. Balch, *Let Wives Be Submissive: The Domestic Code in 1 Peter* (Chico, CA: Scholars Press, 1981), 23–59.

22 See 1 Tim 3:4–5, 12, 15; 5:4, 8, 13–14; 2 Tim 1:14; 2:20; 3:6; Titus 1:7, 11; 2:5. See also Epictetus, *Discourses* 1.9.4, 11; 1.10.10; 1.12.4–9; 1.19.15.

23 Epictetus, 1.12.15–16. Translation is W. A. Oldfather, *Epictetus. Discourses, Books 1–2*, Loeb Classical Library 131 (Cambridge, MA: Harvard University Press, 1925), 91–93.

24 See Epictetus, 1.12.7–10:

> The good and excellent man must, therefore, inquire into all these things [the existence of the gods], before he subordinates [*hypotaxen*] his own will to him who administers [*dioikounti*] the universe, precisely as good citizens submit to the law of the state. And he that is being instructed ought to come to his instruction with this aim, "How may I follow the gods in everything, and how may I be acceptable to the divine administration [*dioikēsei*, note the *oik* root], and how may I become free?" Since he is free for whom all things happen according to his moral purpose, and whom none can restrain.

Translation is Oldfather, *Epictetus. Discourses, Books 1–2*, 89–91.

25 For the political functions of the *ekklēsia* in the classical period, see Mogens H. Hansen, *The Athenian Assembly in the Age of Demosthenes* (Oxford: Blackwell, 1987), 94–124.

26 See Laura S. Nasrallah, "1 Corinthians," in *The Letters and Legacy of Paul: Fortress Commentary on the Bible Study Edition*, ed. Margaret Aymer, Cynthia Briggs Kittredge, and David A. Sánchez (Minneapolis: Fortress, 2016), 428; George H. van Kooten, "Ἐκκλησία τοῦ θεοῦ: The 'Church of God' and the Civic Assemblies (ἐκκλησίαι) of the Greek Cities in the Roman Empire: A Response to Paul Trebilco and Richard A. Horsley," *New Testament Studies* 58, no. 4 (2012): 522–48; and David E. Fredrickson, "Congregations as Communities of Moral Deliberation," in *The Promise of Lutheran Ethics*, ed. Karen L. Bloomquist and John Stumme (Minneapolis: Fortress, 1998), 116–24.

27 Note here the key philosophic term for self-control ("behave," *anastrephesthai*). See 1 Tim 4:12; and Epictetus, *Discourses* 1.7.2–4, 21, 27; 1.9.11; 1.22.13.

28 First Tim 2:11; 3:4; Titus 2:5, 9; 3:1; Col 2:5; 3:18; Eph 1:22; 5:21, 22, 24; 1 Pet 2:13, 18; 3:1, 5, 22; 5:5; 1 Tim 2:11; 3:4; Titus 1:3; 2:8, 15.

29 For the fatherhood of the emperor, see T. R. Stevenson, "The Ideal Benefactor and the Father Analogy in Greek and Roman Thought," *Classical Quarterly* 42, no. 2 (1992): 421–26.

30 See Martha Nussbaum, "The Incomplete Feminism of Musonius Rufus: Platonist,
    Stoic, and Roman," in *The Sleep of Reason: Erotic Experience and Sexual Ethics in
    Ancient Greece and Rome*, ed. Martha Nussbaum and Juha Sihvola (Chicago: Uni-
    versity of Chicago Press, 2002), 283–326.

31 Plutarch, *Advice to Bride and Groom* 142E. Translation is Frank Cole Babbitt,
    Plutarch. Moralia, vol. 2, *How to Profit by One's Enemies. On Having Many Friends.
    Chance. Virtue and Vice. Letter of Condolence to Apollonius. Advice about Keeping Well.
    Advice to Bride and Groom. The Dinner of the Seven Wise Men. Superstition*, Loeb Clas-
    sical Library 222 (Cambridge, MA: Harvard University Press, 1928), 323. For
    a discussion of this passage, see Victoria Wohl, "Scenes from a Marriage: Love
    and *Logos* in Plutarch's *Coniugalia Praecepta*," *Helios* 24, no. 2 (1997): 170–92.

32 See Stowers, "Paul and Self-Mastery," 2:276–78.

33 For a wife's modest clothing as an advertisement of her husband's moral character,
    see Annette Bourland Huizenga, *Moral Education for Women in the Pastoral and
    Pythagorean Letters: Philosophers of the Household* (Leiden: Brill, 2013), 169–200.
    See also Alex C. Purves, *Space and Time in Ancient Greek Narrative* (Cambridge:
    Cambridge University Press, 2010), 209–11.

34 For Arrian's life and career, see P. A. Brunt, "From Epictetus to Arrian," in *Studies
    in Stoicism*, ed. Miriam Griffin and Alison Samuels (Oxford: Oxford University
    Press, 2013), 342–59.

35 Arrian's letter is reminiscent of the proem to Plato's *Theaetetus*. See Sean Alexan-
    der Gurd, *Work in Progress: Literary Revision as Social Performance in Ancient Rome*
    (Oxford: Oxford University Press, 2012), 34.

36 Arrian, *Letter to Lucius Gellius*. Translation is Oldfather, *Epictetus. Discourses, Books
    1–2*, 5–7.

37 See 2 Tim 3:10–13. The living example of the teacher is better than spoken words.
    But spoken words are superior to written words, which lack a stability of reference.

38 See 1 Tim 5:21–22; 2 Tim 2:16; 2 Pet 1:12; Gregory of Nyssa, *Contra Eunomium*
    2.1.106, 302; and Gregory of Nyssa, *De opificio hominis* 224. The historian Papias
    of Hierapolis preferred interviews to writings as sources: "For I did not suppose
    that the things from books would aid me so much as the things from the living and
    continuing voice." Translation is Daniel J. Theron, *Evidence of Tradition* (Grand
    Rapids, MI: Baker Book House, 1957), 29.

39 For another New Testament example of text confused with voice, see 2 Pet
    1:16–21. See also Plato, *Phaedrus* 263E. Lutheran orthodoxy's dogma concern-
    ing Holy Scripture repeats the confusion: "The Holy Scriptures are the Word
    of God reduced to writing, according to His will, by the prophets, evangelists,
    and apostles, perfectly and perspicuously setting forth the doctrine of the nature

and will of God, that men may therefore be brought unto eternal life." Schmid, *Doctrinal Theology*, 59.

40 If writing is so problematic, it might be objected, why would the author exhort Timothy to "give attention to the public reading of scripture" (1 Tim 4:13), as the NRSV translates? Since there are no Greek words standing behind "public" and "of scripture," the exhortation to "give attention to the public reading" might refer instead to personal study at the direction of the teacher.

41 The son listening to his father and reproducing the father's life by reproducing his mind were complementary ideals in the educational system of the ancient world. For actual educational practices, see Ronald F. Hock, "Paul and Greco-Roman Education," in Sampley, *Paul in the Greco-Roman World*, 1:230–53. The father-son setting of 1 Tim is an obvious example of patriarchy. For the connection of patriarchy to phonocentrism, see Jacques Derrida, "Plato's Pharmacy," in *Dissemination*, trans. Barbara Johnson (Chicago: University of Chicago Press, 1981), 73–84.

42 Note how 2 Pet 1:16–21, a passage from a very late writing within the canon of the New Testament, takes readers back to the story of the transfiguration (Mark 9:2–10; Luke 9:28–36; Matt 17:1–9). The pseudonymous author bolsters his authority by claiming to have heard the divine voice.

43 See 2 Tim 1:6: "For this reason I remind you to rekindle the gift of God that is within you through the laying on of my hands." See 1 Pet 1:13; Jas 1:21; Plato, *Republic* 527D; and Marcus Aurelius, *Meditations* 7.2.

44 See Plato, *Theaetetus* 206D.

45 See Plato, *Theaetetus* 154E. In contrast, the orator Aeschines (389–314 BCE) favored the practice of wrestling with words (*In Ctesiphontem* 206). Later evidence associates *logomaxia* with hairsplitting; see Hesychius, *Lexicon* T 521. See also John Heath, *The Talking Greeks: Speech, Animals, and the Other in Homer, Aeschylus, and Plato* (Cambridge: Cambridge University Press, 2005), 272.

46 The praise of concise speech, allegedly a masculine trait, is another form the hatred of women takes in the Pastoral Epistles and in the ancient philosophic tradition. For examples of this praise, see Plutarch, *Concerning Talkativeness* 511B; and Clement of Alexandria, *Stromata* 2.2.4.2; 7.16.104.1. The phrase "old wives' tales" in 1 Tim 4:7 alludes to the Pastoral Epistles' claim that women are insatiable in speech. For this widespread prejudice against women's speech, see Marianne Bjelland Kartzow, *Gossip and Gender: Othering of Speech in the Pastoral Epistles* (New York: de Gruyter, 2009), 67–97. See also Jason König, "Body and Text," in *The Cambridge Companion to the Greek and Roman Novel*, ed. Tim Whitmarsh (Cambridge: Cambridge University Press, 2008), 127–44; Heath, *Talking Greeks*, 171, 185–92; and Elizabeth H. Sutherland, "Writing (on) Bodies: Lyric Discourse and the Production of Gender in Horace Odes 1.13," *Classical Philology* 100, no. 1

(2005): 52–82. For this prejudice in early Christian literature, see Kartzow, *Gossip and Gender*, 133–75.

47 The NRSV has obscured the idea of cutting in its translation: "rightly explaining the word of truth." For better translation options, see Daniele Pevarello, *The Sentences of Sextus and the Origins of Christian Asceticism* (Tübingen, Germany: Mohr Siebeck, 2013), 133.

48 An example of the philosophers' disdain of *endless speaking* (*aperantologia*) is a remark of Antisthenes (*Gnomologium Vaticanum* 12): "He said that brevity of speech is a virtue and endless speech [*aperantologon*] is a vice" (my translation). From the Pastoral Epistles' point of view, the opponents' main characteristic was a lack of discipline reflected in their endless explanations relying upon genealogies (1 Tim 1:4; Titus 3:9).

49 See Plato, *Sophist* 229A–230E; Xenophon, *Memorabilia* 1.2.18–33; and Posidonius, *Fragmenta* 410.80–85.

50 Clement of Alexandria, *Stromata* 4.5.19.1–4. Translation is *Ante-Nicene Fathers*, ed. and trans. Alexander Roberts and James Donaldson (1885; repr., Peabody, MA: Hendrickson, 1994), 2:412.

51 Clement conceived of moral life as Seneca had: the heroic conquest of desire. For Seneca's use of military imagery, see Elizabeth Asmis, "Seneca on Fortune and the Kingdom of God," in *Seneca and the Self*, ed. Shadi Bartsch and David Wray (Cambridge: Cambridge University Press, 2009), 115–38.

52 See Caputo, *Radical Hermeneutics*, 32–35.

53 There must have been a bit of the imp in Paul as he grafted *didaskalia* onto a hoping-against-hope kind of hope. While I use *imp* to describe Paul, with similar admiration, Caputo applies the word *rogue* and the name *Hermes* (as a trickster) to describe figures like Friedrich Nietzsche, Jacques Derrida, Gianni Vattimo, and Richard Rorty. See Caputo, *Hermeneutics*, 15–17, 117–18, 127–32, 164–66, 173–88. Caputo's linking Hermes as a trickster to Derrida's passion for absolute hospitality and to Vattimo's passion for love points to the deep moral seriousness of deconstruction. Thief that I am, I want to steal the word *moral* from moralists both ancient and modern.

54 For this approach to tradition, see Michael Naas, "Earmarks: Derrida's Reinvention of Philosophical Writing in 'Plato's Pharmacy,'" in Leonard, *Derrida and Antiquity*, 43–72.

55 For Paul's way of quoting the Bible, see Steve Moyise, "Does Paul Respect the Context of His Quotations?," in *Paul and Scripture: Extending the Conversation*, ed. Christopher D. Stanley (Atlanta: Society of Biblical Literature, 2012), 97–114.

56 Caputo thinks of this sort of play as "acting within a tradition" in order to "open up the impossible for the other." See Caputo, *Prayers and Tears*, 83–85.

57 Perfect altruism is of course a dream but a very sweet one. For Caputo's reflections on Derrida's realism about self-interest and the latter's proposal for a "more welcoming, hospitable narcissism," see Caputo, 160–61.

58 Orion, *Etymologicum (excerpta e cod. Vat. gr. 1456)* 19 (my translation).

59 Athenaeus, *The Learned Banqueters* 6.66.14: "To flatter [*kolakeuein*] now has the name to please [*areskein*]" (my translation).

60 See 2 Cor 1:19–20.

61 See Plato, *Symposium* 184B–C; Lucian, *Nigrinus* 15; and Lucian, *How to Write History* 61.

62 See Basil, *Asceticon magnum sive Quaestiones (regulae brevius tractatae) MPG* 31.1173.34–41.

63 In 1 Thess 2:5, Paul anticipates that his style of ministry could provoke such a charge. See Abraham J. Malherbe, "'Gentle as a Nurse': The Cynic Background to 1 Thessalonians 2," in Holladay et al., *Light from the Gentiles*, 1:53–67. Paul was right. When he wrote 2 Cor, opponents had recently charged him with flattering his hearers while present but writing severe letters when absent. See David E. Fredrickson, "*Parrēsia* in the Pauline Epistles," in *Friendship, Flattery, and Frankness of Speech: Studies on Friendship in the New Testament World*, ed. John Fitzgerald (Leiden: Brill, 1996), 161–83. Nevertheless, Paul desires that his Roman readers incessantly say yes to one another even if he risks the charge of encouraging flattery. See 1 Cor 9:1–23; 2 Cor 1:17; Gal 1:10; 5:13. For a comparison of Paul with the ancient demagogue, see Dale B. Martin, *Slavery as Salvation: The Metaphor of Slavery in Pauline Christianity* (New Haven, CT: Yale University Press, 1990), 86–116. Dio Cassius's description of a demagogue (*Roman History* 37.22.3) provides an especially illuminating parallel to Paul's self-presentation.

64 The NRSV's translation follows the traditional, Christian interpretation of *bastazein*: to forgive, tolerate, or heal (small) sins. See Basil, *Asceticon magnum sive Quaestiones (regulae brevius tractatae) MPG* 31.1200.44–1201.5; and Ps.-Basil, *Homilia de paenitentia MPG* 31.1484.20–22.

65 See Sophocles, *Electra* 1126–70; and Euripides, *Alcestis* 19, 724.

66 Gennadius (*Orationes et Panegyrici* 5.6.41–42) understood *bastazein* in Rom 15:1 as carrying the dead on one's shoulders.

67 Weakness plays an important role in Paul's report of the emotional aftermath of an abduction into paradise (2 Cor 12:1–12). Caputo has noticed this. See his *Weakness of God*, 7–9, 42–54.

68 See Teun Tieleman, "Wisdom and Emotion: Galen's Philosophical Position in Avoiding Distress," in *Galen's Treatise Περὶ Ἀλυπίας (De indolentia) in Context: A Tale of Resilience*, ed. Caroline Petit (Leiden: Brill, 2019), 205–6; and Christopher

Gill, *The Structured Self in Hellenistic and Roman Thought* (Oxford: Oxford University Press, 2006), 222–24, 254–63, 272, 278, 313.

69 Plutarch (*How to Study Poetry* 17C) worries that texts portraying suffering and weakness will rub off on young persons. See note 1 above.

70 Philo, *That the Worse Is Wont to Attack the Better* 113.

71 For the Stoics, the soul is like a muscle. It has tone (*tonos*) or slackness (*atonia*). See Chrysippus, *Fragmenta moralia* 473.5–7; and Chrysippus, *Fragmenta logica et physica* 876.3–5. See further Gill, *Structured Self*, 284.

72 Plutarch, *Timoleon* 6.4. Translation is Bernadotte Perrin, *Plutarch. Lives*, vol. 6, *Dion and Brutus. Timoleon and Aemilius Paulus*, Loeb Classical Library 98 (Cambridge, MA: Harvard University Press, 1918), 273.

73 See John D. Caputo, "Adieu-sans Dieu: Derrida and Levinas," in *The Face of the Other and the Trace of God: Essays on the Philosophy of Emmanuel Levinas*, ed. Jeffrey Bloechl (New York: Fordham University Press, 2000), 284–87; and Naas, *Taking on the Tradition*, 158–64.

74 See John of Damascus, *Sacra parallela MPG* 95.1200.18: "The nature of love does not know satisfaction" (my translation). See also Gal 5:14. For the infinite call of love, see David E. Fredrickson, "The Justice of Faith," *Dialog* 53, no. 2 (2013): 121–27.

75 See Dio Chrysostom, *Orations* 32.4–13. See also 2 Cor 3:5. On self-commendation among the philosophers, see Malherbe, "'Gentle as a Nurse,'" 1:53–67.

76 John D. Caputo, *Against Ethics: Contributions to a Poetics of Obligation with Constant Reference to Deconstruction* (Bloomington: Indiana University Press, 1993), 7. See also Caputo, *Prayers and Tears*, 210–12.

77 Caputo, *Against Ethics*, 6.

Chapter 4

1 I also find the Stoic philosopher Epictetus exhausting, since like the author of the Pastoral Epistles, he thinks life has a single purpose, to train the soul and thus perfect the self. See Epictetus, *Discourses* 1.1.25; 1.6.35–36; 1.8.4–5; 1 Tim 6:12; 2 Tim 3:10; 4:7.

2 For the mirror as an aid in self-examination and self-formation in ancient philosophy, see Shadi Bartsch, *The Mirror of the Self: Sexuality, Self-Knowledge, and the Gaze in the Early Roman Empire* (Chicago: University of Chicago Press, 2006), 18–28.

3 When I read the Pastoral Epistles—and, for that matter, Col, Eph, Heb, 2 Thess, 1 and 2 Pet, Jas, Jude, Matt, and Rev—I feel the need for a healthy dose of what

John D. Caputo calls "the nihilism of grace." See Caputo, *Hoping against Hope*, 169–200.

4   See Helen Lovatt, *The Epic Gaze: Vision, Gender and Narrative in Ancient Epic* (Cambridge: Cambridge University Press, 2013), 310–17.

5   See Sappho, *Fragments* 112.

6   See Philostratus the Elder, *Love Letters* 25; and Alciphron, *Epistles* 1.11.3; 3.29.3.

7   See Sappho, *Fragments* 16.15–20; Euripides, *Ion* 1550; Musaeus, *Hero and Leander* 55–60; and Achilles Tatius, *Leucippe and Clitophon* 1.19.1–2. For more examples, see Kost, *Musaios, Hero und Leander*, 229–32.

8   Heliodorus, *Aethiopica* 3.5.5. Translation is B. P. Reardon, *Collected Ancient Greek Novels* (Berkeley: University of California Press, 2008), 414.

9   See Paul S. Fiddes and Günter Bader, "Whatever Happened to a Pauline Text? 2 Cor. 3.6 and Its Afterlife," in *The Spirit and the Letter: A Tradition and a Reversal*, ed. Paul S. Fiddes and Günter Bader (London: Bloomsbury, 2013), 3–7.

10 See Achilles Tatius, *Leucippe and Clitophon* 6.6.2–3:

> The expression of her face showed the presence together in her both of grief and fear. For I do not think that it is rightly said that the mind is entirely invisible: it can be accurately discerned in the face as in a mirror. When it is in a state of delight, it causes the appearance of joy to shine from the eyes; when in sorrow, it contracts the face in a manner that tells of the disaster that has occurred.

Translation is S. Gaselee, *Achilles Tatius. Leucippe and Clitophon*, Loeb Classical Library 45 (Cambridge, MA: Harvard University Press, 1969), 315. For a discussion of this passage, see Morales, *Vision and Narrative*, 135–40.

11 This is the logic of ancient physiognomy. See John T. Fitzgerald, "Galen's *De indolentia* in the Context of Greco-Roman Medicine, Moral Philosophy, and Physiognomy," in *Galen's "De indolentia": Essays on a Newly Discovered Letter*, ed. Clare K. Rothschild and Trevor W. Thompson (Tübingen, Germany: Mohr Siebeck, 2014), 213–20; and Ian Redpath, "The *Physiognomy* of Adamantius the Sophist," in *Seeing the Face, Seeing the Soul: Polemon's Physiognomy from Classical Antiquity to Medieval Islam*, ed. Simon Swain (Oxford: Oxford University Press, 2007), 493–547.

12 Eyes are indeed portals to the soul, as a very popular motif in the ancient world claimed. See Euripides, *Hippolytus* 525–29; Musaeus, *Hero and Leander* 93–98; and Philostratus the Elder, *Love Letters* 32. Easy access to the soul through the eyes, however, is not the whole story.

13 See Plato, *Greater Alcibiades* 132E–133A, a crucial passage discussed at length in Bartsch, *Mirror of the Self*, 47–56. See also Patricia A. Rosenmeyer, "Medulla as

a *Locus Eroticus*," *Arethusa* 32, no. 1 (1999): 45–46. For the viewer's experience of an "overpowering otherness" in this circumstance, see Lovatt, *Epic Gaze*, 80–85.

14 This is a problem recognized by Socrates in Xenophon, *Memorabilia* 3.10.5.

15 Caputo, *Weakness of God*, 283. See also Caputo, *Against Ethics*, 95–97.

16 For Maurice Blanchot's alternative to thinking of literature as goal oriented, see Elisabeth M. Loevlie, "Faith in the Ghosts of Literature: Poetic Hauntology in Derrida, Blanchot and Morrison's *Beloved*," *Religions* 4, no. 3 (2013): 340–45.

17 Caputo, *Prayers and Tears*, 333.

18 For Paul's use of the *face-to-face* motif in 1 Cor 13:12, see David E. Fredrickson, "When Enough Is Never Enough: Philosophers, Poets, Peter, and Paul on Insatiable Desire," in Spencer, *Mixed Feelings and Vexed Passions*, 326–29.

19 Sappho, *Fragments* 31. Translation is David A. Campbell, *Sappho, Alcaeus. Greek Lyric*, vol. 1, *Sappho and Alcaeus*, Loeb Classical Library 142 (Cambridge, MA: Harvard University Press, 1982), 79–81; see also Sappho, *Fragments* 23. This is a much-discussed topic in Sappho studies. See Margaret M. Toscano, "The Eyes Have It: Female Desire on Attic Greek Vases," *Arethusa* 46, no. 1 (2013): 1–40; Franco Ferrari, *Sappho's Gift: The Poet and Her Community*, trans. Benjamin Acosta-Hughes and Lucia Prauscello (Ann Arbor: Michigan Classical Press, 2010), 405–8; and Ellen Greene, "Subjects, Objects, and Erotic Symmetry in Sappho's Fragments," in *Among Women: From the Homosocial to the Homoerotic in the Ancient World*, ed. Nancy Sorkin Rabinowitz and Lisa Auanger (Austin: University of Texas Press, 2002), 82–105. If Eros does not bring death, then it does inflict insomnia; see Theocritus, *Idylls* 30.5–10.

20 Apollonius of Rhodes, *Argonautica* 3.287–98. Translation is William H. Race, *Apollonius Rhodius. Argonautica*, Loeb Classical Library 1 (Cambridge, MA: Harvard University Press, 2009), 239–41. See also Apollonius of Rhodes, *Argonautica* 3.1009–10, 1065–67; Chariton, *Callirhoe* 1.1.6; Ovid, *Heroides* 16.103–4; and Musaeus, *Hero and Leander* 100–107, on which see Helen Morales, "Gender and Identity in Musaeus' *Hero and Leander*," in *Constructing Identities in Late Antiquity*, ed. Richard Miles (New York: Routledge, 1999), 46–47.

21 Apollonius of Rhodes, *Argonautica* 3.967–72. Translation is Race, *Apollonius Rhodius*, 293.

22 *The Greek Anthology* 5.255. Translation is W. R. Paton, *The Greek Anthology*, vol. 1, *Book 1: Christian Epigrams. Book 2: Description of the Statues in the Gymnasium of Zeuxippus. Book 3: Epigrams in the Temple of Apollonis at Cyzicus. Book 4: Prefaces to the Various Anthologies. Book 5: Erotic Epigrams*, rev. Michael A. Tueller, Loeb Classical Library 67 (Cambridge, MA: Harvard University Press, 2014), 387. See Ovid, *Amores* 2.16.41–42. See also J. C. B. Petropoulos, *Eroticism in Ancient and Medieval Greek Poetry* (London: Duckworth, 2003), 32–36, 61–73.

23 For the idea of deferral of knowing, see Susan Hammerschlag, "Poetics of
    the Broken Tablet," in Baring and Gordon, *Trace of God*, 61.

24 I have run together the positions of the two great theorists of letter and spirit in the
    Christian tradition, Origen and Augustine. I regret that I have minimized their
    differences. For a more detailed comparison of the two positions, see Morwenna
    Ludlow, "Spirit and Letter in Origen and Augustine," in Fiddes and Bader, *Spirit
    and the Letter*, 87–102.

25 For a similar departure from the traditional, hermeneutical understanding
    of 2 Cor 3:6, see Stephen Westerholm, "'Letter' and 'Spirit': The Foundation of
    Pauline Ethics," *New Testament Studies* 30, no. 2 (1984): 229–48.

26 Translation is Larry J. Perkins, "Exodus," in *A New English Translation of the
    Septuagint: And Other Greek Translations Traditionally Included under That Title*, ed.
    Albert Pietersma and Benjamin G. Wright (Oxford: Oxford University Press,
    2007), 76.

27 Scripture extracts following headings from here to the end of this chapter are my
    translations.

28 Early interpreters thought "some" referred to the superapostles. I agree. See, for
    example, *Catena in epistulam ii ad Corinthios (catena Pseudo-Oecumenii)* 364.19–24.
    In letters of recommendation, the writer asks the recipient to regard the bearer as
    the re-presentation of the sender. See Stowers, *Letter Writing*, 157. In a sense, the
    identity of the letter's bearer disappears into the recommender. See, for example,
    Phlm 17.

29 Diodorus Siculus, *Library of History* 12.13.1. Translation is C. H. Oldfather,
    Diodorus Siculus. Library of History, vol. 4, *Books 9–12.40*, Loeb Classical Library
    375 (Cambridge, MA: Harvard University Press, 1946), 401.

30 Diodorus Siculus, *Library of History* 12.13.1. Translation is Oldfather, *Library of
    History*, 4:401. For the close association of epistles and covenants, see Lucian, *The
    Passing of Peregrinus* 41.

31 Plato condemned writing (*Phaedrus* 274C–277A) because it enfeebles memory
    and cannot stabilize its own meaning; he nevertheless employed writing in a
    metaphorical sense (*Phaedrus* 276A). See Michèle Lowrie, *Writing, Performance,
    and Authority in Augustan Rome* (Oxford: Oxford University Press, 2009), 9–11.

32 Ps.-Diogenes, *Epistles* 18. Translation is Benjamin Fiore, "The Epistles of Dio-
    genes," in *The Cynic Epistles: A Study Edition*, ed. Abraham J. Malherbe (Atlanta:
    Scholars Press, 1977), 111. See also Epictetus, *Discourses* 2.3.1.

33 Philosophers appropriated the figure to explain how perception works. See Paulo
    Togni, "Plato's Soul-Book Simile and Stoic Epistemology," *Méthexis* 26 (2013):
    166–68, 174–77.

34 Achilles Tatius, *Leucippe and Clitophon* 1.9.4–5. Translation is S. Gaselee, *Leucippe and Clitophon*, 315. See also Achilles Tatius, *Leucippe and Clitophon* 5.13.3–4. Several of the epigrams of Meleager associate lovesickness with writing on the heart. See, for example, *The Greek Anthology* 5.212: "The noise of Love sinks ever in my ears, and my eyes in silence yield their sweet tears to Desire; neither night nor daylight lays love to rest, but already the spell has put its stamp [*typos*] visibly in my heart [*kradia*]." Translation is Paton, *Greek Anthology*, 1:349. See also *The Greek Anthology* 5.78, 155; 12.65; Musaeus, *Hero and Leander* 69–80; and Synesius, *Epistles* 123. For the motif of writing on the heart, see Morales, *Vision and Narrative*, 130–35.

35 Plutarch, *The Dialogue on Love* 759C. Translation is Edwin L. Minar, F. H. Sandbach, and W. C. Helmbold, *Plutarch. Moralia*, vol. 9, *Table-Talk, Books 7–9. Dialogue on Love*, Loeb Classical Library 425 (Cambridge, MA: Harvard University Press, 1961), 367.

36 The NRSV obscures Paul's references to slavery in 2 Cor, since it translates *diakonia* (slavery or service) as "ministry" and *diakonos* (slave) as "minister."

37 Ovid, *Amores* 1.2.19–52. Translation is Grant Showerman, *Ovid. Heroides. Amores*, revised by G. P. Goold, Loeb Classical Library 41 (Cambridge, MA: Harvard University Press, 1914), 323–25. The motif occurs predominantly in Latin erotic verse. For other examples, see Ovid, *Amores* 1.7.35–48; 2.18.18; and Propertius, *Elegies* 2.8.40.

38 See Fredrickson, "*Parrēsia* in the Pauline Epistles," 165–66.

39 For an example of this form of *parrēsia*, see Plutarch, *Timoleon* 15.5.

40 The distraught lover does not restrain the expression of pain but speaks openly of it. See Plato, *Symposium* 222C; and Chariton, *Callirhoe* 3.7.4.

41 Paul also claims to be speaking frankly in 2 Cor 4:2: "We speak fully of the things of shame" (my translation). See Hesychius, *Lexicon* Alpha 6097; and Suda, *Lexicon* Alpha 3475.

42 See Aristotle, *Generation of Animals* 781a24–27. For the role of *pneuma* in perception, see Julius Pollux, *Onomasticon* 2.75–77. See also David E. Hahm, *The Origins of Stoic Cosmology* (Columbus: Ohio State University Press, 1977), 157–74.

43 I am *not* claiming, however, that spirit writing communicates the author's intention better than writing in the nonmetaphorical sense. As I will point out, Paul associates the spirit with the face-to-face relation in which perception of the other leads not to knowledge but to a desire to know intensified by the deferral of knowledge.

44 See, for example, Phil 1:9, if *aisthēsis* is translated as "perception" rather than the NRSV's "insight."

45 For contradictory sensations (ghastly and fragrant) emanating from a single source, see Amy Lather, "Olfactory Theater: Tracking Scents in Aeschylus's *Oresteia*," *Arethusa* 51, no. 1 (2018): 33–54.

46 For the face as a mirror of the heart, see note 10 above.

47 See Epictetus, *Discourses* 3.21.11–12; 3.22.2, 8, 52, 95–97; and Dio Chrysostom, *Orations* 33.9; 77/78.38.

48 For the various meanings of *diathēkē*, see *Etymologicum Gudianum* Delta 356; and Suda, *Lexicon* Delta 563.

49 See the introduction.

50 Paul's new covenant was not entirely without precedent. His attempt to rethink political relations apart from writing resembles what ancient political theorists called *synōmosia*, a "solemn league." Solemnity was bestowed by friendship and oath taking. See Hesychius, *Lexicon* Delta 1018; Sigma 2747; and Ps.-Zonaras, *Lexicon* Sigma 1687.10–13. Diodorus describes how written documents testify to the *solemn league*:

> There being no head of the government in Egypt for two years, and the masses betaking themselves to tumults and the killing of one another, the twelve most important leaders formed a solemn league [*synōmosian*] among themselves, and after they had met together for counsel in Memphis and had drawn up agreements setting forth their mutual goodwill and loyalty they proclaimed themselves kings. After they had reigned in accordance with their oaths and promises and had maintained their mutual concord a period of fifteen years, they set about to construct a common tomb for themselves. (Diodorus Siculus, *Library of History* 1.66.1)

See also Plutarch, *Marcius Coriolanus* 9.2–3; and 2 Cor 2:17; 4:2.

51 On this passage, see David E. Fredrickson, "Paul's Sentence of Death (2 Corinthians 1:9)," in *God, Evil, and Suffering: Essays in Honor of Paul R. Sponheim*, ed. Terrence E. Fretheim and Curtis L. Thompson (St. Paul, MN: Word & World, 2000), 99–107. The NRSV and other modern English translations of 2 Cor 1:11 do not translate *prosōpon*, the Greek term for "face."

52 David E. Fredrickson, "'Through Many Tears' (2 Cor 2:4): Paul's Grieving Letter and the Occasion of 2 Corinthians 1–7," in *Paul and Pathos*, ed. Thomas H. Olbricht and Jerry L. Sumney (Atlanta: Society of Biblical Literature, 2001), 161–79.

53 See 2 Cor 2:5–11.

54 The distinction between the two kinds of *doxa* is present in 2 Cor 3:18, although the translation of the NRSV hides it: "And all of us, with unveiled faces, seeing the glory of the Lord as though reflected in a mirror, are being transformed into the same image from one degree of glory to another [*apo doxēs eis doxan*]; for this comes from the Lord, the Spirit." With the introduction of "degree," for which there is no corresponding word in the Greek text, the NRSV fails to communicate the idea of deferral. The fourth-century theologian Gregory of Nyssa, however, understood *apo doxēs eis doxan* quite differently. Gregory wrote about an unceasing, insatiable desire for God without rest and without end, a life (and, for Gregory, an afterlife) lived in blind expectation of the unimaginable. See Ovidiu Sferlea, "On the Interpretation of the Theory of Perpetual Progress (*epektasis*): Taking into Account the Testimony of Eastern Monastic Tradition," *Revue d'histoire ecclésiastique* 109, nos. 3–4 (2014): 564–87.

55 Chariton, *Callirhoe* 4.1.8–10. Translation is G. P. Goold, *Callirhoe*, Loeb Classical Library 481 (Cambridge, MA: Harvard University Press, 1995), 195. See also Chariton, *Callirhoe* 5.9.1–2.

56 For the motif of beauty as a weapon, see Fredrickson, *Eros and the Christ*, 87–89. As an example of the motif's endurance, see Rainer Maria Rilke, *Duino Elegies 1*, in *The Selected Poetry of Rainer Maria Rilke*, ed. and trans. Stephen Mitchell (New York: Vintage International, 1989), 151:

> For beauty is nothing
> but the beginning of terror, which we still are just able to endure,
> and we are so awed because it serenely disdains
> to annihilate us. Every angel is terrifying.

57 Chariton, *Callirhoe* 5.3.9. Translation is Goold, *Callirhoe*, 245. For more on staring in astonishment, see also Helioduorus, *Aethiopica* 3.5.5; Hesychius, *Lexicon* Alpha 8048; and Luke 4:20.

58 *LSJ* 444.

59 For this translation, see Fredrickson, "*Parrēsia* in the Pauline Epistles," in Fitzgerald, *Friendship, Flattery, and Frankness*, 177–79.

60 For negative and positive examples in ancient rhetoric, see Fredrickson, 177–79.

61 Homer, *Odyssey* 8.82–95. Translation is A. T. Murray, *Homer. Odyssey*, vol. 1, *Books 1–12*, revised by George E. Dimock, Loeb Classical Library 104 (Cambridge, MA: Harvard University Press, 1919), 279. See Chariton, *Callirhoe* 1.4.6; 5.2.4.

62 For the approach to language I am invoking here, which Hegel initiated in his reflection on Adam's naming of the animals and Maurice Blanchot developed in a fascinating variation of Hegel's thinking, see Caputo, *Hermeneutics*, 145–70; Sarah Clift, *Committing the Future to Memory: History, Experience, Trauma* (New York: Fordham University Press, 2014), 176–87; and Peter Schwenger, "Words and the Murder of the Thing," *Critical Inquiry* 28, no. 1 (2001): 99–113.

63 The NRSV inexplicably substitutes "one" for "he."

64 In an ancient wedding ritual, as the bride's veil was taken up (*anakalyptein*) or her face was uncovered (*apokalyptein*), the couple would gaze at each other face-to-face and become wife and husband at that moment. See Vermeule, *Aspects of Death*, 146. See also Vassiliki Panoussi, "*Ego Maenas*: Maenadism, Marriage, and the Construction of Female Identity in Catullus 63 and 64," *Helios* 30, no. 2 (2003): 101–26. For a nuptial interpretation of unveiling in 2 Cor 3, see John of Ford, *Sermons* 29.2.

Chapter 5

1 Getting the reader's commitment without the reader's consent is one of the oldest tricks in the book. See the myth of Acontius and Cydippe in Ovid, *Heroides* 20 and 21, on which see Patricia A. Rosenmeyer, "Love Letters in Callimachus, Ovid and Aristaenetus or the Sad Fate of a Mailorder Bride," *Materiali e discussioni per l'analisi dei testi classici* 36 (1996): 9–31.

2 The parallel between reading and watching a play is an ancient one. See Luca Graverini, "The Ass's Ears and the Novel's Voice: Orality and the Involvement of the Reader in Apuleius' *Metamorphoses*," in Rimell, *Seeing Tongues, Hearing Scripts*, 155–57.

3 Caputo, *Weakness of God*, 117 (my emphasis).

4 For a retelling of the biblical story of creation without the presupposition of divine sovereignty, see Caputo, *Weakness of God*, 55–84.

5 See Mark 9:9–10, 34; 10:24–26, 32, 38.

6 For a few examples, compare Matt 16:5–12 with Mark 8:14–21 and Matt 20:20 with Mark 10:35.

7 For a Stoic perspective on the intersection of gift giving, gratitude, and politics, see Inwood, *Reading Seneca*, 65–94. Derrida complained that Marcel Mauss's pioneering study failed to distinguish gift giving and the economic exchange that gifts inevitably fall prey to. See Nick Mansfield, *The God Who Deconstructs Himself: Sovereignty and Subjectivity between Freud, Bataille, and Derrida* (New York: Fordham University Press, 2010), 75–81.

8 The Gospel of Matthew ignored the critique of benefaction in the Gospel of Mark and in so doing set the course of theology for centuries to come. We might say that Matthew elevates Greco-Roman benefaction and the economy of exchange into the *Godhead*. Thanks in part to Matthew, neither of the following statements is the least bit controversial among the vast majority of Christians: God is the great giver of life and of all things; to God all honor and thanksgiving are due.

9 See Pevarello, *Sentences of Sextus*, 104–14. For poverty, shame, and exclusion, see Margaret Atkins and Robin Osborne, eds., *Poverty in the Roman World* (Cambridge:

Cambridge University Press, 2009), 11–15, 35, 69–70. See also the vivid description of the poor in Artemidorus, *Oneirocritica* 3.52:

> A place of prayer and beggars and all people who are bums and wretches and scroungers [*ptōchoi*] foretells grief and worry and the wasting away of the soul for both a man and a woman. The former because no one would go off to a place of prayer unless he was worried, and the latter because bums, being wholly odious and poor and totally unsound, get in the way of every course of action. . . . And beggars signify that the reputations and affairs of the observer will be like their own. But when they receive a coin, it foretells great harm and danger, and often also death for the one providing it or for someone near to him. For they resemble death since, among men, they alone, just like death, do not give back once they have taken.

Translation is Harris-McCoy, *Artemidorus' "Oneirocritica,"* 287.

10 For the poor giving to the poor, see Anneliese Parkin, "'You Do Him No Service': An Exploration of Pagan Almsgiving," in Atkins and Osborne, *Poverty in the Roman World*, 71.

11 Here I have applied to the beggarly widow Caputo's distinction between insistence and existence in *Insistence of God*, 14–19.

12 Caputo also thinks the widow exemplifies Derrida's understanding of the absolute gift. See Caputo, *Prayers and Tears*, 175–77.

13 In the thirteenth century, Jacopone da Todi challenged the economic scheme underlying Christianity's doctrine of redemption; see especially Jacopone da Todi, *Lauds* 65. For an English translation, see Serge Hughes and Elizabeth Hughes, *Jacopone da Todi: The Lauds* (New York: Paulist, 1982), 196–203.

14 This means that a hallowed idea in Christian thought—that Jesus gave his life as a sacrifice for sin—needs to be questioned in the name of the gift, since sacrifice is also a giving in order to get. See Caputo, *Weakness of God*, 232–34.

15 See the essays in John D. Caputo and Michael J. Scanlon, eds., *God, the Gift, and Postmodernism* (Bloomington: Indiana University Press, 1999). For the application of poststructural thinking about the gift to the Christian doctrine of forgiveness, see Caputo, *Weakness of God*, 208–35.

16 Caputo, *Prayers and Tears*, 163.

17 Those who dream of impossible things make very suspicious readers. But they are passionate readers, too, unsatisfied with the possible and the repetition of the same. See Caputo, 219–20. Such suspicion and passion characterize Caputo's longed-for "new species of theologian"; see his *Insistence of God*, 26.

18 Just to be clear, I am not asserting that the women of Mark 12:41–44 and 14:3–9 gave perfect gifts, but their deviation from the traditional pattern of benefaction

challenges the dropped-from-heaven feel the social practice of benefaction had for the ancients and still has today. Their style of giving challenged ancient patronage—and again, I have no idea whether it was intentional, since I am just a reader and not a mind reader. Besides, both women are literary fictions, and fictions do not think, nor do they have intentions. Yet they do have the power to get us dreaming of other ways of giving, ways that struggle to get free from displaying social status and obligating recipients.

19 The Greek here is intriguing: "For all of them have contributed out of their abundance; but she out of her poverty [*hysterēseōs*] has put in everything she had, all she had to live on" (Mark 12:44). The NRSV's "poverty" is misleading. She is certainly poor, but the term *hysterēsis* points in another direction, since the root *hyster* had the sense of "coming too late," "falling short," or "failing to obtain" (*LSJ* 1905–6). The Greek word for "womb," which was conceptualized as an empty space, was related to *hyster*. The point here is that she gives out of her lack, not out of meagre resources. The latter giving is possible; the former is impossible, and that is what makes it a true gift.

20 I am repeating Derrida's reading of the Gospel of Matthew. On the one hand, Derrida thinks Matthew has a profound understanding of the absolute gift, of giving without return ("But when you give alms, do not let your left hand know what your right hand is doing, so that your alms may be done in secret," Matt 6:3–4). On the other hand, Derrida draws attention to the One, the Father, who ruins the gift by calculating rewards ("and your Father who sees in secret will reward you"; 6:4). See Jacques Derrida, *The Gift of Death and Literature in Secret*, trans. David Wills, 2nd ed. (Chicago: University of Chicago Press, 2008), 88–108.

21 For Caputo's analysis (relying on Emmanuel Levinas) of the isolating effects of pain and the salvific power of touch, see *Weakness of God*, 244–52.

22 For the theme of isolation in Mark's crucifixion scene, see David E. Fredrickson, "Nature's Lament for Jesus," *Word & World* 26 (2006): 38–46. Note how Matthew transforms Mark's depiction of a betrayed and abandoned Jesus into a bizarre preview of the resurrection:

> At that moment the curtain of the temple was torn in two, from top to bottom. The earth shook, and the rocks were split. The tombs also were opened, and many bodies of the saints who had fallen asleep were raised. After his resurrection they came out of the tombs and entered the holy city and appeared to many. (Matt 27:51–53)

23 The writer of the Gospel of Matthew fancied the notion that persons whose deeds do not match their words (23:1–3) will fall into utter isolation and suffer for eternity without the possibility of escape (Matt 24:30, 51; 25:30). Notice that

Matthew draws the woman's hands away from Jesus's body. While Mark has the woman anoint (*myrisai*) Jesus's body with myrrh, Matthew has her throw it at him (literally!), although the NRSV's translation, "pouring," obscures the distance the Matthean Jesus wants to maintain between himself and the woman: "By pouring ['throwing,' *balousa*] this ointment on my body she has prepared me for burial" (Matt 26:12).

24 Presumably, it is called *Mini* because it is much shorter than Revelation, which in Greek is *Apokalypsis Iōannou* (Apocalypse of John). I think Mini-Apocalypse is an inappropriate caption for Mark 13. In this chapter, the writer of Mark challenges the logic of retribution, whereas in Revelation, it is affirmed. Actually, the Apocalypse of John is no apocalypse at all because it already knows the end down to the very metrics of the new Jerusalem and tells readers all the details. A secret told is a secret destroyed. See Caputo, *Prayers and Tears*, 88–101.

25 Matthew's version (24:1) tones down the disciples' awe: "As Jesus came out of the temple and was going away, his disciples came to point out to him the buildings of the temple."

26 For the imperial ideology behind impressive buildings, see A. J. Spawforth, *Greece and the Augustan Cultural Revolution* (Cambridge: Cambridge University Press, 2011), 207–11.

27 See Long, *From Epicurus to Epictetus*, 256–82; Susan Sauvé Meyer, "Chain of Causes: What Is Stoic Fate?," in Salles, *God and Cosmos*, 71–90.

28 Cicero, *On Divination* 1.127. Translation is W. A. Falconer, *Cicero. On Old Age. On Friendship. On Divination*, Loeb Classical Library 154 (Cambridge, MA: Harvard University Press, 1923), 361–63. See Richardo Salles, "Chrysippus on Conflagration and the Indestructibility of the Cosmos," in Salles, *God and Cosmos*, 118–31.

29 For Stoics who wanted to toe the orthodox line, the length of rope was ten thousand years. It is not as though the concept of time as a rope is an intellectual mistake, however, and we can just wave a wand and rid our consciousness of it. Western culture counts on repetition; our minds are habituated to causality. And why not? Millions of lives have been saved, or made less painful, by statisticians who must think of time as a rope and point us toward possible causes and probable results and away from speculations based on anecdote or divine intervention. For respect of the predictable while holding out for religion's debt to the impossible, see John D. Caputo, *The Folly of God: A Theology of the Unconditional* (Salem, OR: Polebridge Press, 2016), 38–40.

30 See Vergados, *Homeric Hymn to Hermes*, 561.

31 Unless one counts—although Christian piety is strongly inclined not to—God's disturbing words in Mark 14:27 reinforcing the theme of abandonment in the

Passion Narrative: "You will all become deserters; for it is written, 'I will strike the shepherd, and the sheep will be scattered.'"

32 So Caputo reports in his *Hoping against Hope*, 6–7. For Caputo's struggle to find hope without ignoring the solar system's demise but also without the otherworldly comforts of Platonism, see the rest of his *Hoping against Hope* and *Insistence of God*.

33 For survivors' traditional accusation, uttered at times of burial, that the dead have abandoned the living, see Christine Perkell, "Reading the Laments of *Iliad* 24," in *Lament: Studies in the Ancient Mediterranean and Beyond*, ed. Ann Suter (Oxford: Oxford University Press, 2008), 97–101; Andromache Karanika, "Greek Comedy's Parody of Lament," in Suter, *Lament*, 183; Olga Levaniouk, "Lament and Hymenaios in Erinna's *Distaff*," in Suter, *Lament*, 200; and Ferrari, *Sappho's Gift*, 122, 166.

34 I am not claiming that Jesus's death in the Gospel of Mark *replaces* the so-called apocalypse, only that readers (like us), whose existence is hoped for in Mark 13:14, live open to a Big End in an unknowable future known only to the silent Father *and* open to the isolating pain experienced by others, or by readers themselves, hearing in that pain a call for response. Matthew disallows this temporal complexity that Mark builds into the narrative; see Matt 24:30–31, 45–51; 25:1–30. Time in Matthew's Gospel is for calculation and recompense and not, as in Mark, the occasion for one who faces death—but can make nothing of it—to welcome, as the dawn of a new world, the approach of another who also faces death and can make nothing of it.

35 See Joel Marcus, "Crucifixion as Parodic Exaltation," *Journal of Biblical Literature* 125 (2006): 73–87. For jokes and insults at the time of lament, see Karanika, *Lament*, 191.

36 For ridicule in the Markan scene of crucifixion, see 15:17–20, 26, 29–32, 35–36, 39. It is not only Jesus who is repulsive. Those who make jokes about his death bear a striking resemblance to Theophrastus's (*Characters* 11.1–3) obnoxious individual:

> It is not difficult to define obnoxiousness (*bdelyrian*): it is joking [*paidia*] that is obvious and offensive. The obnoxious man is the sort who, when he meets respectable women, raises his cloak and exposes his genitals. In the theater he claps after others have stopped, and hisses the actors whom the others enjoy watching. When the audience is silent he rears back and belches, to make the spectators turn around.

> Translation is Jeffrey Rusten and I. C. Cunningham, *Theophrastus, Herodas, Sophron. Characters. Herodas: Mimes. Sophron and Other Mime Fragments*, Loeb Classical Library 225 (Cambridge, MA: Harvard University Press, 2003), 87.

37 Did Mark's Jesus die from grief? Perhaps. In Mark 14:34, "even to death" is an addition to the quotation "I am deeply grieved" from Ps 42. Furthermore, Pilate's amazement at Jesus's rapid death suggests that the duration of dying had somehow been cut short. Ancient psychology knew of death from grief. See Fitzgerald, "Galen's *De indolentia*," 209–13.

38 See Buxton, *Forms of Astonishment*, 24, 30, 41, 116, 120–21, 127.

Selected Bibliography

Adamson, Peter, Rotraud Hansberger, and James Wilberding, eds. "Philosophical Themes in Galen." *Supplement, Bulletin of the Institute of Classical Studies*, no. 114 (2014).

Algra, Keimpe. "Stoic Philosophical Theology and Graeco-Roman Religion." In *God and Cosmos in Stoicism*, edited by Ricardo Salles, 224–252. Oxford: Oxford University Press, 2009.

Armstrong, Michael S. *"Hope the Deceiver": Pseudo-Seneca "De Spe" (Anth. Lat. 415 Riese)*. Hildesheim, Germany: Georg Olms, 1998.

Arthur-Montagne, Jacqueline Michelle. "Symptoms of the Sublime: Longinus and the Hippocratic Method of Criticism." *Greek, Roman, and Byzantine Studies* 57, no. 2 (2017): 325–355.

Asmis, Elizabeth. "Seneca on Fortune and the Kingdom of God." In *Seneca and the Self*, edited by Shadi Bartsch and David Wray, 115–138. Cambridge: Cambridge University Press, 2009.

Atkins, Margaret, and Robin Osborne, eds. *Poverty in the Roman World*. Cambridge: Cambridge University Press, 2009.

Aymer, Margaret, Cynthia Briggs Kittredge, and David A. Sánchez, eds. *The Letters and Legacy of Paul: Fortress Commentary on the Bible Study Edition*. Minneapolis: Fortress, 2016.

Babbitt, Frank Cole, trans. *Plutarch. Moralia*. Vol. 1, *The Education of Children. How the Young Man Should Study Poetry. On Listening to Lectures. How to Tell a Flatterer from a Friend. How a Man May Become Aware of His Progress in Virtue*. Loeb Classical Library 197. Cambridge, MA: Harvard University Press, 1927.

———, trans. *Plutarch. Moralia*. Vol. 2, *How to Profit by One's Enemies. On Having Many Friends. Chance. Virtue and Vice. Letter of Condolence to Apollonius. Advice about Keeping Well. Advice to Bride and Groom. The Dinner of the Seven Wise Men. Superstition*. Loeb Classical Library 222. Cambridge, MA: Harvard University Press, 1928.

Balch, David L. "The Areopagus Speech: An Appeal to the Stoic Historian Posidonius against Later Stoics and Epicureans." In *Greeks, Romans, and Christians: Essays in Honor of Abraham J. Malherbe*, edited by David L. Balch, Everett Ferguson, and Wayne A. Meeks, 52–79. Minneapolis: Fortress, 1990.

——, ed. *Homosexuality, Science, and the "Plain Sense" of Scripture*. Grand Rapids, MI: Eerdmans, 2000.

——. *Let Wives Be Submissive: The Domestic Code in 1 Peter*. Chico, CA: Scholars Press, 1981.

Balch, David L., Everett Ferguson, and Wayne A. Meeks, eds. *Greeks, Romans, and Christians: Essays in Honor of Abraham J. Malherbe*. Minneapolis: Fortress, 1990.

Baring, Edward, and Peter E. Gordon, eds. *The Trace of God: Derrida and Religion*. New York: Fordham University Press, 2015.

Bartsch, Shadi. *The Mirror of the Self: Sexuality, Self-Knowledge, and the Gaze in the Early Roman Empire*. Chicago: University of Chicago Press, 2006.

Bartsch, Shadi, and David Wray, eds. *Seneca and the Self*. Cambridge: Cambridge University Press, 2009.

Beard, Mary. "Cicero's 'Response of the Haruspices' and the Voice of the Gods." *Journal of Roman Studies* 102 (2012): 20–39.

Beckett, Wendy Mary. *John of Ford: Sermons on the Final Verses of the Song of Songs*. Vol. 6. Kalamazoo, MI: Cistercian, 1984.

Bennington, Geoffrey. *Not Half No End: Militantly Melancholic Essays in Memory of Jacques Derrida*. Edinburgh: Edinburgh University Press, 2010.

Bettini, Maurizio. *The Ears of Hermes: Communication, Images, and Identity in the Classical World*. Translated by William Michael Short. Columbus: Ohio State University Press, 2011.

——. *The Portrait of the Lover*. Translated by Laura Gibbs. Berkeley: University of California Press, 1999.

Blanton, Ward. *A Materialism for the Masses: Saint Paul and the Philosophy of the Undying Life*. New York: Columbia University Press, 2014.

Bloechl, Jeffrey, ed. *The Face of the Other and the Trace of God: Essays on the Philosophy of Emmanuel Levinas*. New York: Fordham University Press, 2000.

Bloomquist, Karen L., and John Stumme, eds. *The Promise of Lutheran Ethics*. Minneapolis: Fortress, 1998.

Booth, Joan. "All in the Mind: Sickness in Catullus 76." In *The Passions in Roman Thought and Literature*, edited by Susanna Morton Braund and Christopher Gill, 150–168. Cambridge: Cambridge University Press, 1997.

Boynton, Eric, and Martin Kavka, eds. *Saintly Influence: Edith Wyschogrod and the Possibilities of Philosophy of Religion*. New York: Fordham University Press, 2009.

Braceland, Lawrence C. *Gilbert of Hoyland: Sermons on the Song of Songs*. Vol. 2. Kalamazoo, MI: Cistercian, 1979.

Bremmer, Jan N. *Greek Religion and Culture, the Bible and the Ancient Near East*. Leiden: Brill, 2008.

Briggs, Sheila. "Can an Enslaved God Liberate? Hermeneutical Reflections on 2 Philippians 2:6–11." *Semeia* 47 (1989): 137–153.

Brunschwig, Jacques, and Martha Nussbaum, eds. *Passions and Perceptions: Studies in Hellenistic Philosophy of Mind*. Cambridge: Cambridge University Press, 1993.

Brunt, P. A. *Studies in Stoicism*. Edited by Miriam Griffin and Alison Samuels. Oxford: Oxford University Press, 2013.

Burton, Philip. *Language in the Confessions of Augustine*. Oxford: Oxford University Press, 2007.

Buxton, Richard. *Forms of Astonishment: Greek Myths of Metamorphosis*. Oxford: Oxford University Press, 2009.

Cairns, Douglas. "Metaphors for Hope in Archaic and Classical Greek Poetry." In *Hope, Joy, and Affection in the Classical World*, edited by Ruth R. Caston and Robert A. Kaster, 13–44. Oxford: Oxford University Press, 2016.

Cambron-Goulet, Mathilde. "Orality in Philosophical Letters." In *Between Orality and Literacy: Communication and Adaptation in Antiquity: Orality and Literacy in the Ancient World*, edited by Ruth Scodel, 148–174. Vol. 10. Leiden: Brill, 2014.

Campbell, David A., trans. *Sappho, Alcaeus. Greek Lyric*. Vol. 1, *Sappho and Alcaeus*. Loeb Classical Library 142. Cambridge, MA: Harvard University Press, 1982.

Caputo, John D. "Adieu-sans Dieu: Derrida and Levinas." In *The Face of the Other and the Trace of God: Essays on the Philosophy of Emmanuel Levinas*, edited by Jeffrey Bloechl, 276–311. New York: Fordham University Press, 2000.

———. *Against Ethics: Contributions to a Poetics of Obligation with Constant Reference to Deconstruction*. Bloomington: Indiana University Press, 1993.

———. "The Experience of God and the Axiology of the Impossible." In *The Experience of God: A Postmodern Response*, edited by Kevin Hart and Barbara Eileen Wall, 20–41. New York: Fordham University Press, 2005.

———. *The Folly of God: A Theology of the Unconditional*. Salem, OR: Polebridge Press, 2016.

———. "Hearing the Voices of the Dead: Wyschogrod, Megill, and the Heterological Historian." In *Saintly Influence: Edith Wyschogrod and the Possibilities of Philosophy of Religion*, edited by Eric Boynton and Martin Kavka, 161–174. New York: Fordham University Press, 2009.

———. *Hermeneutics: Facts and Interpretation in the Age of Information*. London: Pelican Books, 2018.

———. *Hoping against Hope: (Confessions of a Postmodern Pilgrim)*. Minneapolis: Fortress, 2015.

———. "Hospitality and the Trouble with God." In *Phenomenologies of the Stranger: Between Hostility and Hospitality*, edited by Richard Kearney and Kascha Semonovitch, 94–108. New York: Fordham University Press, 2011.

———. *The Insistence of God: A Theology of Perhaps*. Bloomington: Indiana University Press, 2013.

———. *More Radical Hermeneutics: On Not Knowing Who We Are*. Bloomington: Indiana University Press, 2000.

———. "Postmodern Hope." In *Postmodern Apologetics? Arguments for God in Contemporary Philosophy*, edited by Christina M. Gschwandtner, 242–264. New York: Fordham University Press, 2013.

———. *The Prayers and Tears of Jacques Derrida: Religion without Religion*. Bloomington: Indiana University Press, 1997.

———. *Radical Hermeneutics: Repetition, Deconstruction, and the Hermeneutic Project*. Bloomington: Indiana University Press, 1987.

———. "Temporal Transcendence: The Very Idea of *à venir* in Derrida." In *Transcendence and Beyond: A Postmodern Inquiry*, edited by John D. Caputo and Michael J. Scanlon, 188–203. Bloomington: Indiana University Press, 2007.

———. "Unprotected Religion: Radical Theology, Radical Atheism, and the Return of Anti-religion." In *The Trace of God: Derrida and Religion*, edited by Edward Baring and Peter E. Gordon, 151–177. New York: Fordham University Press, 2015.

———. *The Weakness of God: A Theology of the Event*. Bloomington: Indiana University Press, 2006.

Caputo, John D., and Michael J. Scanlon, eds. *God, the Gift, and Postmodernism*. Bloomington: Indiana University Press, 1999.

———, eds. *Transcendence and Beyond: A Postmodern Inquiry*. Bloomington: Indiana University Press, 2007.

Cary, Earnest, trans. *Dionysius of Halicarnassus. Roman Antiquities*. Vol. 1, *Books 1–2*. Loeb Classical Library 319. Cambridge, MA: Harvard University Press, 1937.

Castelli, Elizabeth A. *Imitating Paul: A Discourse of Power*. Louisville, KY: Westminster John Knox, 1991.

Caston, Ruth R., and Robert A. Kaster, eds. *Hope, Joy, and Affection in the Classical World*. Oxford: Oxford University Press, 2016.

Ceccarelli, Paola. *Ancient Greek Letter Writing: A Cultural History (600 BC–150 BC)*. Oxford: Oxford University Press, 2013.

Clift, Sarah. *Committing the Future to Memory: History, Experience, Trauma*. New York: Fordham University Press, 2014.

Cooke, H. P., and Hugh Tredennick, trans. *Aristotle. Categories. On Interpretation. Prior Analytics*. Loeb Classical Library 325. Cambridge, MA: Harvard University Press, 1938.

de Jonge, Casper C. *Between Grammar and Rhetoric: Dionysius of Halicarnassus on Language, Linguistics and Literature*. Leiden: Brill, 2008.

De Pretis, Anna. "'Insincerity,' 'Facts,' and 'Epistolarity': Approaches to Pliny's *Epistles* to Calpurnia." *Arethusa* 36, no. 2 (2003): 127–146.

Derrida, Jacques. *The Gift of Death and Literature in Secret*. Translated by David Wills. 2nd ed. Chicago: University of Chicago Press, 2008.

———. "Plato's Pharmacy." In *Dissemination*, translated by Barbara Johnson, 61–171. Chicago: University of Chicago Press, 1981.

Dunning, Benjamin, ed. *The Oxford Handbook of New Testament, Gender, and Sexuality*. Oxford: Oxford University Press, 2019.

Enache, Cătălin. "Character, Voice and the Limits of Dietetics in Hippocrates' De victu I 36." *Wiener Studien* 129 (2016): 71–91.

Enns, Diane. *Love in the Dark: Philosophy by Another Name*. New York: Columbia University Press, 2016.

Etzelmüller, Gregor, and Christian Tewes, eds. *Embodiment in Evolution and Culture*. Tübingen, Germany: Mohr Siebeck, 2016.

Eusebius. *The Proof of the Gospel: Eusebius*. Edited and translated by W. J. Ferrar. Eugene, OR: Wipf & Stock, 2001.

Falconer, W. A., trans. *Cicero. On Old Age. On Friendship. On Divination*. Loeb Classical Library 154. Cambridge, MA: Harvard University Press, 1923.

Felton, Debbie, ed. *Landscapes of Dread in Classical Antiquity: Negative Emotion in Natural and Constructed Spaces*. New York: Routledge, 2018.

Ferrari, Franco. *Sappho's Gift: The Poet and Her Community*. Translated by Benjamin Acosta-Hughes and Lucia Prauscello. Ann Arbor: Michigan Classical Press, 2010.

Fiddes, Paul S., and Günter Bader, eds. *The Spirit and the Letter: A Tradition and a Reversal*. London: Bloomsbury, 2013.

———. "Whatever Happened to a Pauline Text? 2 Cor. 3.6 and Its Afterlife." In *The Spirit and the Letter: A Tradition and a Reversal*, edited by Paul S. Fiddes and Günter Bader, 3–7. London: Bloomsbury, 2013.

Fiore, Benjamin. *The Function of Personal Example in the Socratic and Pastoral Epistles*. Rome: Biblical Institute Press, 1986.

FitzGerald, Augustine. *The Letters of Synesius of Cyrene*. London: Oxford University Press, 1926.

Fitzgerald, John T. "Galen's *De indolentia* in the Context of Greco-Roman Medicine, Moral Philosophy, and Physiognomy." In *Galen's "De indolentia": Essays on a Newly Discovered Letter*, edited by Clare K. Rothschild and Trevor W. Thompson, 203–220. Tübingen, Germany: Mohr Siebeck, 2014.

Ford, Andrew. "The Beginnings of Dialogue: Socratic Discourses and Fourth-Century Prose." In *The End of Dialogue in Antiquity*, edited by Simon Goldhill, 29–44. Cambridge: Cambridge University Press, 2008.

Foucault, Michel. *The History of Sexuality*. Vol. 2, *The Use of Pleasure*, translated by Robert Hurley. New York: Pantheon, 1985.

Frede, Michael. "The Case for Pagan Monotheism." In *One God: Pagan Monotheism in the Roman Empire*, edited by Stephen Mitchell and Peter Van Nuffelen, 53–81. Cambridge: Cambridge University Press, 2010.

Fredrickson, David E. "Congregations as Communities of Moral Deliberation." In *The Promise of Lutheran Ethics*, edited by Karen L. Bloomquist and John Stumme, 115–129. Minneapolis: Fortress, 1998.

———. "Ephesians and Stoic Physics." *Word & World* 22, no. 2 (2002): 144–154.

———. *Eros and the Christ: Longing and Envy in Paul's Christology*. Minneapolis: Fortress, 2013.

———. "Hellenistic Philosophy and Literature." In *The Oxford Handbook of New Testament, Gender, and Sexuality*, edited by Benjamin Dunning, 239–256. Oxford: Oxford University Press, 2019.

———. "The Justice of Faith." *Dialog* 53, no. 2 (2013): 121–127.

———. "Natural and Unnatural Use in Romans 1:24–27: Paul and the Philosophic Critique of Eros." In *Homosexuality, Science, and the "Plain Sense" of Scripture*, edited by David L. Balch, 197–222. Grand Rapids, MI: Eerdmans, 2000.

———. "Nature's Lament for Jesus." *Word & World* 26, no. 1 (2006): 38–46.

———. "*Parrēsia* in the Pauline Epistles." In *Friendship, Flattery, and Frankness of Speech: Studies on Friendship in the New Testament World*, edited by John Fitzgerald, 161–183. Leiden: Brill, 1996.

———. "Paul, Hardships, and Suffering." In *Paul in the Greco-Roman World: A Handbook, Volumes 1 and 2*, edited by Paul Sampley, 2:172–197. 2nd ed. New York: T&T Clark, 2016.

———. "Paul's Sentence of Death (2 Corinthians 1:9)." In *God, Evil, and Suffering: Essays in Honor of Paul R. Sponheim*, edited by Terrence E. Fretheim and Curtis L. Thompson, 99–107. St. Paul, MN: Word & World, 2000.

———. "'Through Many Tears' (2 Cor 2:4): Paul's Grieving Letter and the Occasion of 2 Corinthians 1–7." In *Paul and Pathos*, edited by Thomas H. Olbricht and Jerry L. Sumney, 161–179. Atlanta: Society of Biblical Literature, 2001.

———. "When Enough Is Never Enough: Philosophers, Poets, Peter, and Paul on Insatiable Desire." In *Mixed Feelings and Vexed Passions: Exploring Emotions in Biblical Literature*, edited by F. Scott Spencer, 311–330. Atlanta: Society of Biblical Literature, 2017.

Fulkerson, Laurel. "'Torn between Hope and Despair': Narrative Foreshadowing and Suspense in the Greek Novel." In *Hope, Joy, and Affection in the Classical World*, edited by Ruth R. Caston and Robert A. Kaster, 75–91. Oxford: Oxford University Press, 2016.

Gaselee, S., trans. *Achilles Tatius. Leucippe and Clitophon*. Loeb Classical Library 45. Cambridge, MA: Harvard University Press, 1969.

Gill, Christopher. *Naturalistic Psychology in Galen and Stoicism*. Oxford: Oxford University Press, 2010.

———. *The Structured Self in Hellenistic and Roman Thought*. Oxford: Oxford University Press, 2006.

Gill, Christopher, Tim Whitmarsh, and John Wilkins, eds. *Galen and the World of Knowledge*. Cambridge: Cambridge University Press, 2009.

Goldhill, Simon. "Why Don't Christians Do Dialogue?" In *The End of Dialogue in Antiquity*, edited by Simon Goldhill, 1–11. Cambridge: Cambridge University Press, 2008.

Goold, G. P., trans. *Callirhoe*. Loeb Classical Library 481. Cambridge, MA: Harvard University Press, 1995.

Grafton, Anthony, and Megan Williams. *Christianity and the Transformation of the Book: Origen, Eusebius and the Library of Caesarea*. Cambridge, MA: Belknap, 2006.

Graver, Margaret. *Stoicism and Emotion*. Chicago: University of Chicago Press, 2007.

Graverini, Luca. "The Ass's Ears and the Novel's Voice: Orality and the Involvement of the Reader in Apuleius' *Metamorphoses*." In *Seeing Tongues, Hearing Scripts: Orality and Representation in the Ancient Novel*, edited by Victoria Rimell, 137–166. Groningen, Netherlands: Barkhuis, 2007.

Greene, Ellen, ed. *Reading Sappho: Contemporary Approaches*. Berkeley: University of California Press, 1996.

———. "Subjects, Objects, and Erotic Symmetry in Sappho's Fragments." In *Among Women: From the Homosocial to the Homoerotic in the Ancient World*, edited by Nancy Sorkin Rabinowitz and Lisa Auanger, 82–105. Austin: University of Texas Press, 2002.

Grethlein, Jonas. *Experience and Teleology in Ancient Historiography: "Futures Past" from Herodotus to Augustine*. Cambridge: Cambridge University Press, 2013.

Griffin, Miriam. "The Younger Pliny's Debt to Moral Philosophy." *Harvard Studies in Classical Philology* 103 (2007): 451–481.

Griggs, Daniel K., trans. *Divine Eros: Hymns of St. Symeon the New Theologian*. Crestwood, NY: St. Vladimir's Seminary Press, 2010.

Gschwandtner, Christina M., ed. *Postmodern Apologetics? Arguments for God in Contemporary Philosophy*. New York: Fordham University Press, 2013.

Gummere, Richard M., trans. *Seneca. Epistles*. Vol. 1, *Epistles 1–65*. Loeb Classical Library 75. Cambridge, MA: Harvard University Press, 1917.

Gurd, Sean Alexander. *Work in Progress: Literary Revision as Social Performance in Ancient Rome*. Oxford: Oxford University Press, 2012.

Gutzwiller, Kathryn J. *Poetic Garlands: Hellenistic Epigrams in Context*. Berkeley: University of California Press, 1998.

Hahm, David E. *The Origins of Stoic Cosmology*. Columbus: Ohio State University Press, 1977.

Haines, C. R., trans. *Marcus Aurelius*. Loeb Classical Library 58. Cambridge, MA:
  Harvard University Press, 1916.

Hammerschlag, Susan. "Poetics of the Broken Tablet." In *The Trace of God: Derrida
  and Religion*, edited by Edward Baring and Peter E. Gordon, 274–288. New York:
  Fordham University Press, 2015.

Hankinson, James. "Actions and Passions: Affection, Emotion, and Moral Self-
  Management in Galen's Philosophical Psychology." In *Passions and Perceptions: Studies in Hellenistic Philosophy of Mind*, edited by Jacques Brunschwig and
  Martha C. Nussbaum, 198–204. Cambridge: Cambridge University Press,
  1993.

Hansen, Mogens H. *The Athenian Assembly in the Age of Demosthenes*. Oxford: Blackwell,
  1987.

Hanson, John. "*Dreams* and *Visions* in the Graeco-Roman World and Early Christianity."
  In *Aufstieg und Niedergang der römischen Welt 2.23.2*, edited by Hildegard Temporini
  and Wolfgang Haase, 1395–1427. Berlin: de Gruyter, 1972.

Hardie, Philip, ed. *Paradox and the Marvelous in Augustan Literature and Culture*. Oxford:
  Oxford University Press, 2009.

Harris, William V. *Dreams and Experience in Classical Antiquity*. Cambridge, MA: Harvard
  University Press, 2009.

Harris-McCoy, Daniel E. *Artemidorus' "Oneirocritica": Text, Translation, and Commentary*.
  Oxford: Oxford University Press, 2012.

Hart, Kevin. *The Dark Gaze: Maurice Blanchot and the Sacred*. Chicago: University of
  Chicago Press, 2004.

———. *The Trespass of the Sign: Deconstruction, Theology, and Philosophy*. Cambridge: Cambridge University Press, 1989.

Hart, Kevin, and Barbara Eileen Wall, eds. *The Experience of God: A Postmodern Response*.
  New York: Fordham University Press, 2005.

Heath, John. *The Talking Greeks: Speech, Animals, and the Other in Homer, Aeschylus, and
  Plato*. Cambridge: Cambridge University Press, 2005.

Hock, Ronald F. "Paul and Greco-Roman Education." In *Paul in the Greco-Roman
  World: A Handbook, Volumes 1 and 2*, edited by Paul Sampley, 1:230–253. 2nd ed.
  New York: T&T Clark, 2016.

Hodkinson, Owen. "'Novels in the Greek Letter': Inversions of the Written-Oral Hierar-
  chy in the Briefroman 'Themistocles.'" In *Seeing Tongues, Hearing Scripts: Orality and
  Representation in the Ancient Novel*, edited by Victoria Rimell, 257–278. Groningen,
  Netherlands: Barkhuis, 2007.

Holladay, Carl, John T. Fitzgerald, Gregory E. Sterling, and James W. Thompson, eds.
  Light from the Gentiles: Hellenistic Philosophy and Early Christianity. 2 Vols. Leiden:
  Brill, 2014.

Holmes, Brooke. "Euripides' Heracles in the Flesh." *Classical Antiquity* 27, no. 2 (2008): 231–281.

Höschele, Regina. "Meleager and Heliodora: A Love Story in Bits and Pieces?" In *Plotting with Eros: Essays on the Poetics of Love and the Erotics of Reading*, edited by Ingela Nilsson, 99–134. Copenhagen: Museum Tusculanum, 2009.

Hughes, Serge, and Elizabeth Hughes. *Jacopone da Todi: The Lauds*. New York: Paulist, 1982.

Huizenga, Annette Bourland. *Moral Education for Women in the Pastoral and Pythagorean Letters: Philosophers of the Household*. Leiden: Brill, 2013.

Hunter, Richard. *Critical Moments in Classical Literature: Studies in the Ancient View of Literature and Its Uses*. Cambridge: Cambridge University Press, 2009.

———. *Theocritus and the Archeology of Greek Poetry*. Cambridge: Cambridge University Press, 1996.

Hunter, Richard, and Donald Russell, eds. *Plutarch: How to Study Poetry ("De audiendis poetis")*. Cambridge: Cambridge University Press, 2011.

Hurst, Andrea. *Derrida Vis-à-Vis Lacan: Interweaving Deconstruction and Psychoanalysis*. New York: Fordham University Press, 2008.

Inwood, Brad. *Reading Seneca: Stoic Philosophy at Rome*. Oxford: Clarendon, 2005.

James, Sharon L. "Her Turn to Cry: The Politics of Weeping in Roman Love Elegy." *Transactions of the American Philological Association* 133, no. 1 (2003): 99–122.

Jazdzewska, Katarzyna. "From Dialogos to Dialogue: The Use of the Term from Plato to the Second Century CE." *Greek, Roman, and Byzantine Studies* 54, no. 1 (2014): 17–36.

Jipp, Joshua W. "Paul's Areopagus Speech of Acts 17:16–34 as Both Critique and Propaganda." *Journal of Biblical Literature* 131, no. 3 (2012): 567–588.

Jouanna, Jacques. *Hippocrates*. Translated by Malcom B. DeBevoise. Baltimore: Johns Hopkins University Press, 1999.

Kamesar, Adam. "The *Logos Endiathetos* and the *Logos Prophorikos* in Allegorical Interpretation: Philo and the D-Scholia to the Iliad." *Greek, Roman, and Byzantine Studies* 44, no. 2 (2004): 163–181.

Karanika, Andromache. "Greek Comedy's Parody of Lament." In *Lament: Studies in the Ancient Mediterranean and Beyond*, edited by Ann Suter, 181–199. Oxford: Oxford University Press, 2008.

Karlsson, Gustav H. *Idéologie et cérémonial dans l'épistolographie byzantine: textes du Xe siècle analysés et commentés*. Uppsala: Almqvist & Wiksell, 1959.

Kartzow, Marianne Bjelland. *Gossip and Gender: Othering of Speech in the Pastoral Epistles*. New York: de Gruyter, 2009.

Kazantzides, George. "Haunted Minds, Haunted Places: Topographies of Insanity in Greek and Roman Paradoxography." In *Landscapes of Dread in Classical Antiquity:*

Negative Emotion in Natural and Constructed Spaces, edited by Debbie Felton, 226–258. New York: Routledge, 2018.

Kearney, Richard. *Anatheism: Returning to God after God*. New York: Columbia University Press, 2010.

Kearney, Richard, and Kascha Semonovitch, eds. *Phenomenologies of the Stranger: Between Hostility and Hospitality*. New York: Fordham University Press, 2011.

Keck, Leander E., and J. Louis Martyn, eds. *Studies in Luke–Acts*. London: SPCK, 1968.

Kirichenko, Alexander. "Mimesis, Metamorphosis and False Closure in Apuleius' Golden Ass." In *The Door Ajar: False Closure in Greek and Roman Literature and Art*, edited by Farouk F. Grewing, Benjamin Acosta-Hughes, and Alexander Kirichenko, 277–308. Heidelberg, Germany: Universitätsverlag Winter, 2013.

———. "Satire, Propaganda, and the Pleasure of Reading: Apuleius' Stories of Curiosity in Context." *Harvard Studies in Classical Philology* 104 (2008): 339–371.

Knust, Jennifer. *Abandoned to Lust: Sexual Slander and Ancient Christianity*. New York: Columbia University Press, 2006.

König, Jason. "Body and Text." In *The Cambridge Companion to the Greek and Roman Novel*, edited by Tim Whitmarsh, 127–144. Cambridge: Cambridge University Press, 2008.

———. "Conventions of Prefatory Self-Presentation in Galen's *On the Order of My Own Books*." In *Galen and the World of Knowledge*, edited by Christopher Gill, Tim Whitmarsh, and John Wilkins, 35–58. Cambridge: Cambridge University Press, 2009.

Koskenniemi, Heikki. *Studien zur Idee und Phraseologie des griechischen Briefes bis 400 n. Chr.* Helsinki, Finland: Finnish Academy, 1956.

Kost, Karlheinz. *Musaios, Hero und Leander: Einleitung, Text, Übersetzung und Kommentar*. Bonn, Germany: Bouvier, 1971.

Laks, Andre, and Malcolm Schofield, eds. *Justice and Generosity: Studies in Hellenistic Social and Political Philosophy*. Cambridge: Cambridge University Press, 2009.

Lanata, Giuliana. "Sappho's Amatory Language." Translated by William Robins. In *Reading Sappho: Contemporary Approaches*, edited by Ellen Greene, 11–25. Berkeley: University of California Press, 1996.

Lather, Amy. "Olfactory Theater: Tracking Scents in Aeschylus's *Oresteia*." *Arethusa* 51, no. 1 (2018): 33–54.

Lawler, Thomas Comerford. *St. Augustine: Sermons for Christmas and Epiphany*. Westminster, MD: Newman Press, 1952.

Leonard, Miriam, ed. *Derrida and Antiquity*. Oxford: Oxford University Press, 2010.

———. "Derrida between 'Greek' and 'Jew.'" In *Derrida and Antiquity*, edited by Miriam Leonard, 135–158. Oxford: Oxford University Press, 2010.

Levaniouk, Olga. "Lament and Hymenaios in Erinna's *Distaff*." In *Lament: Studies in the Ancient Mediterranean and Beyond*, edited by Ann Suter, 200–232. Oxford: Oxford University Press, 2008.

Lichtman, Maria. "Negative Theology in Marguerite Porete and Jacques Derrida." *Christianity and Literature* 47, no. 2 (1998): 213–227.

Lienhard, Joseph T. *Origen: Homilies on Luke: Fragments on Luke*. Washington, DC: Catholic University of America Press, 1996.

Loevlie, Elisabeth M. "Faith in the Ghosts of Literature: Poetic Hauntology in Derrida, Blanchot and Morrison's *Beloved*." *Religions* 4, no. 3 (2013): 336–350.

Long, A. A. *From Epicurus to Epictetus: Studies in Hellenistic and Roman Philosophy*. Oxford: Oxford University Press, 2006.

Longley, Georgina. "'I, Polybius': Self-Conscious Didacticism?" In *The Author's Voice in Classical and Late Antiquity*, edited by Anna Marmodoro and Jonathan Hill, 175–205. Oxford: Oxford University Press, 2013.

Lovatt, Helen. *The Epic Gaze: Vision, Gender and Narrative in Ancient Epic*. Cambridge: Cambridge University Press, 2013.

Lowrie, Michéle. *Writing, Performance, and Authority in Augustan Rome*. Oxford: Oxford University Press, 2009.

Ludlow, Morwenna. "Spirit and Letter in Origen and Augustine." In *The Spirit and the Letter: A Tradition and a Reversal*, edited by Paul S. Fiddes and Günter Bader, 87–102. London: Bloomsbury, 2013.

Luther, Martin. "The Freedom of a Christian." In *Luther's Works*, edited and revised by Harold J. Grimm, translated by W. A Lambert, 333–377. Vol. 31. Philadelphia: Muhlenberg Press, 1957.

———. *Lectures on Galatians*. Vol. 26 of *Luther's Works*, edited by Jaroslav Pelikan and Walter A. Hansen, translated by Jaroslav Pelikan, 1–461. Saint Louis, MO: Concordia, 1963.

Lyne, R. O. A. M. "*Servitium Amoris*." *Classical Quarterly* 29, no. 1 (1979): 117–130.

Malherbe, Abraham J. *Ancient Epistolary Theorists*. Atlanta: Scholars Press, 1988.

———, ed. *The Cynic Epistles: A Study Edition*. Atlanta: Scholars Press, 1977.

———. "'Gentle as a Nurse': The Cynic Background to 1 Thessalonians 2." In *Light from the Gentiles: Hellenistic Philosophy and Early Christianity*, edited by Carl Holladay, John T. Fitzgerald, Gregory E. Sterling, and James W. Thompson, 53–67. Vol. 1. Leiden: Brill, 2013.

———. *The Letters to the Thessalonians: A New Translation with Introduction and Commentary*. New York: Doubleday, 2000.

———. "'Not in a Corner': Early Christian Apologetic in Acts 26:26." In *Light from the Gentiles: Hellenistic Philosophy and Early Christianity*, edited by Carl Holladay,

John T. Fitzgerald, Gregory E. Sterling, and James W. Thompson, 209–227. Vol. 1. Leiden: Brill, 2013.

———. "Pseudo-Heraclitus, Epistle 4: The Divinization of the Wise Man." In *Light from the Gentiles: Hellenistic Philosophy and Early Christianity*, edited by Carl Holladay, John T. Fitzgerald, Gregory E. Sterling, and James W. Thompson, 597–634. Vol. 2. Leiden: Brill, 2013.

Malherbe, Abraham J., and Everett Ferguson. *Gregory of Nyssa: The Life of Moses*. New York: Paulist, 1978.

Mansfeld, Jaap. "'Illuminating What Is Thought': A Middle Platonist *Placitum* on 'Voice' in Context." *Mnemosyne* 58, no. 3 (2005): 358–407.

Mansfield, Nick. *The God Who Deconstructs Himself: Sovereignty and Subjectivity between Freud, Bataille, and Derrida*. New York: Fordham University Press, 2010.

Marcus, Joel. "Crucifixion as Parodic Exaltation." *Journal of Biblical Literature* 125, no. 1 (2006): 73–87.

Margariti, Katia. "Lament and Death Instead of Marriage: The Iconography of Deceased Maidens on Attic Grave Reliefs of the Classical Period." *Hesperia* 87, no. 1 (2018): 91–176.

Marmodoro, Anna, and Jonathan Hill, eds. *The Author's Voice in Classical and Late Antiquity*. Oxford: Oxford University Press, 2013.

Martin, Dale B. *Inventing Superstition: From the Hippocratics to the Christians*. Cambridge, MA: Harvard University Press, 2004.

———. *Slavery as Salvation: The Metaphor of Slavery in Pauline Christianity*. New Haven, CT: Yale University Press, 1990.

McLeod, A. M. G. "Physiology and Medicine in a Greek Novel: Achilles Tatius' Leucippe and Clitophon." *Journal of Hellenic Studies* 89 (1969): 97–105.

Meeks, Wayne A. *The First Urban Christians: The Social World of the Apostle Paul*. 2nd ed. New Haven, CT: Yale University Press, 2003.

Mendoza, Manuel Villalobos. *When Men Were Not Men: Masculinity and Otherness in the Pastoral Epistles*. Sheffield: Phoenix Press, 2014.

Meyer, Susan Sauvé. "Chain of Causes: What Is Stoic Fate?" In *God and Cosmos in Stoicism*, edited by Ricardo Salles, 71–90. Oxford: Oxford University Press, 2009.

Miles, Richard, ed. *Constructing Identities in Late Antiquity*. New York: Routledge, 1999.

Milnor, Kristina. *Gender, Domesticity, and the Age of Augustus: Inventing Private Life*. Oxford: Oxford University Press, 2005.

Minar, Edwin L., F. H. Sandbach, and W. C. Helmbold, trans. *Plutarch. Moralia*. Vol. 9, *Table-Talk, Books 7–9. Dialogue on Love*. Loeb Classical Library 425. Cambridge, MA: Harvard University Press, 1961.

Mitchell, Stephen, ed. and trans. *The Selected Poetry of Rainer Maria Rilke*. New York: Vintage International, 1989.

Mitchell, Stephen, and Peter Van Nuffelen, eds. *One God: Pagan Monotheism in the Roman Empire*. Cambridge: Cambridge University Press, 2010.

Monks at Saint Bernard Abbey. *Guerric of Igny: Liturgical Sermons*. 2 vols. Spencer, MA: Cistercian, 1970–1971.

Morales, Helen. "Gender and Identity in Musaeus' *Hero and Leander*." In *Constructing Identities in Late Antiquity*, edited by Richard Miles, 41–69. New York: Routledge, 1999.

———. *Vision and Narrative in Achilles Tatius' Leucippe and Clitophon*. Cambridge: Cambridge University Press, 2004.

Morrison, A. D. "Authorship and Authority in Greek Fictional Letters." In *The Author's Voice in Classical and Late Antiquity*, edited by Anna Marmodoro and Jonathan Hill, 287–312. Oxford: Oxford University Press, 2013.

Moyise, Steve. "Does Paul Respect the Context of His Quotations?" In *Paul and Scripture: Extending the Conversation*, edited by Christopher D. Stanley, 97–114. Atlanta: Society of Biblical Literature, 2012.

Murray, A. T., trans. *Homer. Odyssey*. Vol. 1, *Books 1–12*. Revised by George E. Dimock. Loeb Classical Library 104. Cambridge, MA: Harvard University Press, 1919.

———, trans. *Homer. Odyssey*. Vol. 2, *Books 13–24*. Revised by George E. Dimock. Loeb Classical Library 105. Cambridge, MA: Harvard University Press, 1919.

Naas, Michael. "Earmarks: Derrida's Reinvention of Philosophical Writing in 'Plato's Pharmacy.'" In *Derrida and Antiquity*, edited by Miriam Leonard, 43–72. Oxford: Oxford University Press, 2010.

———. *The End of the World and Other Teachable Moments: Jacques Derrida's Final Seminar*. New York: Fordham University Press, 2015.

———. *Taking on the Tradition: Jacques Derrida and the Legacies of Deconstruction*. Palo Alto, CA: Stanford University Press, 2003.

Nasrallah, Laura S. "1 Corinthians." In *The Letters and Legacy of Paul: Fortress Commentary on the Bible Study Edition*, edited by Margaret Aymer, Cynthia Briggs Kittredge, and David A. Sánchez, 427–471. Minneapolis: Fortress, 2016.

Natali, Carlo. "*Oikonomia* in Hellenistic Political Thought." In *Justice and Generosity: Studies in Hellenistic Social and Political Philosophy*, edited by Andre Laks and Malcolm Schofield, 95–119. Cambridge: Cambridge University Press, 2009.

Nelsestuen, Grant A. "*Oikonomia* as a Theory of Empire in the Political Thought of Xenophon and Aristotle." *Greek, Roman, and Byzantine Studies* 57, no. 1 (2017): 74–104.

Nilsson, Ingela, ed. *Plotting with Eros: Essays on the Poetics of Love and the Erotics of Reading* Copenhagen: Museum Tusculanum, 2009.

Nock, Arthur Darby. *Conversion: The Old and the New in Religion from Alexander the Great to Augustine of Hippo*. Oxford: Oxford University Press, 1933.

Norris, Richard A. *Gregory of Nyssa: Homilies on the Song of Songs*. Atlanta: Society of
    Biblical Literature, 2012.

Nussbaum, Martha. "The Incomplete Feminism of Musonius Rufus: Platonist, Stoic,
    and Roman." In *The Sleep of Reason: Erotic Experience and Sexual Ethics in Ancient
    Greece and Rome*, edited by Martha Nussbaum and Juha Sihvola, 283–326. Chicago:
    University of Chicago Press, 2002.

Nussbaum, Martha, and Juha Sihvola, eds. *The Sleep of Reason: Erotic Experience and
    Sexual Ethics in Ancient Greece and Rome*. Chicago: University of Chicago Press, 2002.

Nutton, Vivian. "Rufus of Ephesus in the Medical Context of His Time." In *On Melan-
    choly: Rufus of Ephesus*, edited by Peter E. Pormann, 139–158. Tübingen, Germany:
    Mohr Siebeck, 2008.

O'Connell, Erin. "Derrida and Presocratic Philosophy." In *Derrida and Antiquity*, edited
    by Miriam Leonard, 73–100. Oxford: Oxford University Press, 2010.

Oldfather, C. H., trans. *Diodorus Siculus. Library of History*. Vol. 4, *Books 9–12.40*. Loeb
    Classical Library 375. Cambridge, MA: Harvard University Press, 1946.

Oldfather, W. A., trans. *Epictetus. Discourses, Books 1–2*. Loeb Classical Library 131.
    Cambridge, MA: Harvard University Press, 1925.

———, trans. *Epictetus. Discourses, Books 3–4. Fragments. The Encheiridion*. Loeb Classical
    Library 218. Cambridge, MA: Harvard University Press, 1928.

O'Sullivan, Timothy M. *Walking in Roman Culture*. Cambridge: Cambridge University
    Press, 2011.

Padel, Ruth. *In and Out of the Mind: Greek Images of the Tragic Self*. Princeton, NJ:
    Princeton University Press, 1992.

Parker, Robert. *On Greek Religion*. Ithaca, NY: Cornell University Press, 2011.

Parkin, Anneliese. "'You Do Him No Service': An Exploration of Pagan Almsgiving."
    In *Poverty in the Roman World*, edited by Margaret Atkins and Robin Osborne,
    60–82. Cambridge: Cambridge University Press, 2006.

Parsons, Sister Wilfrid. *Saint Augustine: Letters*. Washington, DC: Catholic University
    of America Press, 1951.

Paton, W. R., trans. *The Greek Anthology*. Vol. 1, *Book 1: Christian Epigrams. Book 2:
    Description of the Statues in the Gymnasium of Zeuxippus. Book 3: Epigrams in the
    Temple of Apollonis at Cyzicus. Book 4: Prefaces to the Various Anthologies. Book 5: Erotic
    Epigrams*. Revised by Michael A. Tueller. Loeb Classical Library 67. Cambridge,
    MA: Harvard University Press, 2014.

———, trans. *The Greek Anthology*. Vol. 3, *Book 9: The Declamatory Epigrams*. Loeb Clas-
    sical Library 84. Cambridge, MA: Harvard University Press, 1917.

Peirano, Irene. *The Rhetoric of the Roman Fake: Latin Pseudepigrapha in Context*. Cam-
    bridge: Cambridge University Press, 2012.

Perkell, Christine. "Reading the Laments of *Iliad* 24." In *Lament: Studies in the Ancient Mediterranean and Beyond*, edited by Ann Suter, 93–117. Oxford: Oxford University Press, 2008.

Perkins, Larry, trans. "Exodus." In *A New English Translation of the Septuagint: And Other Greek Translations Traditionally Included under That Title*, edited by Albert Pietersma and Benjamin G. Wright, 43–81. Oxford: Oxford University Press, 2007.

Perrin, Bernadotte, trans. *Plutarch. Lives*. Vol. 6, *Dion and Brutus. Timoleon and Aemilius Paulus*. Loeb Classical Library 98. Cambridge, MA: Harvard University Press, 1918.

Petit, Caroline, ed. *Galen's Treatise Περὶ Ἀλυπίας (De indolentia) in Context: A Tale of Resilience*. Leiden: Brill, 2019.

Petropoulos, J. C. B. *Eroticism in Ancient and Medieval Greek Poetry*. London: Duckworth, 2003.

Pevarello, Daniele. *The Sentences of Sextus and the Origins of Christian Asceticism*. Tübingen, Germany: Mohr Siebeck, 2013.

Pietersma, Albert, and Benjamin G. Wright, eds. *A New English Translation of the Septuagint: And Other Greek Translations Traditionally Included under That Title*. Oxford: Oxford University Press, 2007.

Pormann, Peter E. "Appendix 2: Isḥāq ibn 'Imrān on 'Scholarly Melancholy.'" In *On Melancholy: Rufus of Ephesus*, edited by Peter E. Pormann, 289–293. Tübingen, Germany: Mohr Siebeck, 2008.

———, ed. *On Melancholy: Rufus of Ephesus*. Tübingen, Germany: Mohr Siebeck, 2008.

Prins, Yopie. "Sappho's Afterlife in Translation." In *Re-reading Sappho: Reception and Transmission*, edited by Ellen Greene, 36–67. Berkeley: University of California Press, 1996.

Purves, Alex C. *Space and Time in Ancient Greek Narrative*. Cambridge: Cambridge University Press, 2010.

Rabinowitz, Nancy Sorkin, and Lisa Auanger, eds. *Among Women: From the Homosocial to the Homoerotic in the Ancient World*. Austin: University of Texas Press, 2002.

Race, William H., trans. *Apollonius Rhodius. Argonautica*. Loeb Classical Library 1. Cambridge, MA: Harvard University Press, 2009.

Ramsby, Teresa R., and Beth Severy. "Gender, Sex, and the Domestication of the Empire in Art of the Augustan Age." *Arethusa* 40, no. 1 (2007): 43–71.

Reardon, B. P. *Collected Ancient Greek Novels*. 2nd ed. Berkeley: University of California Press, 2008.

Redpath, Ian. "The *Physiognomy* of Adamantius the Sophist." In *Seeing the Face, Seeing the Soul: Polemon's Physiognomy from Classical Antiquity to Medieval Islam*, edited by Simon Swain, 493–547. Oxford: Oxford University Press, 2007.

Richter, Daniel S. *Cosmopolis: Imagining Community in Late Classical Athens and the Early Roman Empire*. Oxford: Oxford University Press, 2011.

Rimell, Victoria, ed. *Seeing Tongues, Hearing Scripts: Orality and Representation in the Ancient Novel*. Groningen, Netherlands: Barkhuis, 2007.

Rist, John M. "Stoic Detachment." In *The Stoics*, edited by John M. Rist, 259–272. Berkeley: University of California Press, 1978.

Roberts, Alexander, and James Donaldson, eds. and trans. *Ante-Nicene Fathers*. Vol. 2. 1885. Reprint, Peabody, MA: Hendrickson, 1994.

Rosati, Gianpiero. "'Latrator Anubis': Alien Divinities in Augustan Rome, and How to Tame Monsters through Aetiology." In *Paradox and the Marvelous in Augustan Literature and Culture*, edited by Philip Hardie, 268–287. Oxford: Oxford University Press, 2009.

Rosenmeyer, Patricia A. "Love Letters in Callimachus, Ovid and Aristaenetus or the Sad Fate of a Mailorder Bride." *Materiali e discussioni per l'analisi dei testi classici* 36 (1996): 9–31.

———. "Medulla as a *Locus Eroticus*." *Arethusa* 32, no. 1 (1999): 19–47.

Ross, William A. "'Ὦ ἀνόητοι καὶ βραδεῖς τῇ καρδίᾳ': Luke, Aesop, and Reading Scripture." *Novum Testamentum* 58, no. 4 (2016): 369–379.

Rothschild, Clare K., and Trevor W. Thompson, eds. *Galen's "De indolentia": Essays on a Newly Discovered Letter*. Tübingen, Germany: Mohr Siebeck, 2014.

Rusten, Jeffrey, and I. C. Cunningham, trans. *Theophrastus, Herodas, Sophron. Characters. Herodas: Mimes. Sophron and Other Mime Fragments*. Loeb Classical Library 225. Cambridge, MA: Harvard University Press, 2003.

Salles, Ricardo. "Chrysippus on Conflagration and the Indestructibility of the Cosmos." In *God and Cosmos in Stoicism*, edited by Richardo Salles, 118–131. Oxford: Oxford University Press, 2009.

———, ed. *God and Cosmos in Stoicism*. Oxford: Oxford University Press, 2009.

Sampley, Paul, ed. *Paul in the Greco-Roman World: A Handbook, Volumes 1 and 2*. 2nd ed. New York: T&T Clark, 2016.

Schmid, Heinrich. *The Doctrinal Theology of the Evangelical Lutheran Church*. Translated by Charles A. Hay and Henry E. Jacobs. 3rd ed., rev. Minneapolis: Augsburg, 1899.

Schmitz, Thomas A., and Nicolas Wiater, eds. *The Struggle for Identity: Greeks and Their Past in the First Century BCE*. Stuttgart, Germany: Franz Steiner, 2011.

Schwenger, Peter. "Words and the Murder of the Thing." *Critical Inquiry* 28, no. 1 (2001): 99–113.

Sedly, David. "Chrysippus on Psychophysical Causality." In *Passions and Perceptions: Studies in Hellenistic Philosophy of Mind*, edited by Jacques Brunschwig and Martha Nussbaum, 313–331. Cambridge: Cambridge University Press, 1993.

Sferlea, Ovidiu. "On the Interpretation of the Theory of Perpetual Progress (*epektasis*): Taking into Account the Testimony of Eastern Monastic Tradition." *Revue d'histoire ecclésiastique* 109, nos. 3–4 (2014): 564–587.

Shaner, Katherine A. "Seeing Rape and Robbery: ἁρπαγμός and the Philippians Christ Hymn (Phil. 2:5–11)." *Biblical Interpretation* 25 (2017): 342–363.

Sharrock, Alison. *Seduction and Repetition in Ovid's "Ars Amatoria II."* Oxford: Clarendon, 1994.

Showerman, Grant, trans. *Ovid. Heroides. Amores.* Revised by G. P. Goold. Loeb Classical Library 41. Cambridge, MA: Harvard University Press, 1914.

Singer, Peter N. "Galen and the Philosophers: Philosophical Engagement, Shadowy Contemporaries, Aristotelian Transformations." In "Philosophical Themes in Galen," edited by Peter Adamson, Rotraud Hansberger, and James Wilberding. Supplement, *Bulletin of the Institute of Classical Studies*, no. S114 (2014): 7–38.

———. "The Mockery of Madness: Laughter at and with Insanity in Attic Tragedy and Old Comedy." *Illinois Classical Studies* 43, no. 2 (2018): 7–38.

Sommerstein, Alan H., trans. *Aeschylus. Persians. Seven against Thebes. Suppliants. Prometheus Bound.* Loeb Classical Library 145. Cambridge, MA: Harvard University Press, 2009.

Sourvinou-Inwood, Christiane. "The Young Abductor of the Locrian Pinakes." *Bulletin of the Institute of Classical Studies* 20, no. 1 (1973): 12–21.

Spawforth, A. J. S. *Greece and the Augustan Cultural Revolution.* Cambridge: Cambridge University Press, 2011.

Spencer, F. Scott. "Getting a Feel for the 'Mixed' and 'Vexed' Study of Emotions in Biblical Literature." In *Mixed Feelings and Vexed Passions: Exploring Emotions in Biblical Literature*, edited by F. Scott Spencer, 1–41. Atlanta: Society of Biblical Literature, 2017.

———, ed. *Mixed Feelings and Vexed Passions: Exploring Emotions in Biblical Literature.* Atlanta: Society of Biblical Literature, 2017.

Squires, John T. *The Plan of God in Luke–Acts.* Cambridge: Cambridge University Press, 1993.

Star, Christopher. *The Empire of the Self: Self-Command and Political Speech in Seneca and Petronius.* Baltimore: Johns Hopkins University Press, 2012.

Stevenson, T. R. "The Ideal Benefactor and the Father Analogy in Greek and Roman Thought." *Classical Quarterly* 42, no. 2 (1992): 421–436.

Stolorow, Robert D. "Friendship, Fidelity, and Finitude: Reflections on Jacques Derrida's *The Work of Mourning*." *Comparative and Continental Philosophy* 2, no. 1 (2010): 143–146.

Stowers, Stanley K. *Letter Writing in Greco-Roman Antiquity.* Philadelphia: Westminster Press, 1986.

———. "Paul and Self-Mastery." In *Paul in the Greco-Roman World: A Handbook, Volumes 1 and 2*, edited by Paul Sampley, 2:270–300. 2nd ed. New York: T&T Clark, 2016.

Strelan, Rick. "A Note on *Asphaleia* (Luke 1.4)." *Journal for the Study of the New Testament* 30, no. 2 (2007): 163–171.

Suter, Ann, ed. *Lament: Studies in the Ancient Mediterranean and Beyond*. Oxford: Oxford University Press, 2008.

Sutherland, Elizabeth H. "Writing (on) Bodies: Lyric Discourse and the Production of Gender in Horace *Odes* 1.13." *Classical Philology* 100, no. 1 (2005): 52–82.

Swain, Simon, ed. *Seeing the Face, Seeing the Soul: Polemon's Physiognomy from Classical Antiquity to Medieval Islam*. Oxford: Oxford University Press, 2007.

———. "Social Stress and Political Pressure: *On Melancholy* in Context." In *On Melancholy: Rufus of Ephesus*, edited by Peter E. Pormann, 113–138. Tübingen, Germany: Mohr Siebeck, 2008.

Temporini, Hildegard, and Wolfgang Haase, eds. *Aufstieg und Niedergang der römischen Welt 2.23.2*. Berlin: de Gruyter, 1972.

Theron, Daniel J. *Evidence of Tradition*. Grand Rapids, MI: Baker Book House, 1957.

Thom, Johan C., ed. *Cosmic Order and Divine Power: Pseudo-Aristotle, "On the Cosmos."* Tübingen, Germany: Mohr Siebeck, 2014.

Thraede, Klaus. *Grundzüge griechisch-römisher Brieftopik*. Munich: C. H. Beck, 1970.

Thumiger, Chiara. "Aretaeus's 'Stomachic' Patients: Comic Features in a Medical Discussion?" *Illinois Classical Studies* 43, no. 2 (2018): 473–487.

———. "Mental Insanity in the Hippocratic Texts: A Pragmatic Perspective." *Mnemosyne* 68, no. 2 (2015): 210–233.

Tieleman, Teun. "Wisdom and Emotion: Galen's Philosophical Position in Avoiding Distress." In *Galen's Treatise Περὶ Ἀλυπίας (De indolentia) in Context: A Tale of Resilience*, edited by Caroline Petit, 199–216. Leiden: Brill, 2019.

Tilg, Stefan. *Chariton of Aphrodisias and the Invention of the Greek Love Novel*. Oxford: Oxford University Press, 2010.

Togni, Paulo. "Plato's Soul-Book Simile and Stoic Epistemology." *Méthexis* 26 (2013): 163–185.

Toohey, Peter. *Melancholy, Love, and Time: Boundaries of the Self in Ancient Literature*. Ann Arbor: University of Michigan Press, 2004.

———. "Rufus of Ephesus and the Tradition of the Melancholy Thinker." In *On Melancholy: Rufus of Ephesus*, edited by Peter E. Pormann, 221–244. Tübingen, Germany: Mohr Siebeck, 2008.

———. "Some Ancient Histories of Literary Melancholia." *Illinois Classical Studies* 15, no. 1 (1990): 143–144.

Toscano, Margaret M. "The Eyes Have It: Female Desire on Attic Greek Vases." *Arethusa* 46, no. 1 (2013): 1–40.

Twomey, Jay. *The Pastoral Epistles through the Centuries*. Chichester, UK: Wiley-Blackwell, 2009.

van Geytenbeek, Anton Cornelis. *Musonius Rufus and Greek Diatribe*. Assen, Netherlands: Van Gorcum, 1962.

van Kooten, George H. "Ἐκκλησία τοῦ θεοῦ: The 'Church of God' and the Civic Assemblies (ἐκκλησίαι) of the Greek Cities in the Roman Empire: A Response to Paul Trebilco and Richard A. Horsley." *New Testament Studies* 58, no. 4 (2012): 522–548.

Vergados, Athanassios. *The Homeric Hymn to Hermes: Introduction, Text and Commentary*. Berlin: de Gruyter, 2013.

Vermuele, Emily. *Aspects of Death in Early Greek Art and Poetry*. Berkeley: University of California Press, 1979.

Vielhauer, Philipp. "On the 'Paulinism' of Acts." In *Studies in Luke–Acts*, edited by Leander E. Keck and J. Louis Martyn, 33–50. London: SPCK, 1968.

Volk, Katharina. "Letters in the Sky: Reading the Signs in Aratus' *Phaenomena*." *American Journal of Philology* 133, no. 2 (2012): 209–240.

Wack, Mary Frances. *Lovesickness in the Middle Ages: The "Viaticum" and Its Commentaries*. Philadelphia: University of Pennsylvania Press, 1990.

Walsh, P. G. *Pliny the Younger: Complete Letters*. Oxford: Oxford University Press, 2006.

Walzer, Richard. *Galen on Jews and Christians*. Oxford: Oxford University Press, 1949.

Webb, Ruth. "Imagination and the Arousal of the Emotions in Greco-Roman Rhetoric." In *The Passions in Roman Thought and Literature*, edited by Susanna Morton Braund and Christopher Gill, 112–127. Cambridge: Cambridge University Press, 1997.

Westerholm, Stephen. "'Letter' and 'Spirit': The Foundation of Pauline Ethics." *New Testament Studies* 30, no. 2 (1984): 229–248.

White, John Lee. *The Form and Function of the Body of the Greek Letter: A Study of the Letter-Body in the Non-literary Papyri and in Paul the Apostle*. Missoula, MT: Society of Biblical Literature, 1972.

Whitmarsh, Tim, ed. *The Cambridge Companion to the Greek and Roman Novel*. Cambridge: Cambridge University Press, 2008.

——, ed. *Local Knowledge and Microidentities in the Imperial Greek World*. Cambridge: Cambridge University Press, 2010.

Wiater, Nicholas. "Writing Roman History—Shaping Greek Identity: The Ideology of Historiography in Dionysius of Halicarnassus." In *The Struggle for Identity: Greeks and Their Past in the First Century BCE*, edited by Thomas A. Schmitz and Nicolas Wiater, 61–91. Stuttgart, Germany: Franz Steiner, 2011.

Wilcox, Amanda. *The Gift of Correspondence in Classical Rome: Friendship in Cicero's "Ad Familiares" and Seneca's "Moral Epistles."* Madison: University of Wisconsin Press, 2012.

Wilken, Robert. *The Christians as the Romans Saw Them.* 2nd ed. New Haven, CT: Yale University Press, 2003.

Wohl, Victoria. "Scenes from a Marriage: Love and *Logos* in Plutarch's *Coniugalia Praecepta.*" *Helios* 24, no. 2 (1997): 170–192.

Wood, David. "Things at the Edge of the World." In *Phenomenologies of the Stranger: Between Hostility and Hospitality*, edited by Richard Kearney and Kascha Semonovitch, 67–79. New York: Fordham University Press, 2011.

Wood, Sarah. *Derrida's "Writing and Difference."* London: Continuum, 2009.

Wright, Wilmer C., trans. *Julian. Orations 6–8. Letters to Themistius, to the Senate and People of Athens, to a Priest. The Caesars. Misopogon.* Loeb Classical Library 29. Cambridge, MA: Harvard University Press, 1913.

Zimmerman, Clayton. *The Pastoral Narcissus: A Study of the First Idyll of Theocritus.* Lanham, MD: Rowman & Littlefield, 1994.

Index